HANDBOOK O

PRACTICAL WOODWORKING TECHNIQUES

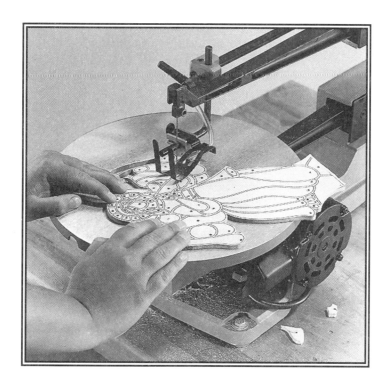

Robert Lento

Sterling Publishing Co., Inc.
New York

For Robert and Jenna Perazzo and Zachary and Simon Dokouzian

CIP Data Available

10 9 8 7 6 5 4 3 2 1

Published by Sterling Publishing Company, Inc.
387 Park Avenue South, New York, N.Y. 10016
© 1999 by Robert Lento
Distributed in Canada by Sterling Publishing
℅ Canadian Manda Group, One Atlantic Avenue, Suite 105
Toronto, Ontario, Canada M6K 3E7
Distributed in Great Britain and Europe by Cassell PLC
Wellington House, 125 Strand, London WC2R 0BB, England
Distributed in Australia by Capricorn Link (Australia) Pty Ltd.
P.O. Box 6651, Baulkham Hills Business Centre, NSW 2153, Australia
Manufactured in the United States of America
All rights reserved

Sterling ISBN 0-8069-1351-7

CONTENTS

INTRODUCTION

■ ■ ■ ■ ■ ■ ■ ■ ■ ■ ■ ■ ■ ■

In spite of great advances in technology and manufacturing that have made high-tech devices like computers common, many folks remain interested and involved with relatively low-tech crafts of all kinds. Woodworking still attracts and holds the interest of many of these craftspeople.

This interest can be attributed to many factors. Working with wood allows individual creativity to flourish. The availability of wood and wood-working equipment and the relative ease with which wood can be worked can also promote this area of activity. Woodworking skills are valuable to the home owner and the apartment dweller alike. Many folks find that the ability to make minor repairs to furniture or other wood pieces can be empowering and rewarding. The beginner can become involved in woodworking with a rel-atively small investment in tools and equipment.

This book can be used as a reference source for craftspeople, home owners, or do-it-your-selfers. It is structured in such a way that begin-ners can quickly understand the information in the first chapter and apply it to that found in other parts of the book. And the text is heavily illustrated so that the reader can easily visualize what is being described.

This book can also be used as an answer guide to common woodworking problems. The self-taught woodworker will find information on the "correct" way to do things, with special emphasize given to using equipment and materials safely.

Chapter One, "Project Planning and Material Selection," will help the craftsperson at any level better understand wood as a material and appre-ciate how its properties affect project design.

The second chapter, "Tool Selection and Use," deals with common hand tools and discusses how to select, care for, and use them.

Chapter three, "Handheld Power Tools," describes how and when to use portable power tools in place of hand tools and more expensive stationary power equipment.

The fourth chapter, "Stationary Power Tools," introduces and provides detailed instruction on the safe and effective use of stationary power equipment like the table saw. Information on what to look for when buying this equipment is also provided.

Chapter five, "Step-by-Step Project-Making," instructs the beginner and advanced woodwork-er on how to make a typical project once a plan is in hand. This chapter can help the woodwork-er select and use tools more wisely when actual-ly making a project.

Chapter six, "Furniture and Carcass Con-struction," discusses how larger and more com-plicated projects like cabinets and other furni-ture are handled. Hardware, non-wood materi-als and cabinet joinery are discussed. This part of the book describes to the reader how to apply much of the information given in other parts of the book.

The last chapter, "Finishing Techniques," describes a variety of finishes for the woodwork-er to select from. Many easy-to-apply and rela-tively "foolproof" finishing materials are dis-cussed. Detailed how-to-do-it information and a step-by-step approach to finishing are provided. The emphasis is on simple systematic finishing procedures.

1

PROJECT PLANNING & MATERIAL SELECTION

■ ■ ■ ■ ■ ■ ■ ■ ■ ■ ■ ■ ■ ■

DECIDING ON A PROJECT DESIGN

Many people are attracted to woodworking because they expect to get great satisfaction from the experience of creating a "project." This anticipation can cause the craftsperson to rush through the hard work of finding or creating a good design for the project. Furniture styles that have remained popular over the years are usually considered good designs. They have a certain universal visual appeal that many people find pleasing. Often, a well-constructed piece made by an obviously skilled woodworker doesn't look quite "right" and many poorly designed pieces can't be categorized as colonial, modern, etc., because they don't fit into any category (1–1).

Commercial furniture manufacturers often produce basic pieces, like dressers, in several identifiable styles, even though the dimensions of the basic forms are the same. They attempt to stylize the pieces by varying finishes, hardware,

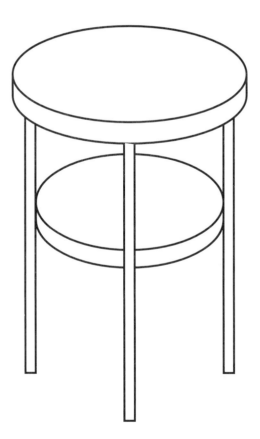

■ *1–1. This poorly designed table has no recognizable style.*

and trimming. Even though some of this work does not represent quality construction, it can be recognized as belonging to a category such as Modern or Early American. Many woodworker-designed pieces don't appear to fit into any recognizable style group.

Since almost any project requires a considerable investment in time and materials, the effort spent in designing or selecting a design is well spent. Adapting an existing design is often a good route for the inexperienced designer to follow.

The first and most important step for the woodworker is to create or find a design that will meet his or her functional and aesthetic requirements. In other words, if a file cabinet is required, it should hold standard-size file folders and allow easy access to them. If the cabinet is to be placed in an office with a contemporary look, it should fit in visually. Perhaps it will have clean lines with little or no added decoration.

The search for a good design should include looking at work that is recognized as being well designed. Magazines devoted to woodworking design or interior decoration can be good sources of information. Shops that sell handmade or "high-end" contemporary furniture are worth visiting. Dimensioned furniture plans are available. If these plans defy assignment to a style category, keep searching.

How can an effective design be identified? First, and most important, the viewer should like the piece. The shape or form of the work helps to generate this feeling. Also, the piece should be functionally sound. For example, a chair must provide both comfort and support.

Some designers feel that form should follow function. In simple terms, this means that a chair should look like a device that is designed to support a human being of average size and shape.

BASIC ELEMENTS OF DESIGN

Effective designs are not produced by using a recipe or formula. Understanding some of the basic elements of design can help to produce a better design.

Balance is one of these elements. The piece in 1–2 illustrates symmetrical balance. If this illustration is divided into two equal parts by a vertical line, each half will be the mirror image of the other. One reason why symmetrical designs are appealing is that they are so common in nature. Regular geometric shapes like squares and circles are also symmetrical. But though symmetrical forms are "safe," they are often considered to be visually boring.

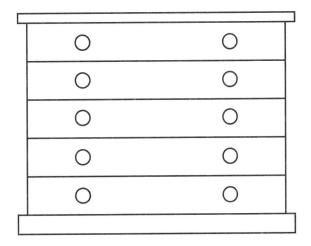

■ *1–2. A chest that was symmetrically designed.*

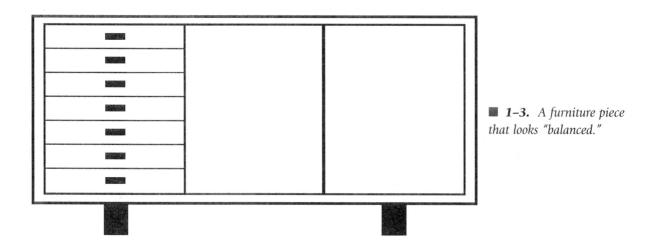

■ *1–3.* *A furniture piece that looks "balanced."*

Asymmetrical or *informal balance* is an alternative that can result in more visually interesting designs. If the project in 1–3 were to be divided in half vertically, the result would be two halves that were not balanced. This piece, however, still *looks* balanced. That is because the forms and shapes on the left appear to equal those on the right in visual weight and interest. Hanging a group of dissimilar pictures in a grouping on a wall is a good example of this process.

When considering designs suitable for use as woodworking projects, we are really dealing with three-dimensional forms that have volume. This concept is especially important in analyzing more complex pieces that are made up of many parts. A bench with a thick top supported by very thin legs might appear top-heavy, with its top being out of proportion to its base. The examination of commercial pieces that are similar to the design being considered can often be helpful in determining good proportion. Many designers construct full-sized mockups of proposed pieces using cardboard or other easily fabricated materials.

All but the simplest designs are made up of several parts that are brought together to form a whole. In an effective design, these parts must "harmonize," or go well together. The piece in 1–4 is a table with round legs, curved rails, and circular decorations. These curved components go well together visually.

Designers can use contrasting shapes, colors, and forms to call attention to or emphasize a particular area. A white circular draw pull on a dark cabinet drawer is an example of this technique.

Up to this point, the main focus of the discussion has been on visual/aesthetic qualities of design. Now let's consider the functional prop-

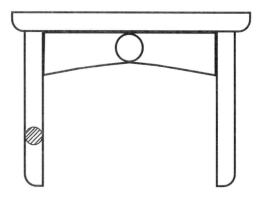

■ *1–4.* *The round legs, curved rails, and circular decorations on this table go well together visually.*

erties of a design that help to make the piece "user friendly." One very helpful first step in designing a functional piece is to identify how the piece will be used. For example, identifying a piece as a coffee table rather than simply as a table helps the designer to focus more effectively on its size. A coffee table is usually used in conjunction with a sofa. The dimensions of the coffee table should be related to the sofa it will be used with. It shouldn't be longer than the sofa or much higher than the sofa cushions (1–5). The height of a table to be used next to a sofa could be determined by considering the

table's function. In 1–6, the table supports a lamp in a way that makes it useful for reading. The table could also serve as a place for a drink or snack. If this table were to be constructed of wood, the finish and material used on the tabletop would be taken into account in its design. For example, plastic laminate might be used to protect the tabletop.

Once the proportions and general form of the design have been established, the *style* of the piece should be considered. A modern or contemporary style is usually characterized by straight lines and simple geometric forms, as

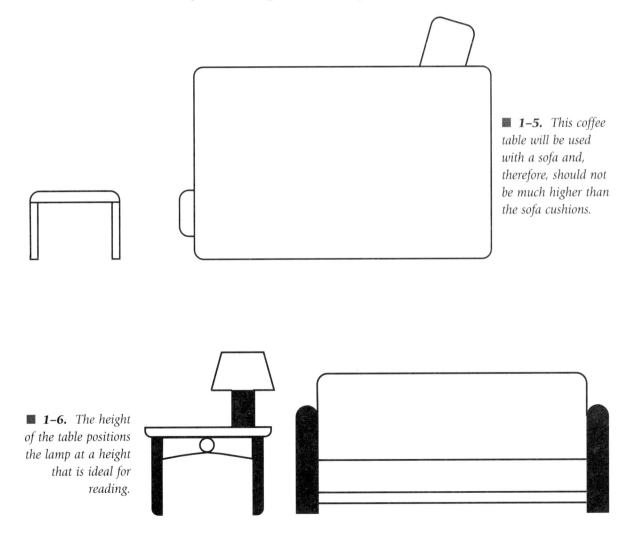

■ *1–5. This coffee table will be used with a sofa and, therefore, should not be much higher than the sofa cushions.*

■ *1–6. The height of the table positions the lamp at a height that is ideal for reading.*

shown in 1–7. An Early American piece might have turned parts and curved elements (1–8).

If the designer is working from a set of dimensioned drawings, much of the design work has already been done. However, minor changes can be made on tracing paper placed over the existing drawing. If a dimensioned drawing is not available, one should be made. For a simple piece, a full-sized drawing made on graph paper will suffice (1–9). If a dimensioned scale drawing is being used, consideration should be given

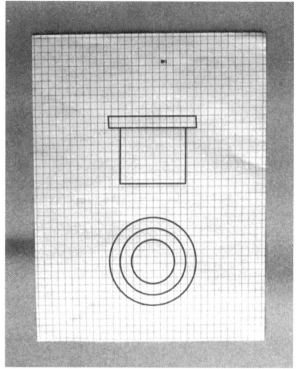

■ *1–9. A full-sized drawing on graph paper.*

■ *1–7. The prevalent characteristics of modern furniture are straight lines and simple form.*

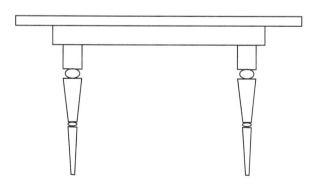

■ *1–8. This Early American table has turned parts and curved elements.*

to make a full-sized version of the drawing. A full-sized drawing can be used to advantage in laying out the actual parts of the piece. Measurements can be "picked off" the full-sized drawing using dividers, as shown in 1–10. This saves time and helps to reduce measuring errors.

Though drawings should be as detailed as possible, some design decisions can be postponed until part of the project is completed. The shape of a tabletop, for example, can be experimented with once the leg-rail system is complete. Cardboard mockup tops can be tried out on the legs, as shown in 1–11.

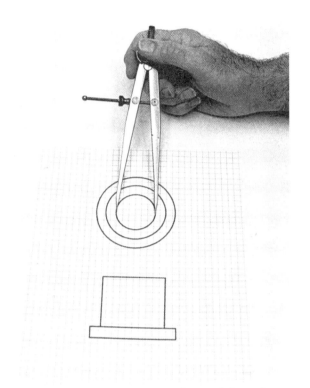

■ *1-10.* *Copying measurements from a full-sized drawing using dividers.*

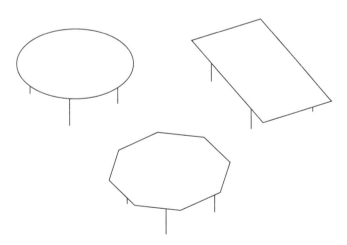

■ *1-11.* *Tabletop mockups on table legs help the designer determine the shape of the top.*

WOOD: THE MATERIAL OF CHOICE

Woodworkers generally don't think very much about why the material they choose to work with is so popular. Wood has been widely used for thousands of years and is often the material of choice today in spite of the availability of metals and synthetic materials. The popularity of wood is largely due to two facts: It is widely available, and it is relatively easy to work with.

Among all commonly used materials, wood is the only one that is renewable. All other materials, such as metals, plastics, and ceramics, are available in finite quantities. Wood can be grown and harvested like any other crop.

Wood is relatively easy to shape. Shaping is accomplished using commonly available tools and equipment. Pieces can be assembled and fastened using joinery, glue, and simple hardware.

Woods that are most suitable for woodworking are dimensionally stable. Unlike metals, they don't shrink or expand very much when heated or cooled. Wood is composed of cells shaped like tiny soda straws (1-12). These straw-like cells swell when they absorb moisture and

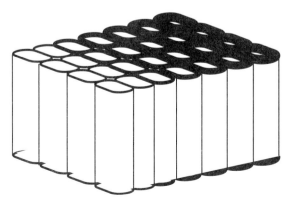

■ *1-12.* *Wood cells.*

shrink when they dry out. This swelling and shrinking affects the diameter or thickness of the cells much more than their length. This is the reason why wood expands and contracts much more across the grain, from edge to edge, than it does with the grain, from end to end (1–13). Though individual species vary, it is common to allow ⅛ of an inch per foot of width for expansion and contraction in solid-wood fabrication.

If the most important characteristics of wood to a woodworker are that it is readily available, easy to shape, and dimensionally stable, *durability* concerns the consumer. Under ideal conditions, wood that is protected from excessive moisture, strong sunlight, and insects can last for thousands of years. Pieces of furniture discovered in burial vaults in the Near East have been found in near-perfect condition. Among the reasons for the durability of wood is its resistance to oxidation or corrosion.

Even though wood is used as a fuel, pieces with large cross sections do not burn rapidly. Thick logs, for example, can take many hours to burn in a fireplace. Wood heated to about 550 degrees F. decomposes at about 0.03 inches per hour. While this is happening, charcoal is formed. Charcoal tends to act as an insulator. Unprotected metal beams, by comparison, transmit heat rapidly and sag (1–14), and this can quickly lead to structural collapse. The relatively low heat conductivity of wood makes it fire resistant and helps to conserve

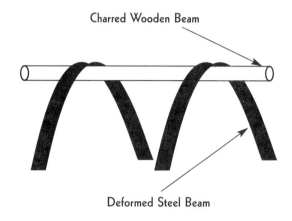

Charred Wooden Beam

Deformed Steel Beam

■ *1–14. In a fire, wooden members resist collapse longer than metal beams.*

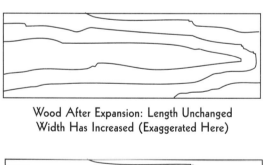

Wood After Expansion: Length Unchanged
Width Has Increased (Exaggerated Here)

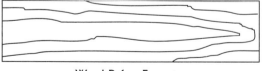

Wood Before Expansion

■ *1–13. Wood expands much more across the grain (from end to end) than with the grain.*

energy in wooden structures. By comparison, brick loses heat six times faster than wood, glass eight times faster, concrete 15 times faster, steel 390 times faster, and aluminum 1,700 times faster. This quality also makes wood comfortable to sit on and to touch.

In structural applications wood has other advantages. Its ability to flex under impact allows a wooden structure to momentarily support a load twice as heavy as it was designed for. Structures made of steel or concrete have little or no ability to support loads greater than their design strength under momentary impact.

Wood is a sound choice from an ecological point of view. The only energy necessary to produce it is sunlight. Materials like steel or concrete require large amounts of heat energy in their production. Most of this comes from the burning of fossil fuels, such as gas or oil. These pour carbon and sulfur oxides into the atmosphere, leading to air pollution. Wood is also biodegradable and, unlike many other materials, does not have to be deposited in the limited landfill space available.

Though wood seems to be a very solid, it is actually made up of hollow, straw-like cells, as shown in 1–15. In the growing part of the tree— the *sapwood*—some of the cells act as tiny pipes that allow sap and other liquids to travel from the tree roots to the leaves. Other cells, the *vessels*, provide support for the tree. In conifers such as fir and pine, a third type of cell, *tracheids*, conducts sap and provides support. Woods like pine and fir that contain these long tracheid cells are widely used for papermaking.

Trees grow by adding a layer of new wood under the bark each year. The sticky *cambium* layer is located under the bark of the tree. The wood on the outside of the trunk makes up the

sap-conducting area of the tree and is known as the *sapwood*. Each year the new layer of wood forms an *annual ring*. These rings are visible at the end of a log or on the surface of a tree stump (1–16).

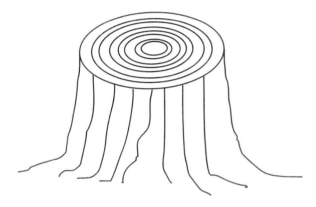

■ **1–16.** *Annual rings on a tree stump.*

With continued growth, the tree trunk increases in diameter, and the center portion of the tree, the *heartwood*, stops conducting sap and water and serves as an internal support to the tree. Heartwood changes chemically; it usually becomes darker than the sapwood. This color difference is very apparent in American walnut, where the heartwood is dark brown while the sapwood is almost white.

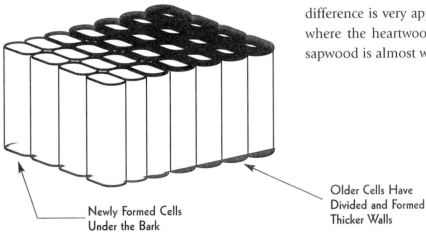

Newly Formed Cells
Under the Bark

Older Cells Have
Divided and Formed
Thicker Walls

■ **1–15.** *A look at the hollow, straw-like cells that comprise wood.*

Another example of color contrast in wood can been seen in woods like fir, where the grain pattern is very pronounced (1–17). The light portion of the wood is formed in the spring, when water is abundant and growth is rapid. This *springwood*, or *earlywood*, is softer than the darker, harder wood formed later in the year when growing conditions are not as favorable. The denser dark wood is known as *latewood*.

■ *1–17.* *Fir has a very pronounced grain pattern.*

■ *1–18.* *This pinecone is from a coniferous tree.*

Softwoods and hardwoods are the two principal types of wood available to the woodworker. Though most hardwoods are relatively hard and most softwoods are relatively soft, these names are used to identify the type of tree the wood comes from. Softwoods, like pine, redwood, and fir, come from trees that have needle-like leaves. They produce seeds in cones and are know as *coniferous* (cone-bearing) trees (1–18). Hardwoods, on the other hand, have broad leaves and produce seeds from true flowers that are enclosed in pods (1–19), like those of the locust tree. These trees are known as *deciduous* trees.

Grain is one of the most visible features of wood. Fir, as shown in 1–17, has characteristic dark, wavy lines typical of relatively fast-growing wood. Grain becomes visible when a log is sawed into boards (1–20). Aesthetically, grain is one of the properties of wood that makes it an attractive material.

■ *1–19.* *Leaves and seeds produced from a hardwood tree.*

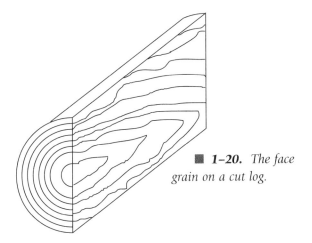

■ *1–20.* *The face grain on a cut log.*

carry weight. The straight-grained piece shown in 1–23 is the best choice for use as a stool rail, which often serves as a footrest.

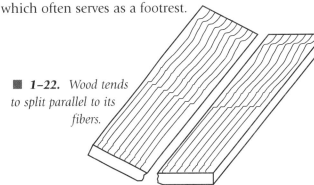

■ *1–22.* *Wood tends to split parallel to its fibers.*

Grain has to be considered when selecting tools for a specific task. The type of saw chosen depends on whether it will be used to make rip cuts—cuts with the grain—or crosscuts—cuts across the grain (1–21). Grain direction can be determined by inspection and/or test cutting. Cutting with the grain generally produces the smoothest cut.

Wood failure is also related to grain direction. Since wood is made up of bundled fibers, it tends to split parallel to these fibers (1–22). Grain orientation also affects wood's ability to

Will Support Light Load

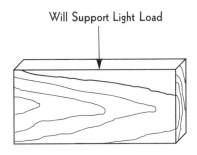

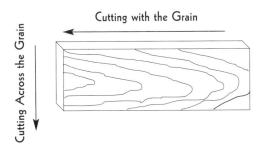

■ *1–21.* *Rip cuts are cuts made with the grain. Crosscuts are cuts made across the grain.*

Will Support Heavier Load

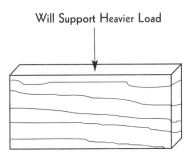

■ *1–23.* *The orientation of wood's grain affects its ability to sustain heavy loads.*

In an ideal world, all of the material used by woodworkers would be defect-free. Any abnormality that makes the wood less desirable aesthetically or functionally is a defect. Defects can affect wood strength and workability. The most common growth or natural defect is the knot (1–24). Knots are formed when branches develop on a tree trunk. The sections of the branch that were alive when the trunk formed around them are sound or interwoven knots. The parts of the branch that were dead as the tree trunk continued to grow around them are loose knots.

Loose knots leave holes that weaken the surrounding area. This weakened wood can fail when a load is applied to it. Tight or interwoven knots are less of a failure threat.

Knots are harder and contain more sap than does the surrounding wood. They also cause grain irregularities. Knots can interfere with cutting and finishing operations such as sanding and staining.

Seasoning defects are the result of the seasoning process. These defects develop during the drying of green or newly harvested wood. Wood in freshly cut trees contains a large amount of water. For most purposes, the level of moisture in the wood must be reduced before the wood can be used. This is accomplished by air-drying after the logs have been cut into boards and stacked. Additional drying in a drying kiln can bring the level of water in the wood down to 12 percent or lower.

During drying, the straw-like wood cells shrink as they loose water (1–25). The cells shrink in width much more than they do in length. Even after seasoning, wood can shrink or

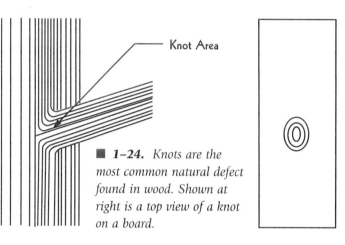

■ *1–24.* Knots are the most common natural defect found in wood. Shown at right is a top view of a knot on a board.

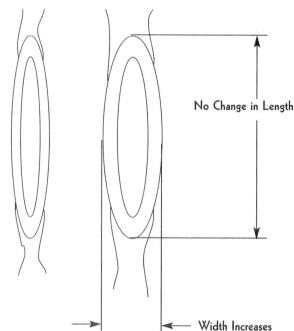

■ *1–25.* This enlarged view of wood cells shows that their width shrinks more drastically than their length when they loose water.

expand as much as ⅛ inch per foot across the grain. Woodworkers must allow for this shrinkage when designing and fabricating pieces.

Warping often develops as wood dries. The most common type is cup warp. As the long cells along the curved annual rings of the board shrink, the board curves up, as shown in 1–26.

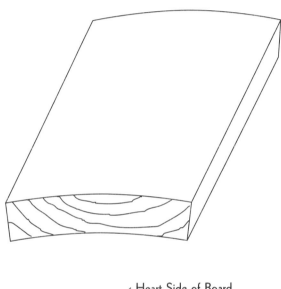

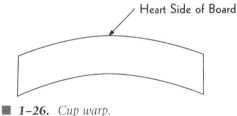

Heart Side of Board

■ *1–26.* *Cup warp.*

Crooking (1–27) is another form of warping. The board remains relatively flat but it curves along its edges.

Bowing (1–28) is a type of warping that produces a board with a curved face that resembles a chair rocker.

Winding or *twisting* can develop during drying. This gives the piece a propeller-like shape.

When purchasing wood, the buyer should select the most defect-free material he or she can afford. Most defects result in a significant increase in processing time and reduce the percentage of the material that is usable.

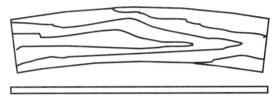

■ *1–27.* *Crooking is a form of warping in which the board remains flat but curves along its edges.*

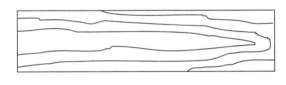

■ *1–28.* *When a board undergoes bowing, its face curves.*

LUMBER-BUYING GUIDELINES

Once the seasoning process is complete, the wood is cut and shaped into the familiar material available at the lumber dealer. *Hardwood lumber* such as maple and oak is rough-sawed into one-inch-thick boards. Craftspeople who use a large volume of wood often buy hardwood lumber in this rough, unsurfaced condition. Surfaced material is usually the only kind of hardwood available to the low-quantity buyer. This material has been surfaced and cut to standard sizes.

Softwood lumber such as pine and fir is usually available in lengths beginning with six feet and increasing in two-foot increments to 12 or 18 feet. Various thicknesses and widths are available. Thickness and width dimensions are usually given in nominal form. A two-by-four is actually 1½ by 3½ inches. The actual dimensions can be found by subtracting a half an inch from the nominal dimensions.

In addition to the standard-sized material described above, a large variety of moldings, casings, and other shaped products are available in both hard and softwoods. These shaped products are known as *worked lumber* (1–29).

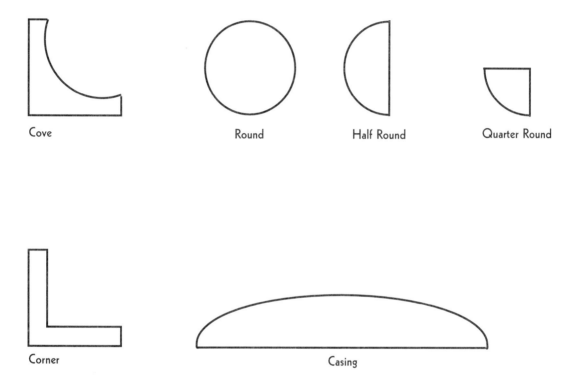

Cove   Round   Half Round   Quarter Round

Corner   Casing

■ *1–29. Moldings and casings are examples of worked lumber.*

Lumber grades such as *select* or *common* are often mentioned in lumber advertisements. These terms are used in grading lumber so that the consumer will have a clearer understanding of the quality of the material being bought.

In softwood grading, the term "select" is used to describe material of the highest quality. Very few defects are permitted in this most expensive grade of lumber. Further down in the select category are the grades B and better, C, and D. Each of these grades allows additional minor defects in the material. All of the select grades are suitable for quality work such as furniture-making.

Numbers 1 and 2 common represent the next-lower step in the grading scale. Additional defects are permitted in these grades. For example, a minimum of two-thirds of the number-1 material must be clear (knot-free), while only half of the material in the number-2 grade has to be clear.

Common is the lowest grade in the softwood system. Many more defects, including larger knots and checks, are permitted. In the common category, five subgrades are included, numbered 1 to 5. One is the highest common grade and 5 is the lowest.

Hardwoods are graded under a system established by the American Hardwood Lumber Association. In this system, the best material is graded as firsts and seconds, commonly referred to as FAS. This material will be at least 83 percent clear, that is, free of all but the most minor defects. Minimum width and length standards also apply.

The next-lowest category is *select*. More defects are permitted here than in the firsts and seconds category, and minimum length and width dimensions are lower.

Dealers often quote lumber prices in terms of board feet. A *board foot* is a piece that is one inch thick, 12 inches wide, and one foot in length. This is actually ¹⁄₁₂ of a cubic foot of material (1–30). The following formula can be used to calculate board feet:

THICKNESS IN INCHES × WIDTH IN INCHES × LENGTH IN FEET

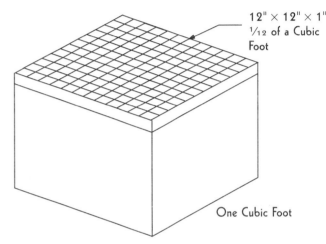

■ 1–30. *A board foot.*

Lumber dealers who permit the buyer to select the material being purchased are preferable to those who do not permit inspection. The material selected should look clean and be free of stains or obvious mold growth. This helps to ensure that the material has been stored correctly. Following are some examination procedures:

1. Check for straightness by holding individual pieces up to the eye for sighting. Badly curved pieces should be rejected.

2. Check the piece for flatness from edge to edge. Cup warp, especially in relatively wide pieces, is not desirable.

3. Pieces that feel unusually heavy for their size may contain an excess amount of sap or pitch. This will make finishing more difficult.

4. If the material is to be finished with a transparent finish like lacquer, it should be as blemish-free as possible. In applications where an opaque finish-like paint is to be used, pieces made up of smaller units jointed together may be acceptable (1–31).

■ *1–31. This finger-jointed board can accept an opaque paint finish.*

PLYWOOD, HARDBOARD, AND OTHER SHEET STOCK

When oversized material is required, plywood becomes an option. Plywood is made by gluing layers or plies of wood together in a sandwich-like fashion. The grain in each layer of wood runs at right angles to the layers above and below it (1–32). This type of assembly allows large sheets to be produced. The alternate grain direction of the plies makes the material dimensionally stable. It will not expand or contract as much as solid wood of similar dimensions would. Among the negative characteristics of plywood are its unsightly edges and its reduced ability to hold screws and nails driven into its edges.

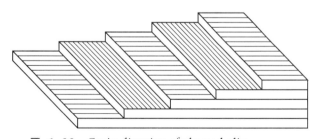

■ *1–32. Grain direction of plywood plies.*

Plywood is most commonly available in sheets measuring four feet wide and eight feet long. The thicknesses available are ¼, ⅜, ½, ⅝, and ¾ inch.

Plywood is available with one side covered with a hardwood veneer such as cherry or maple. This material is often used in cabinet construction and wall paneling.

The outer layers of the plywood are usually assigned one of the letter grades: A, B, C, or D. The A grade allows the fewest defects, while D grade allows the most. An A surface can be finished with a transparent coating; C-and D-grade plywood is usually used in applications where it is covered.

A panel stamped CDX indicates that one face is covered with C- grade material, the other face covered with D-grade material, and that a glue suitable for exterior (X) applications has been used in the assembly (1–33).

■ *1–33. Plywood designation stamp.*

Softwood plywood is made of woods such as fir. When waterproof glue is used to adhere the plies, it is known as exterior plywood. Otherwise, it is designated as interior grade.

Hardwood plywood is usually made of a wood such as birch and is graded with the numbers 1 through 4. Number-1 grade is the best quality, while the number-4 grade is least desirable. Hardwood plywood can often be identified by the uniformity and relative thinness of its layers (1–34).

■ 1–35. *Hardboard (bottom) and particleboard shown for contrast.*

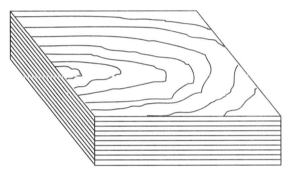

■ 1–34. *Hardwood plywood has uniform, relatively thin layers.*

Another form of hardboard is perforated with holes drilled in a grid pattern on one-inch centers (1–36). This material is often used for tool and equipment panels. A variety of hooks and holders are made to fit into the holes in the board.

Hardboard is a uniformly dark brown material that is made from the waste products of paper-making (1–35). It is often used for cabinet backs and drawer bottoms. Two types are available: standard and the moisture-resistant tempered. Hardboard is most commonly available in 4 × 8-foot sheets. Thicknesses range from ⅛ to 5/16 inch. The most common form of hardboard is smooth on one side and rough on the reverse. The material is somewhat abrasive and tends to dull cutting tools. Hardboard is harder and denser than plywood; carbide-edged tools are recommended for cutting operations. The material is difficult to glue or fasten.

■ 1–36. *Hardboard perforated with holes.*

Particleboard, or *flake board,* is another sheet material manufactured from recycled wood byproducts (1–37). It is available in four by eight-foot sheets ranging in thickness from about ½ to ¾ inch. Most particleboard surfaces are relatively smooth. The standard material is

■ *1–37. Particleboard, also known as flake board.*

■ *1–38. This kitchen cabinet is covered with plastic laminate.*

not water-resistant. When covered with a thin plastic laminate, the material is often used in the manufacture of kitchen cabinets and low-end furniture (1–38). The procedures described for cutting and fastening hardboard can be used when working with flake board.

Oriented strand board (OSB) is a flake-board-like sheet material made of relatively large pieces of wood that have been formed into sheets (1–39). This material is used primarily in building construction because of its rough exterior. It is water-resistant.

Medium-Density Fiberboard (MDF) is another type of sheet material used by woodworkers. This board is sold in sheets like plywood and hardboard, and comes in a variety of thicknesses ranging from ⅛ to 2 inches. Among the principal advantages of this product are its flatness and smoothness. Its flatness makes it desirable

as substrate for veneers. Its smoothness allows it to take an opaque paint finish well. MDF is very dense, and carbide-edged tools are recommended for cutting operations. It does accept glue well, but like hardboard it doesn't fasten well with screws and nails (1–39).

■ *1–39. Top: Oriented Strand Board (OSB). Bottom: Medium-density fiberboard (MSB).*

CHAPTER 2

HAND TOOL SELECTION & USE

■ ■ ■ ■ ■ ■ ■ ■ ■ ■ ■ ■ ■ ■

The typical woodworker has a variety of hand tools available for use in his or her shop. Which of the many tools available in the market are the most essential? How are quality tools selected and cared for? How and when are these hand tools used? These are some of the questions that will be addressed in this chapter.

Some inexperienced woodworkers question the value of hand tools when power tools are available. Why have a set of chisels when a router is available? Why own a handsaw when portable circular saws abound?

One way to answer these questions is to look at the tool kit of the professional woodworker. These woodworkers usually have a large assortment of hand tools available. The reason for this is that in many situations a hand-powered tool is the best tool for the job. In the hands of an experienced user, hand tools offer a high degree of control and precision. These tools are also easily taken to the job site. A door that needs a bit of trimming can't be easily brought to a jointer in a shop. A hand plane can be brought to the work. Many portable power tools require an electrical outlet for use. Hand tools don't.

The tools considered in this chapter will be those that are most commonly used by wood-workers. (Highly specialized tools will not be discussed.) Not all of the tools discussed are essential. Each woodworker should make his or her selections based on experience, need, and resources. Used tools are often viable options to new ones. A well-maintained 50-year-old plane is often made of materials that are superior to those being used today. Many communities have used tool dealers who can be sought out as a source of such equipment.

MEASURING TOOLS

Measuring is one of the most common tasks performed by the woodworker. Accurate measurements are essential for a job like making a replacement drawer part. Measurements should be made with as much precision as time allows. In rough carpentry, ⅛-inch tolerances may be acceptable. In cabinetwork, the minimum tolerance should be not more than ¹⁄₁₆ inch. When several identical pieces are required, they can often be cut one after the other, using the same machine setting. In this way, pieces like square frame components will all end up being identical in length and width.

Measuring tapes are commonly used by wood-workers because they are convenient and compact (2–1). Their flexibility allows them to be used in measuring curved surfaces (2–2).

Tapes are available in a variety of lengths, commonly ranging from 6 to 25 feet. Wide tapes are more rigid than narrow ones; this rigidness allows the tape to be extended out to reach distant locations when necessary.

Measuring tapes often highlight all 12- and 16-inch intervals (2–3). Tapes with 16-inch intervals are used in building-construction work, where many of the structural components are spaced at 16-inch on-center intervals.

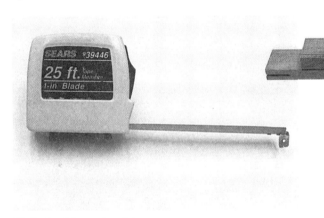

■ *2–1. Measuring tape.*

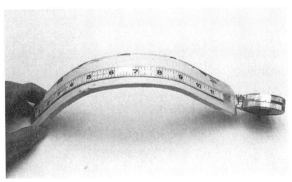

■ *2–2. This measuring tape is being used to measure a curved surface.*

■ *2–3. The 12- and 16-inch intervals on this measuring tape are highlighted.*

Tape hooks must be firmly attached to tape ends. Loose hooks can slide on the tape, giving an inaccurate measurement.

Inside measurements are made by adding the length of the tape case to the tape measurement (2–4). For example, if a measurement is made of an opening and the tape reads " 21¼ inches" and the tape case is 2¾ inches long, the opening is 24 inches wide.

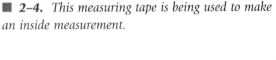

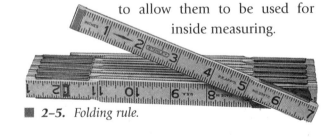

■ *2–4. This measuring tape is being used to make an inside measurement.*

Folding or zigzag rules that are six or eight feet long are often used by carpenters (2–5). Rulers of this type are relatively rigid and can be used for making horizontal measurements without sagging or collapsing. Many folding rules have an extendible section at one or both ends to allow them to be used for inside measuring.

■ *2–5. Folding rule.*

Bench rules, made of wood or metal, are also useful in the shop. These rules are usually manufactured in one-, two-, three-, and four-foot lengths. Markings or calibrations are usually given in sixteenths of an inch on one edge and eighths of an inch on the other. Wooden rules are a good choice for use around machines because they will not damage the machine if they accidentally come into contact with a cutter. In addition to their use in measuring, bench rules can be used to test for flatness (2–6) and in the laying out of straight lines.

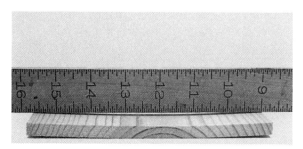

■ **2–6.** *Testing a board's flatness with a folding rule.*

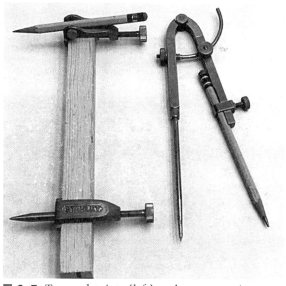

■ **2–7.** *Trammel points (left) and compass points.*

LAYOUT TOOLS

Compasses are used to lay out circles and circle segments. Large circles can be drawn using *trammel points* (2–7). One of the trammels has a removable point. This trammel is fitted with a screw that can be used to hold a pencil in place of the metal point.

Squares are simple tools that consist of a handle and calibrated blade set at 90 degrees to each other (2–8). Try squares are used to test surfaces to determine whether or not adjacent surfaces form a right, or 90-degree, angle. They are also used to draw lines at right angles to surfaces.

When adjacent surfaces form a 90-degree, or right, angle they are said to be square to each other. This concept is important to the woodworker because most project parts are assembled so that they are square to each other (2–9). A square is used to test these surfaces to make sure they form a 90-degree angle.

■ **2–8.** *Try square.*

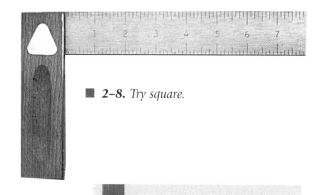

■ **2–9.** *Checking the squareness of two pieces with a try square.*

Combination squares are used to perform a variety of testing, layout, and measuring operations (2–10). Though these tools were originally designed as metalworker's tools, they are widely used by woodworkers.

■ *2–10.* *The combination square has many uses, ranging from testing the flatness of the board to laying out parallel lines.*

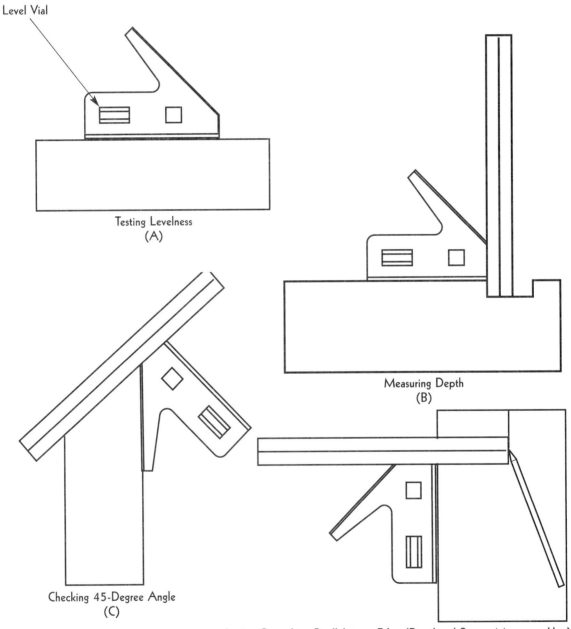

Level Vial

Testing Levelness
(A)

Measuring Depth
(B)

Checking 45-Degree Angle
(C)

Laying Out a Line Parallel to an Edge (Pencil and Square Move as a Unit)
(D)

Triangular squares (2–11) are also used by woodworkers. This tool can be used in place of the try square. It has additional calibrations that are used in house-framing layouts.

■ *2–11. Triangular square.*

T—bevels, or bevel squares (2–12), are an adjustable version of the try square. This tool is used in much the same way a try square is. The angle formed by the handle and blade is variable. It can be set by adjusting the tool to fit an existing pair of surfaces or by using a protractor.

■ *2–12. T-bevel.*

Spirit levels (2–13) are used to test surfaces for levelness or plumbness. The principle involved with these tools is that a level surface is one that is parallel to the horizon or parallel to the surface of a liquid at rest. Spirit levels contain glass vials filled with an alcohol–water solution. When a bubble in the vial comes to rest between the two indicator lines on the vial, the surface being tested is level.

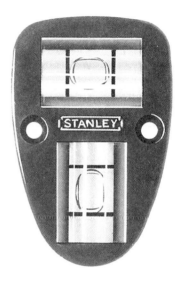

■ *2–13. Spirit levels. When the bubble on the level's vial rests between the two indicator lines on the vial, the surface that is being tested is level.*

Spirit levels are used to install fixed objects such as wall shelves. They are also used to test surfaces to determine whether they are level or plumb. A surface is *plumb* or *vertical* when it is at right angles to a level surface (2–14).

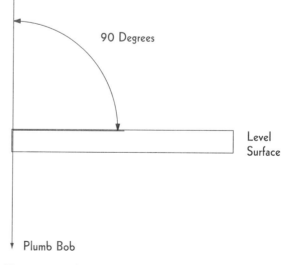

■ *2–14. A plumb surface is square to a level surface.*

Calipers are used for indirect measuring. After the calipers have be adjusted to fit an object, the distance from one leg to another is measured with a rule (2–15). Outside calipers can be used to measure the diameters of round objects (2–16). This measuring tool is frequently used during wood turning to measure the diameters of work being turned on the wood lathe. Inside calipers (2–17) are used to make internal measurements. In wood turning, inside calipers are used to measure the diameter of the hollowed-out area of a bowl.

Protractors are used to measure and lay out angles. The tool shown in 2–18 has an adjustable leg that can be used to lay out angles. Protractors can also be used to measure existing angles.

Up to this point, the focus has been on layout tools, which are used to prepare wood for processing with cutting tools. The following section discusses handsaws and knives, the two primary cutting tools.

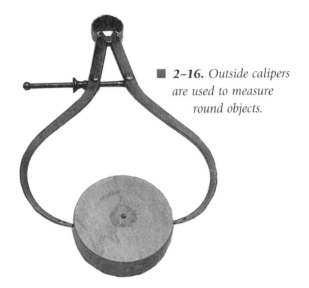

■ *2–16. Outside calipers are used to measure round objects.*

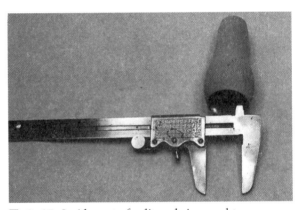

■ *2–17. Inside part of calipers being used to measure a recess.*

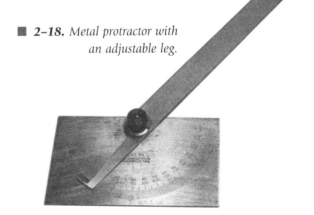

■ *2–18. Metal protractor with an adjustable leg.*

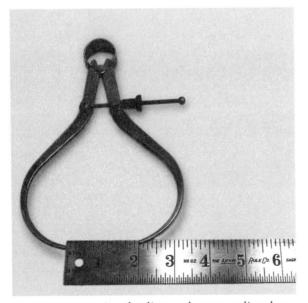

■ *2–15. Measuring the distance between caliper legs.*

HANDSAWS

Handsaws (2–19) consist of a handle of wood or plastic holding a toothed steel blade. The teeth act like a row of tiny chisels or knife points as they cut a path or kerf through the wood.

Crosscut saws are the most common type of handsaw. These saws are designed for cutting across the grain of the workpiece. Crosscut saws have teeth that cut like a row of knife points (2–20, middle).

Ripsaws have teeth that cut like a row of chisels. They are used to cut with the grain (2–20, top).

Crosscut saws can be used for ripping, although they cut more slowly than ripsaws. Ripsaws are not used for crosscutting because they would produce an unacceptably rough surface.

Toolbox saws have teeth with a less traditional shape (2–20, bottom). These saws are fast-cutting and leave a rough-cut surface. Toolbox saws have hardened teeth that allow the saws to be used to cut materials like hardboard and flake board. These hardened teeth help the saw to stay sharp longer. Toolbox saws are used to cut with or across the grain. They are sized to be stored in the typical toolbox.

All handsaws have *set* teeth that are bent alternately from side to side so that the groove or kerf made by the teeth is wider than the blade is thick (2–21). This helps to keep the saw from binding during cutting.

■ *2–19.* Handsaw.

Ripsaw Teeth

Crosscut Saw Teeth

Toolbox Saw Teeth

■ *2–20. At top, a close-up of the teeth on a crosscut saw. At bottom, the teeth on a toolbox saw.*

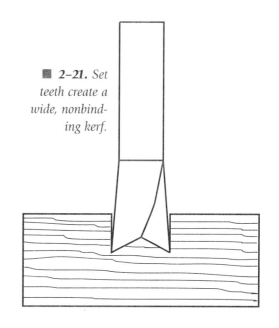

■ *2–21. Set teeth create a wide, nonbinding kerf.*

Using a Handsaw

Follow these step-by-step procedures when using handsaws:

1. Make a layout line to locate the saw cut. Use a try square to draw lines for crosscutting. Approximately ⅛ inch of extra material should be left for smoothing and squaring the cut surface.

2. Secure the workpiece in a vise or clamp it to a bench or other suitable surface.

3. Hold the saw down along your leg, with the leg in a relaxed position. Move your body to the right or left until the saw is in line with the cutting line. This helps to keep the saw from twisting and binding during cutting.

4. Place the saw teeth on the line to be cut. Place the thumb of the free hand down on the work and against the saw blade (2–22). The thumb helps to keep the saw on the layout line. With the thumb in place, pull the saw upward. Repeat this until a starting groove is formed.

5. Remove the thumb from the workpiece before starting any downward sawing.

6. If the saw bends, stop cutting and move it back to the starting position. Take short strokes until the saw begins to move more freely.

7. If the saw begins to stray away from the layout line, bend it slightly in the direction desired. Continue to move the saw up and down while doing this.

8. When approaching the end of the cut, support the piece being cut off to help prevent it from breaking before the cut is complete.

The steps described above apply to ripping and crosscutting. When sawing obliquely, the cut should be made as shown in 2–23, so that any splitting will be limited to the scrap area of the piece being cut.

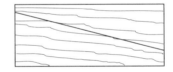

■ *2–23. Making an oblique rip cut.*

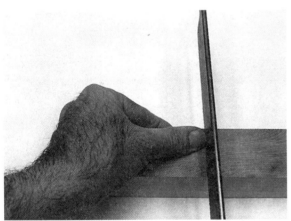

■ *2–22. The position of the thumb when using a handsaw to crosscut.*

BACKSAWS

Backsaws or dovetail saws (2–24) are used for finer and more precise work such as joinery. These saws have thin blades and small teeth. The blades are kept rigid by a metal back. The back limits cut depth to the distance from the back to the teeth. Backsaws are generally used to cut pieces that are three inches or less in width. Starting notches (2–25) and guide blocks (2–26) can be used as aids in controlling the cutting angles and position of the saw.

■ **2–26.** *A guide block, clamped to the workpiece, that will aid when making cuts with a backsaw.*

■ **2–24.** *Backsaw (top) and dovetail saw (bottom).*

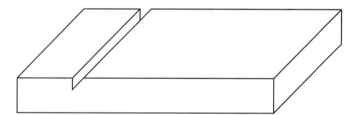

■ **2–25.** *A starting notch can be used to help control the cutting angle and position of a backsaw.*

COPING SAWS

Coping saws (2–27) are used for making curved cuts. The saw blade is held rigid in a frame tensioned by turning the saw handle while the frame is held in a fixed position. The pin-ended blades are usually about six inches long. The blade is installed in the frame with the teeth pointing downward. This helps to keep the

■ **2–27.** *Coping saw.*

blade rigid as the saw is pulled down into the work (2–28). Internal cuts are made by placing the blade in a hole drilled into the area to be removed before assembling the saw (2–29). The saw blade should be square to the work during cutting. Keeping the saw moving up and down during cutting prevents blade binding and allows the saw to follow the curved layout lines.

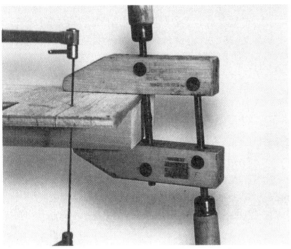

■ *2–28. Vertically cutting a workpiece with a coping saw.*

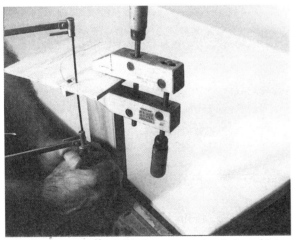

■ *2–29. Coping-saw blade in a starting hole ready to make internal cuts. This is also referred to as pierced work.*

KNIVES

Knives are among the earliest cutting tools invented by man. A knife consists of a steel blade mounted in a handle to improve grip and control. *Utility knives* (2–30) have disposable blades. This helps to ensure that the tool is sharp and ready for use. Knives can be used for a variety of jobs, including cutting layout lines into a workpiece, cutting veneer, and trimming. Fixed and retractable blade models are available.

■ *2–30. Utility knife.*

CHISELS

Chisels are shaping and smoothing tools. Wood chisels can be thought of as a refinement of the knife, having cutting edges on their ends. Chisels are manufactured with several different types of handles.

Socket chisels (2–31, center) have a wooden handle that fits into a recess or socket formed by the upper end of the chisel. This allows the chisel to be used with a mallet.

Chisels with tang-in handles (2 -31, top) have a pointed end or tang that fits into a wooden handle. A leather washer is usually attached to the end of the handle to protect it. A metal ferrule or ring at the other end of the handle helps to keep the handle from splitting. Chisels with tang-in handles are not designed to be used with a mallet.

Chisels with molded-plastic handles (2–31, bottom) have durable plastic handles that allow the chisels to be used with or without a mallet.

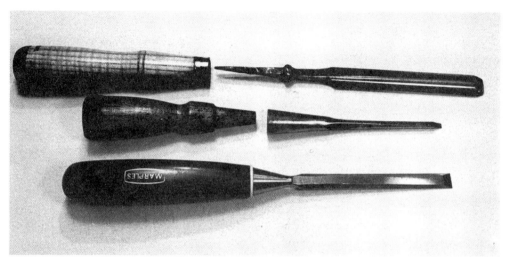

2-31. *A variety of wood chisels. At top is a chisel with a tang-in handle. In the middle is a socket chisel. On the bottom is a chisel with a molded-plastic handle.*

Chisels with different blade designs include the flat *firmer chisel,* the *paring chisel,* and the cup-shaped *gouge.* Firmer chisels are all-purpose cutting tools. These chisels can be used for almost any chiseling job. Paring chisels have beveled edges that help to prevent binding when cutting recesses like mortises or grooves. Gouges are used to scoop material out when cutting recesses in a piece like a bowl.

Even though many chiseling operations can be done with a router, the chisel is often used for trimming in jobs like hinge installation or in locations that are not accessible to a router.

Chisel cutting edges are ground according to use. A 50-degree angle is ground when the chisel is intended for use on hard materials like maple (2–32). A 25-degree angle is used when the tool is to be used on softer materials like pine. The relatively thin 25-degree edge is fragile and can be nicked if the tool is used on hard materials. Though chisels with cutting edges that are ground to 50 degrees are less likely to nick, they do not cut as efficiently as those ground to 25 degrees.

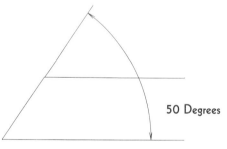

2-32. *A chisel cutting angle of 25 degrees is used when the chisel cuts softer woods. A 50-degree angle is used on harder woods.*

Safety Techniques

These safety techniques should be followed when using chisels:

1. Read and follow the tool manufacturer's safety instructions.
2. Always wear approved eye protection during chiseling.
3. Check chisel sharpness and the condition of the handle before using the chisel.
4. Secure workpieces in a vise or with a clamp whenever possible.
5. Keep both hands on the chisel during chiseling.
6. During cutting, move the chisel in a direction that is away from your body.

Using a Chisel

In rough work, when a lot of material has to be removed quickly, the chisel is used bevel side down as it cuts with the grain of the workpiece (Illus. 2–33).

■ *2–33. Using a chisel bevel-side down to "hog out" a rabbet.*

The cutting is completed using the chisel with its bevel side up. This allows the removal of small amounts of wood with maximum tool control. In 2–34, the vise liner is being used to guide a chisel that is cutting a mortise.

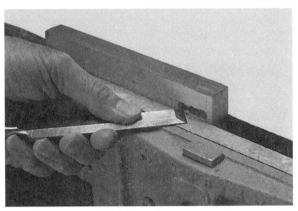

■ *2–34. Using a chisel bevel-side up to trim a mortise. Notice that the vise liner limits the depth of cut.*

Chiseling *across the grain* is necessary for jobs like making dadoes. A dado is a recess that goes across the grain. The first step is to cut knife lines on each side of the recess. The knife cuts are used to guide a dovetail saw, which is used to make cuts on each side of the dado. The saw cuts help to limit splitting during chiseling (2–35). If a shallow recess is being cut, the knife cuts alone can be used to prevent splitting.

Chiseling *end grain* requires the use of a very sharp chisel. The chisel must be moved in a sideways direction to provide a shearing cutting action (2–36). Chiseling end grain can crush the wood fibers. This is especially true when softwoods are being cut. A sharp chisel and shear cutting can help to minimize crushing. Additional information on chisel use can be found in Chapter 6.

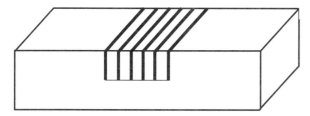

■ *2–35. Saw cuts used to establish dado depth.*

■ *2–36. Vertically cutting end grain with a chisel to form the sides of a dado.*

HAND PLANES

The plane can be thought of as a tool that is used to hold and control a chisel-like blade or iron during cutting. This tool enables the woodworker to better control the blade when cutting than would be possible using the hands alone. The plane represents a refinement of the chisel, just as the chisel represents a refinement of the knife.

The plane is designed to remove a thin shaving each time it travels over the surface. When used and set properly, it produces a smooth and flat surface. The resulting surface is often smoother than one that can be produced by sanding.

Planes are made up of a number of parts (2–37), including a chisel-like cutter called a *plane iron.* The bottom, or *sole,* of the plane is machined flat and true. A slot or *throat* cut through the sole allows the plane iron to project through the bottom of the plane. The plane iron rests on a metal "ramp" called a *frog.* The *adjusting nut* moves the plane iron up or down the frog in order to adjust cut thickness. The *adjusting lever,* attached to the frog, is used to move the plane iron from side to side so that its cutting edge can be set parallel to the sole of the plane.

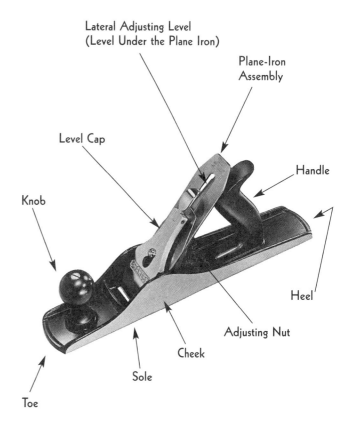

Lateral Adjusting Level
(Level Under the Plane Iron)

Plane-Iron Assembly

Level Cap

Handle

Knob

Heel

Adjusting Nut

Cheek

Sole

Toe

■ *2–37. Plane parts.*

Planes are held, by a right-handed user, with the right hand on the handle and the left hand on the knob (2–38). The hands are reversed for left-handed users. To prevent blade damage, planes are placed on their sides when not in use.

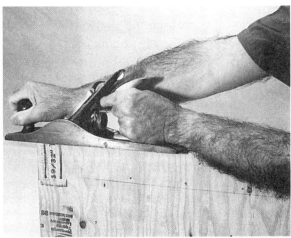

■ **2–38.** *Planing a long surface. Notice the position of the hands. The right hand (of this right-handed operator) is on the handle, and the left is on the knob.*

Planes are made in a variety of lengths. Long surfaces, such as door edges, require the use of a long plane such as the *jointer* (2–39). Jointer planes are about 24 inches long and are held with both hands.

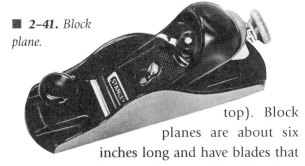

■ **2–39.** *Jointer.*

Long planes remove high spots as they bridge low areas. This results in a straight and flat surface (2–40, bottom).

Short planes, such as the *block plane* (2–41), can't be used to flatten long surfaces because they tend to follow surface irregularities (2–40,

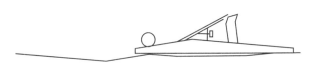

■ **2–40.** *Straight, flat surface being produced by a long hand plane.*

■ **2–41.** *Block plane.*

top). Block planes are about six inches long and have blades that are set at about 20 degrees to the sole or bottom of the place. They are usually held with one hand, and are primarily used for smoothing ends, short edges, and curved surfaces.

Jack planes (2–42) are the most commonly used planes. This tool is about 14 inches long and two inches wide. It is an all-purpose tool that can be used in place of a variety of longer or shorter planes.

■ **2–42.** *Jack plane.*

Using a Plane

PRE-USE PROCEDURE

The first step in using a plane is to check the position of the cap by removing the plane-iron assembly (the plane iron and cap) from the plane. This is done by lifting the cam on the lever cap. (Refer to 2–37.) The end of the cap must be about ⅟₁₆ inch from the cutting edge of the plane iron (2–43). Loosening the cap screw allows the cap to be adjusted. The cap stiffens the plane iron and helps to control wood splitting.

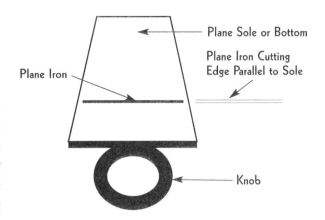

■ *2–44. The blade on this plane has been set parallel to the bottom of the plane.*

■ *2–43. The iron cap on a plane must be approximately ⅟₁₆ inch from the iron's cutting edge.*

The second step is to check the condition of the plane iron's cutting edge. It must be razor-sharp and nick—or chip-free. Nicks produce ridges on planed surfaces. A dull plane will not cut smoothly and encourages the user to adjust the plane for a heavy cut. This can result in the throat of the plane becoming clogged.

Once the plane-iron assembly is back in place, the plane iron's cutting edge is checked to see that it is parallel to the plane bottom or sole (2–44). The lateral adjusting lever is used for this adjustment. The adjusting nut is used to set the plane iron for a *very light* cut.

■ *2–45. When you are planing an edge or other long surface, pressure should be exerted on the knob at the start of a cut.*

EDGE-PLANING TECHNIQUES

Follow these step-by-step procedures when edge-planing an edge or other long surface:

1. Secure the workpiece so that it will not move during planing. A bench vise should be used whenever possible.
2. Place the toe of the plane on the edge to be planed (2–45). Apply maximum pressure to the plane knob with the left hand. Push the plane forward with the right hand, which should be on the handle of the plane. *Do not apply downward pressure to the handle until it is over the workpiece.*

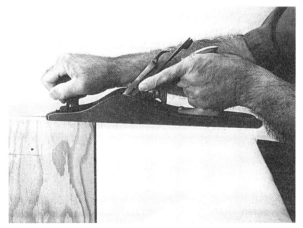

3. When the front of the plane reaches the end of the piece, reduce pressure on the knob.

This procedure will result in an even or uniformly thick cut. The shaving produced should be onionskin thick. This requires a sharp blade and uniform downward pressure on the plane. With practice, this method of cutting will become automatic and natural. The cut surface should be very smooth. If the surface appears to be rough, the direction of planing should be reversed.

The straightness of a planed edge should be tested with a rule. In 2–46, the center area touching the rule is high. This high area should be marked with a soft pencil and planed until it is flat. Frequent checking with the rule is recommended. When the rule and the surface make continuous contact, the edge is straight.

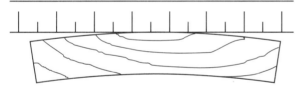

■ *2–46. Testing the straightness of a planed edge. The center area of the board shown here is high, so it will be marked with a soft pencil and planed until it is flat.*

The squareness of a planed edge to the face of a piece is checked with a try square (2–47). An edge is square to a face when the corner made by the edge and the face form a 90-degree angle. A try square placed on a square corner will not allow any light to show under its blade. The handle of the try square must be held firmly against the face of the workpiece during testing. The try square is moved from one end of the piece to the other. High spots are indicated by areas of con-

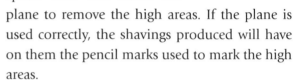

■ *2–47. Checking the squareness of a planed edge with a try square.*

tact between the blade of the square and the edge of the workpiece. These high spots are marked with a pencil.

During planing, the plane is tilted slightly in the direction of the marked high spots. This will cause the plane to remove the high areas. If the plane is used correctly, the shavings produced will have on them the pencil marks used to mark the high areas.

The squaring process should be carried out slowly and methodically, with frequent testing with a try square. The object is to square the edge by removing as little wood as possible.

Ends cut with a backsaw or table saw are often smooth and square enough to use without any additional processing. The ends of wide pieces and those cut with handsaws often require smoothing and squaring. Block planes are suitable for use on most ends. Longer planes can be substituted when longer ends are being processed.

Follow these step-by-step procedures when planing the ends of stock:

1. Check the end for squareness with a try square. Mark high areas with a soft pencil.

2. Secure the workpiece by placing it in a vise.

3. Move the plane from the edges of the piece

to the center (2–48). Maximum pressure must be applied to the plane during cutting. Ends must be checked for squareness to faces and edges.

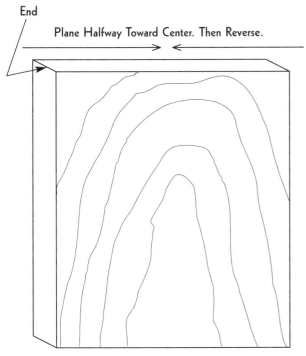

■ *2–48. End-planing technique involves planing from both edges.*

Smoothing Convex Surfaces

Convex, or "positive," curved surfaces like those found on bowls or model boat hulls can be smoothed with a block plane (2–49). Smoothing concave, or "negative," curved surfaces with a block plane can be done as long as the curve is not too deep.

Very deep concave surfaces can be smoothed with a spokeshave (2–50). The spokeshave is a plane that has a very short sole or bottom. This allows the plane's blade to remain in contact with the wood in deeply curved surfaces.

The spokeshave is held with two hands. The thumbs are placed against the rests on each side of the cutter. The cutter is adjusted by turning the knurled nuts on each side of the blade.

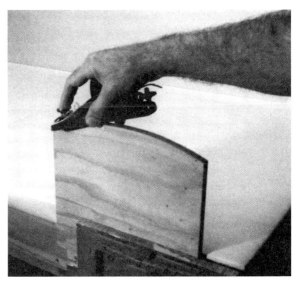

■ *2–49. Smoothing a convex surface with a block plane.*

■ *2–50. Spokeshave.*

Scrapers and Other Smoothing Tools

Hand scrapers (2–51) are simple handheld tools that are used to smooth wood surfaces. Scrapers are useful in smoothing surfaces that cannot be smoothed easily by planing. They can also be used to scrape away glue residue. Eye protection should be worn when scraping glue residue to guard against injury from flying glue chips.

Swan scrapers are used for concave surfaces. A burr, formed during grinding, provides the sharp edge that allows scrapers to remove material. After grinding, the burr is set, or bent, using a burnishing tool (2–52).

Files are also used for smoothing and shaping wood. A file is made by cutting ridges into the surface of a steel bar (2–53). Files produce a somewhat rough, shredded surface. Therefore, they are useful in smoothing and shaping when a high degree of smoothness is not required. Cabinet files are specifically designed for woodworking.

One end of the file is usually shaped into a narrow pointed tang. Handles are slipped onto this tang to provide an improved grip and to prevent hand injury. *Files should never be used without a handle.*

Half-round files are all-purpose tools that are popular with woodworkers. The flat side of the file is used to file flat and convex surfaces, and the round side is used to file concave surfaces.

Rat-tail files have a circular cross-sectional shape and are used to smooth and shape small concave curves like those produced by a coping saw.

Metal-working files can be used on wood, although they tend to clog more quickly than cabinet files.

File cards are stiff brushes used to clean file surfaces.

■ **2–51.** *Hand scrapers. At top is a swan scraper. At bottom is a rectangular scraper.*

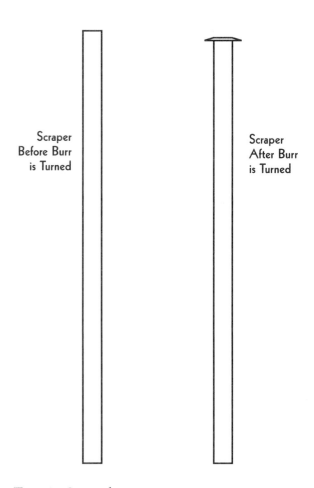

Scraper Before Burr is Turned

Scraper After Burr is Turned

■ **2–52.** *Scraper burr.*

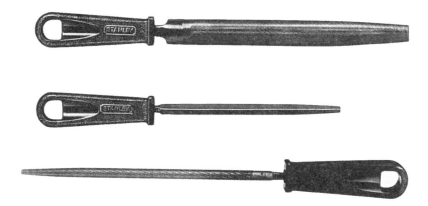

■ *2–53. Files. At top: half-round file. In middle: **triangular file**. At bottom: rat-tail file.*

■ **2–54.** *Perforated rasp.*

Rasps are used for wood-shaping. They look like and are used in much the same way that files are. Their coarse teeth roughen the wood surface as they rapidly remove material.

Perforated rasps are rasp-like tools that have replaceable cutting surfaces. These tools are used in much the same way a regular rasp is. Some models resemble files, while others are similar to wood planes (2–54).

more control. A properly sharpened plane or chisel is capable of producing an onionskin-thick shaving.

Grinding is required when the cutting edge is nicked or the bevel is rounded (2–55). If grinding is required, the tool is sharpened on a grinding wheel. It is then whetted on an oil- or water-stone.

Sharpening Chisels and Plane Irons

The cutting efficiency of planes and chisels is directly related to their sharpness. Dull tools tend to slip over the surface. Sharp tools are safer to use because they cut with less effort and allow

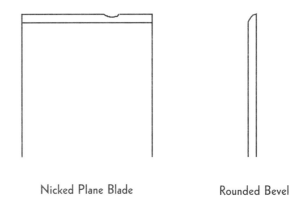

Nicked Plane Blade   Rounded Bevel

■ *2–55. At left, a nicked plane blade. At right, a cross-section view of a blade with a rounded bevel. Both conditions require grinding.*

The following steps are recommended for sharpening chisels and plane irons:

1. Adjust the angle of the grinder rest to match the angle of the tool to be ground (2–56).

■ *2–56. Sharpening a chisel edge or plane iron involves grinding the tool with it on a grinder tool rest.*

2. Use the hand to hold the tool to steady it as you move it across the grinding wheel from side to side.
3. Keep the surface being ground as cool as possible by dipping the tool in a water bath.

   When the bevel has been flattened and / or all nicks have been removed, the tool is reading for whetting.

Whetting Chisels and Plane Irons

Whetting is a process that removes any thread-like burrs formed during grinding. Several different types of "stones" can be used for whetting (2–57). Oilstones are flat, rectangular slabs of natural or manufactured stone. This type of stone, as the name indicates, is lubricated during whetting with a light oil. Waterstones are usually natural stones that use water as a lubricant. Diamond stones consist of a metal plate mounted on a plastic base. Holes in the plate contain diamond particles. Water is used to lubricate diamond stones. These stones are more durable than oil- or waterstones and they retain their shape.

Sharpening-stone grades are used to indicate relative coarseness of the stones. Oil- and water-stones are usually assigned grades like fine, medium, and coarse. Diamond stones are graded numerically, a number 400 being relatively coarse and a number 800 relatively fine. In most cases, a medium or number-500 stone is used for whetting after grinding.

■ *2–57. Diamond stone and oilstone.*

Stones must be flat to function properly. Diamond stones stay flat because they have a durable steel surface that does not wear down. Oil- and waterstones can lose their flatness in use. Follow these step-by-step procedures when whetting tools:

1. Lubricate the stone and anchor it to a suitable surface.

2. Place the tool's bevel on the surface of the stone. The bevel must be in full contact with the stone. The lubricant can often be seen moving away from under the tool when the bevel is against the stone's surface.

3. Move the tool back and forth over the stone's surface while keeping the bevel in full contact with it. A rocking motion is to be avoided, as this will tend to round the bevel. Various tool sharpeners are available to hold the tool at a constant angle to the stone during whetting (2–58).

4. After passing the tool over the stone several times, reverse it and rub the flat face of the tool opposite the bevel back and forth on

■ *2–58. Plane iron holder.*

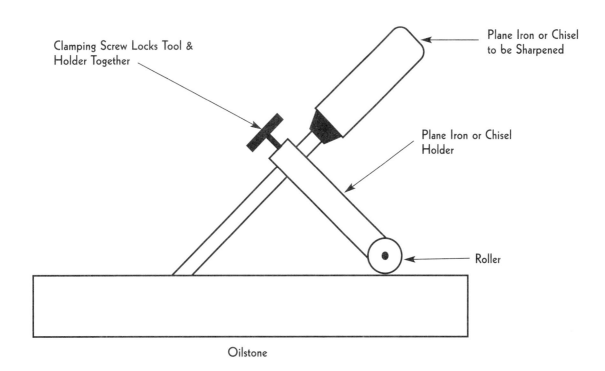

the stone (2–59). It is important to keep the tool absolutely flat while this is being done or a double bevel will develop.

Repeat steps three and four until the burr on the cutting edge is removed.

5. Strop the tool by pulling it across a piece of leather several times. After each pass, reverse the tool so each side of the edge is brought into contact with the strop. During stropping, hold the tool at about a 45-degree angle to the strop (2–60).

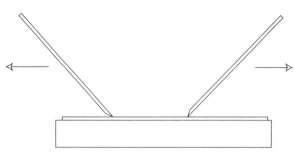

■ *2–60. Stropping technique.*

Sharpness can be tested by making a cut on a piece of scrap securely clamped to a bench. Both hands must be kept on the tool during testing, to avoid injury.

Shaped stones, or *slipstones,* are made in a variety of shapes for use in whetting gouges and other tools that can't be sharpened on a flat stone (2–61).

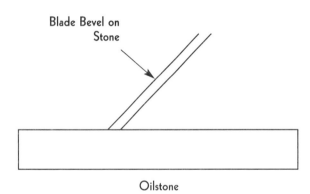

Blade Bevel on Stone

Oilstone

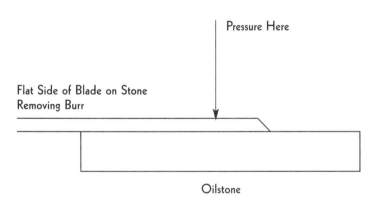

Pressure Here

Flat Side of Blade on Stone Removing Burr

Oilstone

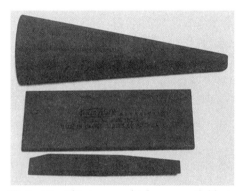

■ *2–61. Slipstones, which are available in many different shapes, are used to whet tools that can't be sharpened on a flat stone.*

■ *2–59. Whetting a tool on an oilstone.*

HOLE-MAKING HAND TOOLS

Round holes are required in a variety of wood-working procedures including doweling, mortising, and fastening.

Small holes, ranging in size from ¹⁄₁₆ to ¼ of an inch, can be made with a hand drill or a push drill (2–62). Hand drills are used with drill bits. Drill bits are sold singly and in sets. High-speed drill bits can be used for wood or metal.

■ **2–62.** *Hole-making drills and bits. At top: drill. In middle: push drill bits. At bottom: hand drill.*

Large holes can be made using auger bits held in a bit brace. The *ratchet bit brace* (2–63) is designed to hold square-shanked auger bits (2–64). The ratchet allows the bit brace to be used when a full handle swing is not possible or

■ **2–63.** *Ratchet bit brace.*

■ **2–64.** *Auger bit.*

is too difficult. The cam ring, located between the handle and chuck shell, is used to regulate the ratchet. When set in the center position, the cam ring allows the chuck to rotate in either direction. With the cam set against the right stop, the bit and chuck rotate as a unit when *clockwise* rotation occurs. When the brace is rotated in the opposite direction, the bit and chuck do not move. When the cam ring is set against the other stop, the brace and bit rotate as a unit when turned counterclockwise. The bit will not rotate when the handle is turned in the opposite direction.

Auger bits are available in diameters ranging from ¼ to 1 inch in ¹⁄₁₆-inch steps. Auger bits bore smooth, accurately sized holes without tearing up the surface of the material around

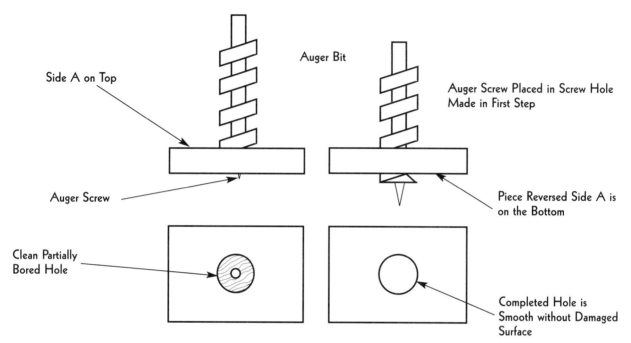

Side A on Top

Auger Bit

Auger Screw

Clean Partially
Bored Hole

Auger Screw Placed in Screw Hole
Made in First Step

Piece Reversed Side A is
on the Bottom

Completed Hole is
Smooth without Damaged
Surface

■ *2–65. Partially bored hole produced by an auger bit.*

the hole (2–65). Through holes should be bored in two steps, to prevent splitting on the reverse surface.

The first hole is bored until the screw on the auger bit breaks through on the opposite side of the piece. Then the bit is withdrawn and the work reversed. The screw on the auger bit is placed in the hole and the second part of the hole is bored.

When the piece cannot be reversed, a piece of scrap can be clamped to the back of the piece being bored. This will allow the bit to come through the piece without splitting the surface.

Blind-hole depth can be controlled by attaching a bit gauge to the bit (2–66). Masking tape can be substituted for the bit gauge when close depth control is not required.

Doweling jigs (2–67) can be used to center holes on a surface. When a doweling jig is used properly, the bored holes will be at a right or 90-degree angle to the surface into which the holes are bored.

Doweling jigs have guide holes to fit a variety of bit diameters ranging from ¼ to ½ inch.

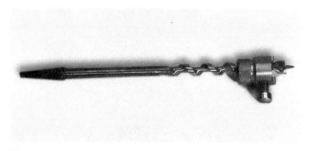

■ *2–66. Auger bit attached to a bit gauge. The gauge is a means of controlling the depths of blind holes.*

■ *2-67. Doweling jig.*

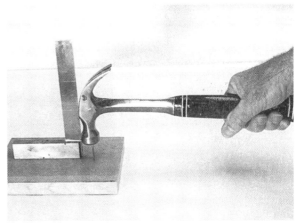

■ *2-68. Hammer head at right angle to the surface.*

HAMMERS

Almost every household has a claw hammer. Hammers are used for driving in and pulling out nails. These tools are available in various weights ranging from 10 to 16 ounces. Heavier hammers are used to drive large nails.

Hammers are available with wooden, metal, and fiberglass handles. The best hammers have forged-steel heads.

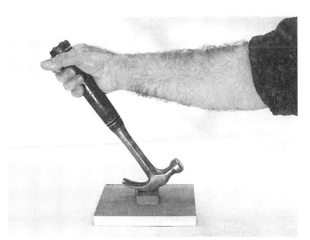

■ *2-69. Technique for pulling up a long nail. Notice the block under the hammer head.*

Safety Techniques

These safety techniques should be followed when using hammers:

1. Wear approved eye protection.
2. Do not use hammers with loose heads.
3. Woodworking hammers should be used exclusively for pulling up and driving in nails.
4. Keep hammer faces clean. This will help to prevent nails from bending.
5. Hold the hammer by the lower end of the handle when using it.
6. Use only the face of the hammer to drive nails.
7. Keep the hammer head at right angles to the surface the nail is being driven into (2–68). This will help to keep the nail from bending.
8. Place a block under the hammer head when pulling up a long nail (2–69). This will help to keep the handle from breaking.

MALLETS, TACK HAMMERS, AND NAIL SETS

Mallets (2–70) are used to drive chisels and to tap project pieces together during assembly.

Magnetic tack hammers (2–70) have a magnetized end that is used for holding starting small nails. Once a nail is started, the nonmagnetic end of the hammer is used to drive it in.

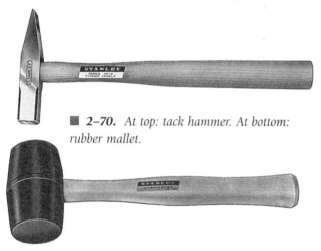

■ *2–70.* *At top: tack hammer. At bottom: rubber mallet.*

Nail sets (2–71) are used to sink the heads of finishing nails and brads below the surface. They are made in a variety of sizes to fit various-sized nails. Holes left after setting can be filled, making the nail "invisible."

■ *2–71.* *Nail sets are used to sink finishing-nail and brad heads below a board's surface.*

SCREWDRIVERS

Screwdrivers are used to drive screws. The two most commonly used types of screws are *slotted* and *Phillips head.* Slotted screws are driven with a standard screwdriver (2–72). Standard screwdriver blades should fit screw slots closely to avoid slipping and screw-head damage.

Phillips screwdrivers (2–72) are used to drive Phillips head screws. Phillips screwdrivers are made in several numbered sizes, including # 1 and # 2. The lower-numbered screwdrivers are designed to be used with small screws, while the higher-numbered ones are used for larger screws. Matching screwdrivers to screw-head sizes helps to prevent damaging screw heads.

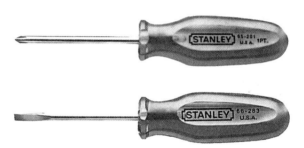

■ *2–72.* *Top: Phillips-head screwdriver. Bottom: Standard screwdriver.*

Screwdrivers are available in lengths ranging from 2 to 18 inches. Short screwdrivers are used with small screws or where working space is limited. Long screwdrivers are used with large screws or when screws are difficult to drive. Additional length adds leverage to a screwdriver, making screw-driving easier. Both hands should be kept on the screwdriver once a screw starts into the wood. This will help the user avoid injury if the screwdriver slips during use. Additional information on screws can be found in the section on fastenings, pages 173 to 179.

HOLDING AND CLAMPING EQUIPMENT

Safety and convenience often require that work-pieces be securely held while being worked on. The *bench vise* (2–73) is often used for this purpose.

Vise size is designated by jaw width. The distance between the jaws when the vise is opened to its maximum is also important. The typical 7-inch vise can open to a maximum of 11 inches. A vise of this size is a good choice for the typical woodworker.

Hardwood vise liners, which are attached to the vise jaws, are installed to protect the work from being marred by the metal vise jaws. The most useful vises have dogs built into the movable vise jaw. The dog can be used, together with a bench stop, to hold over-sized work.

Rapid-action vises have jaws that can be pushed closed and tightened with a half turn of the vise handle. Rotating the handle in a coun-terclockwise direction until it is vertical releases the jaw from the screw so that it can be pushed closed. Turning the handle in a clockwise direction engages the jaw and screw, allowing the vise to be tightened against the workpiece.

Clamps, like vises, are holding devices. They can be used to hold work to a benchtop or to hold pieces together while glue sets or holes are drilled. Though *C-clamps* are metalworking tools, woodworkers use them because they are versatile and have great holding power. Work held in C-clamps should be protected from damage with wooden blocks (2–74).

■ *2–74.* The wood blocks are protecting the work-piece.

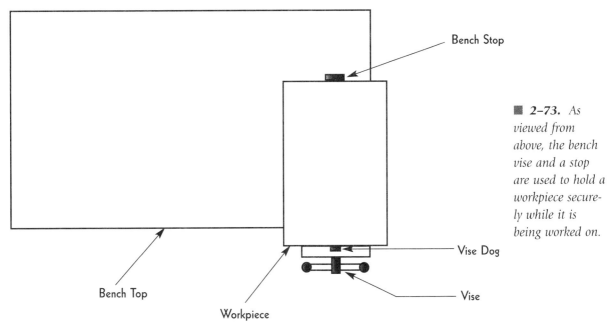

Bench Stop

■ *2–73. As viewed from above, the bench vise and a stop are used to hold a workpiece securely while it is being worked on.*

Vise Dog

Bench Top

Vise

Workpiece

Hand-screw clamps, or *hand screws,* are wooden parallel clamps that are specifically designed for woodworking (2–75). Large wooden jaws provide damage-free holding pressure over a large area.

The numbers stamped into the end of each clamp jaw designate screw size and capacity. The smallest clamp, #5/0, has four-inch-long jaws that open to a maximum of two inches. The largest, #5, has 18-inch-long jaws that open to a maximum of 14 inches.

Hand-screw clamp jaws hold best when they are parallel. Jaws can be kept parallel, during opening or closing, by holding the inside clamp handle stationary while the outside handle is cranked through a circular path. Hand screws can be tightened by alternately turning each handle until the jaws are securely positioned on the work.

Spring clamps are used to clamp small assemblies. The model shown in 2–76 has movable jaw pieces that help to distribute pressure over a wide area. An alternate form of clamp for small holding jobs can be made in the workshop by using a one-inch-long ring of PVC pipe cut once in a lengthwise direction (2–77).

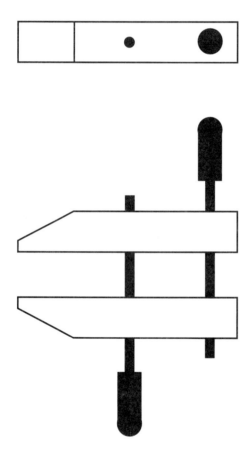

■ *2–75. Hand-screw clamp.*

■ *2–76. Spring clamp with movable jaw pieces.*

■ *2–77. This shop-made clamp is a piece of PVC pipe.*

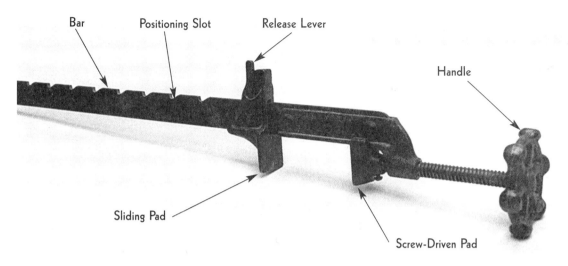

Bar   Positioning Slot   Release Lever

Handle

Sliding Pad

Screw-Driven Pad

■ **2–78.** *Bar clamps.*

Bar clamps (2–78) are used to clamp large assemblies like tabletops. These clamps usually range in length from 24 to 72 inches. The work being clamped must be protected from the steel clamp jaws. Wooden blocks are commonly used for this purpose.

Pipe clamps (2–79) are an inexpensive alternative to bar clamps. A pipe clamp is made by screwing a fixture onto the threaded end of a piece of ¾-inch steel pipe. Both bar and pipe clamps are adjusted by releasing a stop on the movable clamp component and sliding it to the desired position on the bar or pipe. The handle on the opposite end of the bar or pipe is turned to provide the amount of pressure required.

Strap, or *web, clamps* (2–80) are used to clamp closed assemblies like chairs or stool legs. They are tightened by turning a shaft that pulls the strap in around the assembly being clamped. A built-in handle, wrench, or screwdriver is used for this purpose.

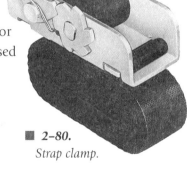

■ **2–80.**
Strap clamp.

■ **2–79.** *A shop-made pipe clamp.*

Hold-down clamps (2–81) are used to hold work down against the benchtop. These clamps are bolted to the benchtop. They allow a clamp to be positioned wherever an appropriate hole is located.

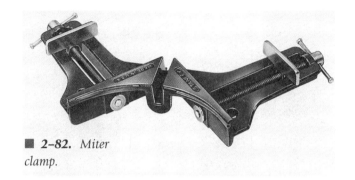

■ **2–82.** *Miter clamp.*

■ **2–81.** *Hold-down clamp.*

■ **2–83.** *Miter vise.*

Miter, or *corner,* clamps (2–82) or *miter vises* (2–83) can be used to clamp or hold small mitered pieces together at right angles.

Portable folding benches, such as the one shown in 2–84, have tops that double as vises. The model in 2–84 is about 30 inches tall and has a top measuring 9 × 24 inches. When used with bench stops, it can hold a piece that is 11 inches wide. Benches of this type are convenient because they can be brought to the work site. When used in pairs, this kind of equipment can be used to hold large doors on edge for processing.

■ **2–84.** *A portable folding bench that is approximately 30 inches tall and with a 9 x 24-inch top.*

3

HANDHELD POWER TOOLS

■ ■ ■ ■ ■ ■ ■ ■ ■ ■ ■ ■ ■ ■

Handheld power tools are often used when a hand tool would be too slow or where the nature of the workpiece precludes the use of a stationary power tool. Drilling a hole in a door can be accomplished easily and quickly with a portable power drill. Bringing the door to a drill press would not be practical in most cases. Sometimes the appropriate stationary power tool may not be available. A woodworker may have access to a router but not to a shaper. Finally, the woodworker may not have the skill necessary to perform an operation with a hand tool.

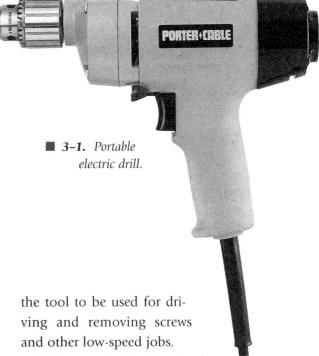

■ **3–1.** *Portable electric drill.*

ELECTRIC DRILLS

Portable electric drills (3–1) are among the most commonly owned power tools. The least-expensive models can hold bits of up to ¼ of an inch in diameter. The most useful models can accommodate a bit or device having a ½-inch-diameter shank. Variable speed and reversible drills allow the tool to be used for driving and removing screws and other low-speed jobs.

Drill power is directly related to a tool's amperage rating. Higher amperage usually means more power. Drills having a speed range of 0 to 760 rpm (revolutions per minute) are ideal for woodworking.

Rechargeable battery-operated electric drills (3—2) are convenient because they do not involve the use of potentially troublesome electrical extension cords. Drills having removable battery packs allow longer work intervals when extra batteries are available. Many rechargeable drills are reversible and have two speeds, 300 and 500 rpm. Battery voltages range from about 6 to 14 volts. Higher-voltage models deliver the most power.

■ *3–2. A rechargeable electric drill. Drills of this type have removable battery packs.*

Safety Techniques

These safety techniques should be followed when using electric drills:

1. Wear approved eye protection when using any power tool, including the drill.
2. If an extension cord is used, it must be grounded unless the drill is double-insulated.
3. Unplug the drills before making any adjustments or bit changes.
4. Never leave chuck keys in the drill.
5. Make sure that the drill's power switches are in the "off" position before plugging the drill in.

PORTABLE JIGSAWS

Portable jigsaws (3–3) are used for curved cutting. The saw is equipped with a narrow blade that is installed with the teeth pointing up toward the base. In this position, the reciprocating blade tends to keep the work against the base of the saw during cutting.

Blade strokes range from ⅝ to 2 inches. Blades that are designed to cut metals and other non-wood materials are available. These blades work best when they are used in variable-speed jigsaws. Cutting capacity is determined by maximum cutting depth, which is usually about two inches.

■ *3–3. Jigsaw.*

Safety Techniques

These safety techniques should be followed when using jigsaws:

1. Always wear eye protection when using any power tool, including the jigsaw.
2. Make sure that the jigsaw's switch is in the "off" position before plugging the saw in.
3. Unplug the saw when making adjustments such as changing blades.
4. Check the blade to ensure that it is correctly installed and in good condition.
5. Check the workpiece to ensure that it is properly secured prior to cutting.
6. Make sure that the saw blade is clear of the workpiece when turning the unit on.

Using the Jigsaw

Follow these step-by-step procedures when using a portable jigsaw:

1. During cutting, make sure that the saw base is kept firmly against the workpiece.
2. Make curves by gradually turning the saw as it is moved forward.
3. If the saw begins to labor or slow down, reduce the cutting rate.
4. Make internal cutouts by inserting the saw blade into a hole drilled into the area to be cut out (3–4).

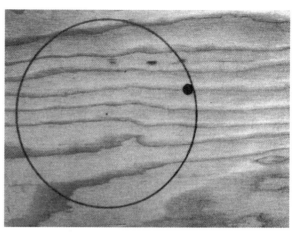

■ *3–4. When a jigsaw is used to make internal cutouts, a hole is drilled into the area to be cut out. The jigsaw blade is then inserted into this hole.*

PORTABLE CIRCULAR SAWS

Portable circular saws (3–5) are used for making straight cuts in wood when the use of a table saw is not possible and when a high degree of accuracy is not required. The saw's cutting capacity is determined by blade diameter. The most common size is 7¼ inches. A saw blade of this diameter can cut to a depth of about 2¼ inches.

■ *3–5. Portable circular saw.*

Most saws have an adjustable base that permits the cut depth and angle to be changed (3–6).

Circular saws usually rotate at about 5,000 rpm. Since these machines draw between 10 and 15 amps during cutting, an adequate power source is essential. If extension cords are used, they must be rated to carry the amount of electricity required by the saw they are used with.

Safety Techniques

These safety techniques should be followed when using circular saws:

1. Wear eye protection when using any power tool, including portable circular saws.
2. Make sure that the power supply and extension cord match the power requirements of the saw being used.
3. Adjust the depth of cut so that no more than ¼ inch of saw blade will protrude from the material being cut.
4. Securely anchor and support the workpiece so that cutoffs will not bind or pinch the blade as the cut is completed.
5. Make sure that the saw's base is resting on the work with the blade clear of the piece when the saw is turned on.
6. Make sure the blade comes to a complete stop before lifting the saw off the work.

■ *3–6.* *Top: Portable circular saw set up so that the blade is extending ¼ inch beyond the wood to be cut. Middle: Circular saw set up for a square cut. Bottom: Circular saw set up for a 15-degree cut.*

Using the Circular Saw

Follow these step-by-step procedures when using a circular saw:

1. Draw a layout line for the saw to follow.
2. With the workpiece secured and supported, place the toe of the saw base on the work and align the blade with the cutting line (3–7).
3. With the blade free of the work, start the saw and make the cut. Straight-edged guides clamped to the work can be used to guide the saw during cutting (3–8).

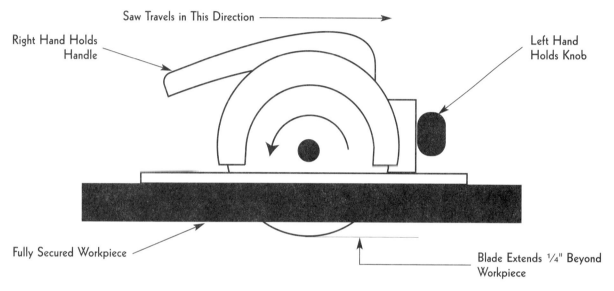

Saw Travels in This Direction

Right Hand Holds Handle

Left Hand Holds Knob

Fully Secured Workpiece

Blade Extends ¼" Beyond Workpiece

3–7. *Cutting with a circular saw involves placing the toe of the saw base on the workpiece and aligning the base with the cutting line.*

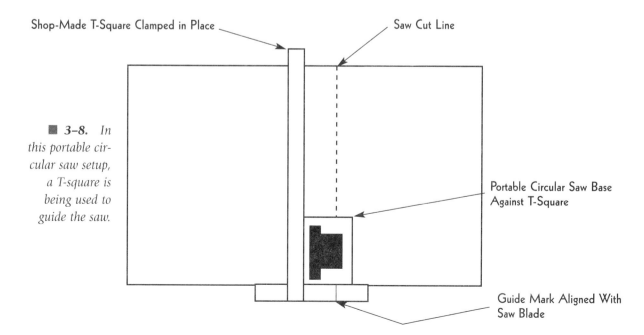

Shop-Made T-Square Clamped in Place

Saw Cut Line

3–8. *In this portable circular saw setup, a T-square is being used to guide the saw.*

Portable Circular Saw Base Against T-Square

Guide Mark Aligned With Saw Blade

4. When the cut is complete, release the saw switch.
5. When the saw blade stops rotating, lift the saw off the work. Remember to keep the saw base in place on the work until the blade stops rotating. This is very important, because a rotating blade can easily snag and cut the saw's power cord.

PLATE JOINERS

Plate, or biscuit, joiners (3–9) are used to make a joint that resembles the spline joint, and which takes less time to make than spline or dowel joints.

■ **3–9.** *Plate, or biscuit, joiner.*

Plate-joiner cutters rotate at about 4,000 rpm and employ a movable faceplate to control the cutting depth. A four-inch-diameter cutter is used to make a round-bottomed groove or slot in the workpiece. A matching slot is cut into the mating piece. The curved slots accept a close-fitting wooden biscuit that aligns the pieces. Glue

applied to the biscuit causes it to swell, locking the pieces together (3–10). Several sizes of biscuits are available (3–11).

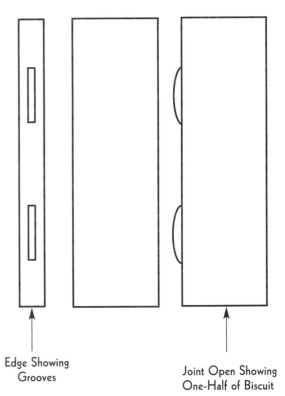

Edge Showing
Grooves

Joint Open Showing
One-Half of Biscuit

■ **3–10.** *Plate-joint assembly.*

■ **3–11.** *Plate-joiner biscuits are available in several sizes.*

Safety Techniques

These safety techniques should be followed when using plate joiners:

1. Always wear eye protection when using any power tool, including plate joiners.
2. Securely anchor the workpiece so that it cannot move.
3. Make all adjustments with the machine unplugged.
4. Retract the cutter when turning the plate joiner on.
5. Make sure the cutter comes to a complete stop before removing the plate joiner from the work.

Using a Plate Joiner

Follow these step-by-step procedures when using a plate joiner:

1. Place the workpieces in the positions they will be in when they are assembled.
2. Starting three inches in from each end, draw layout lines at six-inch intervals across the grain with a try square.
3. Set the depth of the plate joiner to match the biscuit to be used.
4. Adjust the fence depth so that the slots will be centered on the edges of the pieces being joined. For example, if the pieces are ¾ inch thick, set the fence to ⅜ inch.
5. Align the machine's witness line (the line cut into the top of the fence) with each of the layout lines, and cut the slots.
6. Make a trial assembly with the biscuits in place. Make adjustments, if these are necessary.
7. Disassemble the work, apply the glue, and reassemble and clamp the pieces.

PORTABLE BELT SANDERS

Portable belt sanders (3–12) are used for a variety of heavy-duty sanding operations on work that cannot be brought to a stationary unit. Belt sanders consist of an endless abrasive belt traveling over two drums. The rear driving drum is rubber-covered, for additional traction. The front drum is crowned (that is, it is larger in diameter in the middle) to help keep the belt from moving sideways during sanding. The front drum is spring-loaded and adjustable, so that belts can be tensioned and tracked on it.

The size of a belt sander is determined by the width and length of its belt. A sander utilizing a belt measuring 4 × 24 inches is known as a 4 × 24-inch sander. This sander has a sanding area of about four by six inches.

Grit numbers are used to grade the belts. A #36 belt is extremely coarse and fast cutting, while a #80 belt is much less coarse and equivalent to medium sandpaper.

■ *3–12. Portable belt sander.*

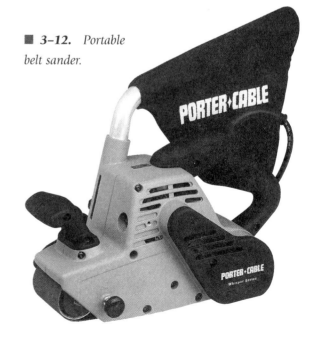

Most portable sanders are equipped with trigger switches that can be locked in the "on" position. A built-in dust-collecting system is a highly desirable feature.

Safety Techniques

Follow these safety techniques when using belt sanders:

1. Always wear approved eye protection and a dust mask when operating a sanding machine.
2. Unplug the belt sander when making any adjustments except belt tracking.
3. Replace worn or damaged belts. Worn belts are difficult to track and can cause the sander to overheat.
4. Secure the workpiece to keep the work from moving during sanding.
5. Make sure the sander is not in contact with the work when the power is turned on.
6. After using the sander, place it on its side to prevent it from running off the work or bench.
7. Use moderate pressure on the machine while sanding. The weight of the sander should be allowed to do the work.
8. Keep power cables away from the sander during sanding.
9. Remove sharp objects (like nails or screws) that might damage the sanding belt.

Using a Portable Belt Sander

Follow these procedures and guidelines when using a portable belt sander:

1. Secure the piece to be sanded in a manner that will keep it from shifting while allowing it to be sanded with the grain.
2. Draw pencil lines across the surface to be sanded to use as sanding indicators.
3. Turn the power on with the sander held directly above and clear of the area to be sanded.
4. Lower the sander to the work with the rear handle raised slightly. This helps to counteract the tendency of the front end of the sander to lift as the sander contacts the surface. Begin sanding at the rear left end of the piece (3–13). Move the sander across the work slowly.

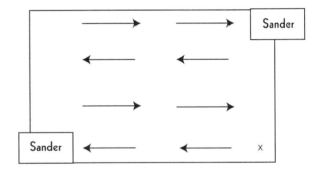

Starting
Point

■ *3–13. The directions followed when sanding a large surface with a portable belt sander.*

5. Move the sander forward until the pressure plate on the machine extends over the edge of the work by about one inch (3–14).
6. Move the sander to the right about three inches and then back to the starting edge. Repeat this until the surface is completely sanded.
7. Sanding can be interrupted by turning the power off and allowing the belt to stop moving before lifting the sander off the work.

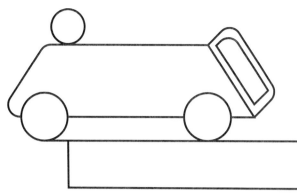

■ *3-14.* *The belt sander is moved along the workpiece until its pressure plate passes over the edge of the piece.*

8. Belt selection is determined by the amount of material to be removed. When a relatively large amount of material is to be removed, a fairly coarse belt like a #60 would be used. Later, when smoothing rather than material removal is important, a #80 or #100 belt might be used.

FINISHING SANDERS

Finishing sanders are designed to remove scratches, dirt, and other minor blemishes. These sanders have soft-abrasive backing pads and must be used with care to avoid rounding surfaces and corners.

Random-orbit sanders (3–15) are especially useful in situations where the surface being sanded has an irregular grain pattern that makes sanding with the grain difficult. The most convenient models have built-in dust-collection systems. The circular abrasive sanding discs used on these machines have holes punched in them to allow the dust to be drawn into a collector (3–15).

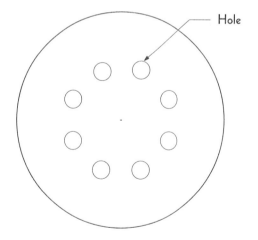

Hole

■ *3-15.* *Top: Random-orbit sander. Bottom: Random-orbit sander discs have holes that allow for dust collection.*

Palm sanders (3–16) can use quarter sheets of sandpaper measuring 4¼ × 4¼ inches. These sanders have an oscillating rate of 14,000 OPM (oscillations per minute).

Some sanders use quick-change discs that have Velcro-like hook and loop backings. These discs can be peeled off and replaced very quickly.

Various grades of sandpaper are used in finishing sanding, starting with #100 or #120 and working up to #220 or higher.

■ *3–16.* *Palm sander.*

Safety Techniques

Follow these safety techniques when using a finishing sander:

1. Wear approved eye protection and a dust mask when operating a sanding machine.
2. Unplug the sander when removing or installing abrasive sheets.
3. Replace worn or damaged abrasive sheets. Worn abrasives can clog rapidly.
4. Secure pieces to keep them stable during sanding.

5. Lift the sanders off the work before turning the power on.

Using a Finishing Sander

Follow these step-by-step procedures when using a finishing sander:

1. Most finishing sanders, including random-orbit and straight-line models, are held with two hands.
2. Turn the finishing sander on and place it on the workpiece.
3. Move the sander over the surface of the work until the desired degree of smoothness is obtained.
4. Keep the sander in motion to reduce surface scratching.

ROUTER

The router (3–17) is a high-speed rotary power tool that can be used for a variety of cutting operations. These include: edge-shaping, groove- and dado-cutting, making joinery, and laminate-trimming. The machine consists of a high-speed motor that usually runs at 25,000 rpm. A chuck mounted on the motor shaft is used to hold a variety of router bits.

Routers are rated by horsepower. For standard use, a one horsepower machine is adequate. Heavy-duty routers are usually rated from one and a half to three horsepower.

Router chucks accept ¼-, ⅜-, and ½-inch round-shanked cutting tools, called bits (3–18). The motor unit is mounted on a circular base that allows it to be held in a fixed position above the work. Holes in the router base allow the workpiece to be seen during cutting.

■ *3-17.* *Routers are power tools that can be used to shape edges, cut grooves and dadoes, trim laminates, and perform many other cutting operations.*

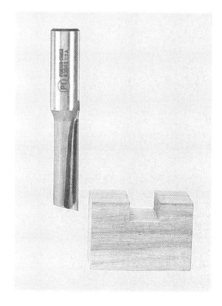

■ *3-18.* *There are many different types and sizes of router bit.*

Fences or edge guides (3–19) are used to guide the router when making straight cuts parallel to adjacent straight surfaces. These edge guides are usually mounted on the router base.

■ 3–20. *Plunge router. The motor on this type of router plunges into the workpiece to a preset depth.*

■ 3–19. *Fences, or edge guides, guide the router when it is making straight cuts. They are usually mounted on the router base.*

Types of Router

Plunge routers (3–20) have bases that are designed to allow the router motor to plunge a preset distance into the workpiece. These machines are usually rated at about 1½ horsepower and turn at 23,000 rpm. Variable-speed models have speed ranges of 12,000 to 25,000 rpm. Plunge routers can usually plunge downward a maximum of two inches.

The plunge feature is especially useful when routing recesses like mortises or blind dadoes. Various types of release devices are used to initiate router plunge. A lever release allows the

machine to be held securely with both hands during the plunge (3–21).

Fixed-based routers have bases that clamp directly to a removable motor, making the router a "fixed" unit.

Veneer trimmers (3–22) are small routers that are used to trim veneers and plastic laminates. These machines are usually rated at about ⅓ horsepower and turn at about 30,000 rpm.

Types of Bit

Router bits are used for a variety of cutting operations. The two principal types of router bit are those having carbide steel cutting surfaces and those made of tool steel. Though carbide bits cost more than tool-steel bits, they last up to ten times longer and can be used to cut a variety of non-wood materials like plastic laminates.

■ **3–21.** *Two hands are used to hold the router during a plunge cut.*

■ **3–22.** *Veneer trimmer. These small routers are used to trim veneer and plastic laminates.*

Straight router bits are used to cut grooves (3–23), dadoes, and other flat-bottomed recesses or gains. When this type of bit is being used to cut, the router is usually controlled by an external guiding device like an edge guide.

■ **3–23.** *Straight groove-cutting bit.*

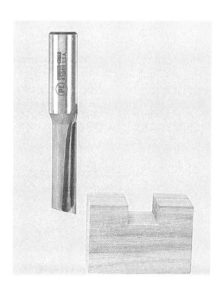

Piloted router bits (3–24) are generally used for edge-shaping. The pilot limits the depth of the cut as it travels along the edge of the workpiece. Bits with ball-bearing pilots are recommended because they will not cause surface burning. Plain-piloted bits can burn into the workpiece edge and cause an irregular cut (3–25).

■ **3–24.** *Ball-bearing-piloted bit.*

■ **3–25.** *The irregular cut and burn marks on this workpiece were made by a plain bit, one without a ball-bearing pilot.*

Safety Techniques

These safety techniques should be followed when using a router:

1. Always wear approved eye protection and a dust mask when using a router.
2. Make sure the power switch is in the "off" position before plugging the machine in.
3. Unplug the router while making adjustments or installing bits.
4. Keep power cables away from areas to be routed.
5. Make sure the router bit is clear of the workpiece when turning the power on.
6. Hold the router securely with both hands while turning the power on, to prevent it from twisting out of control.
7. Secure the work so that it cannot shift position during cutting.
8. A grounded outlet and extension cord must be used unless the router is double-insulated.

Using a Router

DETERMINING CUTTING DEPTH

First the bit is installed in the router, and then the cutting depth is set. To do this, place the base of the machine on top of two strips of wood that are equal in thickness to the required depth of cut (3–26). Then move the motor downward until the router bit touches the surface between the wood strips. At this point, clamp the motor to the router base. The cut made by the router will equal the thickness of the wood strips.

Hinge leaves can be substituted for the wood strips when hinge gains are being cut.

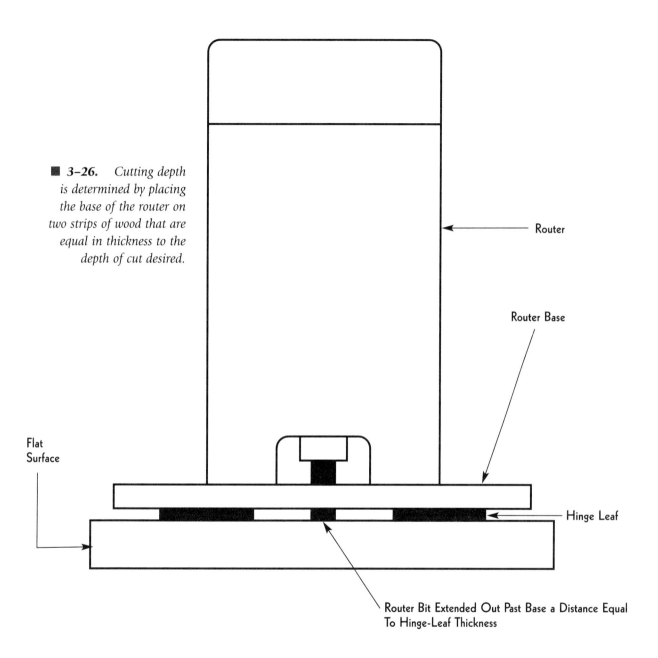

■ *3–26. Cutting depth is determined by placing the base of the router on two strips of wood that are equal in thickness to the depth of cut desired.*

Router

Router Base

Flat
Surface

Hinge Leaf

Router Bit Extended Out Past Base a Distance Equal
To Hinge-Leaf Thickness

EDGE-SHAPING WITH A PILOTED BIT

Follow these step-by-step procedures when edge-shaping:

1. Check the edge to be shaped to make sure that it is clean and free of irregularities. Router bits will reproduce and enlarge any imperfections in the edge being shaped.

2. Select a router bit that will produce the desired shape, and install it in the router. All but ¼ inch of the shank of the bit should be inside the router chuck.

3. Adjust the router so that the bit extends

beyond the router base the distance necessary for making the required cut (3–27). The bit should remove about ¼ inch of material on the first cut.

4. Secure the work to the benchtop or work surface. Small pieces can be secured by placing them on a router mat (3–28).

5. Secure the router by placing one hand on each of the router handles. The router bit must be clear of the workpiece when the power is turned on.

6. Place the router on the workpiece and move it until the pilot on the bit contacts the edge of the piece. At this point, one of the router handles should be over the workpiece, as shown in 3–29.

7. Move the router to the right, in a counter-clockwise direction. This helps to ensure a smooth cut.

8. If both ends and edges are to be shaped, do the ends first, to reduce splitting.

■ *3–28.* *Small workpiece on router mat.*

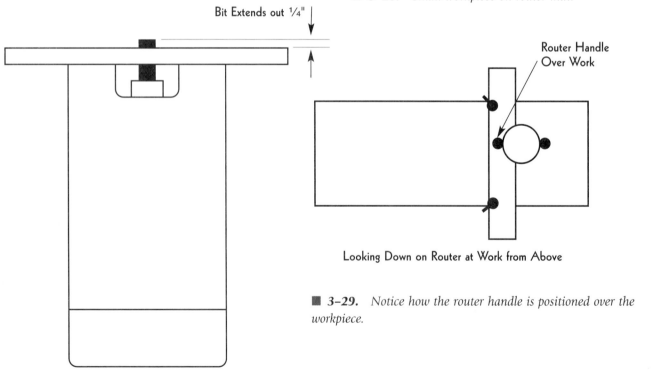

Looking Down on Router at Work from Above

■ *3–29.* *Notice how the router handle is positioned over the workpiece.*

■ *3–27.* *The bit should extend from the router base the distance needed to make the required cut.*

CUTTING GROOVES, DADOES, AND RABBETS

Follow these step-by-step procedures when cutting grooves, dadoes, and rabbets:

1. Lay out the area to be cut. This can be done with a sharp pencil or a utility knife. Knife cuts help to limit surface splitting.

2. Select a router bit that will produce the desired cut and install it in the router. Each cut should remove ¼ inch of material.

3. Clamp a shop-made router guide to the workpiece (3–30). Turn the router on and make the cut by moving the router to the right. The router base must be kept against the guide strip during cutting.

4. Rabbets and dadoes can be made using a shop-made T-square-like device. Use the groove cut into the "T" to position the guide on the work (3–31).

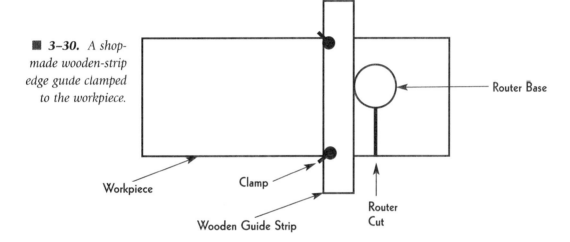

■ **3–30.** *A shop-made wooden-strip edge guide clamped to the workpiece.*

Router Base

Workpiece

Clamp

Wooden Guide Strip

Router Cut

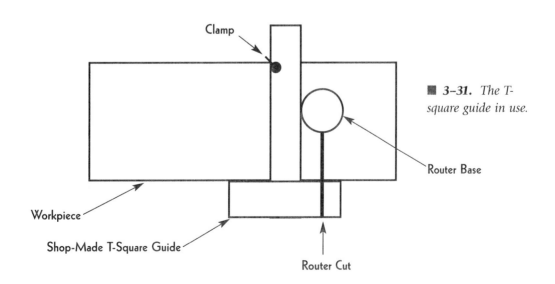

Clamp

■ **3–31.** *The T-square guide in use.*

Router Base

Workpiece

Shop-Made T-Square Guide

Router Cut

Manufactured edge guides that fasten to the base of the router can also be used to cut grooves parallel to the grain of the piece (3–32). Some of these edge guides are provided with a pin that allows the router to make circular cuts (3–33).

Template guides (3–34) allow the router to be used with templates like those on the dovetail fixture (3–35). The template guide prevents the router bit from cutting into the template.

■ **3–34.** *Dovetail-fixture template guide.*

■ **3–32.** *Metal edge guides can also be used to make certain cuts.*

■ **3–35.** *Dovetail fixture.*

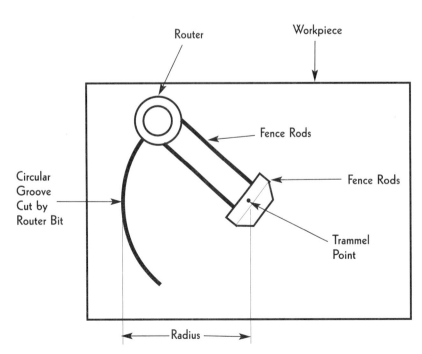

Router
Workpiece
Fence Rods
Fence Rods
Circular Groove Cut by Router Bit
Trammel Point
Radius

■ **3–33.** *Making a circular cut with the trammel, or pin, provided with a metal edge guide.*

TRIMMING PLASTIC LAMINATES

Plastic laminates are often applied to surfaces, like desktops, that are subject to heavy use. Laminates can also be used to add color or a pattern to a surface and/or to mask the underlying material.

Laminates are sold in sheets two to four feet wide and three to twelve feet long. Two thicknesses are commonly available: $\frac{1}{32}$ inch for light-duty and $\frac{1}{16}$ inch for heavy-duty applications.

Plastic laminates can be cut to rough size on the table saw using a small-toothed carbide-tipped blade designed for that purpose. They can also be cut using a router and an appropriate bit.

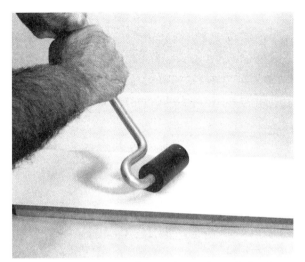

■ *3–36.* *Using a J-roller on the surface of plastic laminate.*

Applying Plastic Laminate to a Tabletop

Follow these step-by-step procedures when applying plastic laminate to a tabletop:

1. Clean the surface of the workpiece and the back of the laminate with a suitable solvent like lacquer thinner. Be sure to follow the safety directions on the thinner and contact cement containers.

2. Apply two coats of contact cement to the cleaned surfaces with a brush or roller. Any excess contact cement can be removed with lacquer thinner.

3. When the cement is dry to the touch, bring the pieces together. Adhering is immediate and the pieces cannot be repositioned.

4. Use a rubber J-roller to roll over the surface of the laminate (3–36). This helps to flatten the surface by forcing out any air trapped under the laminate.

5. Trim the laminate using a router and a carbide veneer-trimming router bit (3–37). The ball-bearing pilot travels along the top surface of the workpiece as the router bit

■ *3–37.* *This veneer trimmer with a laminate-trimming router bit can be used to trim plastic laminate.*

trims the laminate flush with that surface.

6. Complete all of the edges before laminating the top.

7. Apply contact cement to the tabletop and the back of the laminate and allowed them to dry.

8. Cover the tabletop with a sheet of kraft paper, which is standard brown wrapping paper. Dry contact cement will not adhere to the paper. Position the plastic laminate on the paper and slowly slide the paper out from between the tabletop and the plastic laminate (3–38).

9. Apply pressure to the laminate with a mallet and wooden block or a J-roller.

10. Trim the excess laminate off with the router. A beveled router bit (3–39) is often used for trimming table and countertops. This type of bit produces a more durable corner.

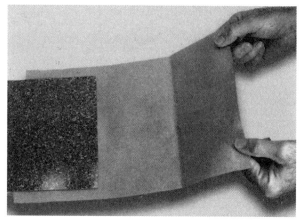

■ *3–38. After the tabletop and the back of the laminate have been glued with contact cement, slowly slide the kraft paper out from between them.*

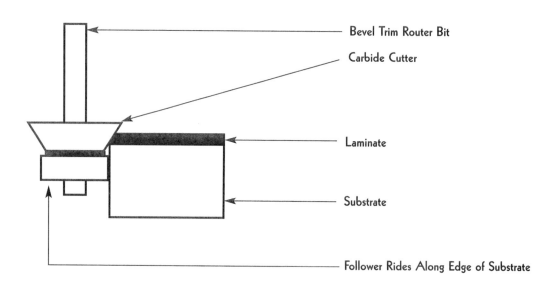

Bevel Trim Router Bit

Carbide Cutter

Laminate

Substrate

Follower Rides Along Edge of Substrate

■ *3–39. A beveled bit can be used to trim plastic laminate.*

PORTABLE PLANERS

Portable planers (3–40) are powered hand planes. They use the same operating principle that stationary jointers use.

A high-speed motor is used to drive a rotating cutter head. The base of the machine is made up of two sections. One section is fixed and the other is movable. The movable section, the *shoe*, is used to control the depth of cut.

Cutting depth is changed by turning the knob on the front of the planer. The depth of cut is equal to the vertical distance between the adjustable shoe and the fixed-base section (3–41). The maximum depth of cut is usually about ⁹⁄₆₄ of an inch.

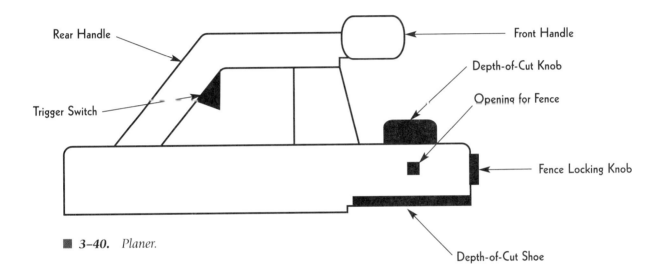

■ *3–40.* *Planer.*

Rear Handle
Trigger Switch
Front Handle
Depth-of-Cut Knob
Opening for Fence
Fence Locking Knob
Depth-of-Cut Shoe

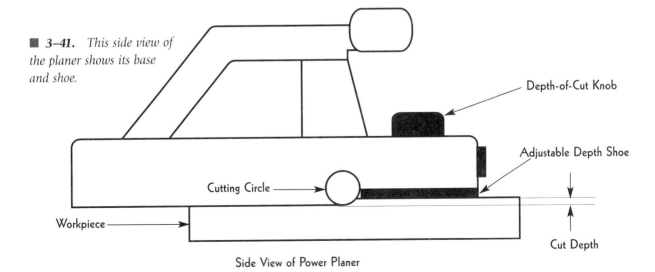

■ *3–41.* *This side view of the planer shows its base and shoe.*

Depth-of-Cut Knob
Adjustable Depth Shoe
Cut Depth
Cutting Circle
Workpiece

Side View of Power Planer

Planer fences are used to keep the cut square to the surface that the fence is in contact with (3–42). In edge-planing, the fence is in contact with the face of the piece.

Rabbets can be made when the fence is adjusted so that part of the surface is cut by the cutter head. This produces a rabbet, or stepped-shaped, cut.

Using a Planer

A planer is used in much the same way a hand plane is. At the beginning of a cut, downward pressure is applied to the knob. When the rear handle reaches the work, downward pressure is applied to the handle and the knob. When the knob moves forward off the work surface, pressure on the knob is reduced.

The surface produced by a planer is made up of shallow parallel ridges. Reducing the speed at which the planer is moved over the work will reduce the size of these ridges. The resulting surface will look and feel smoother than one produced by a faster-moving planer.

For specific operations with each brand of planer, follow the directions provided by the planer manufacturer.

■ *3–42.* *This front view of the planer shows the fence.*

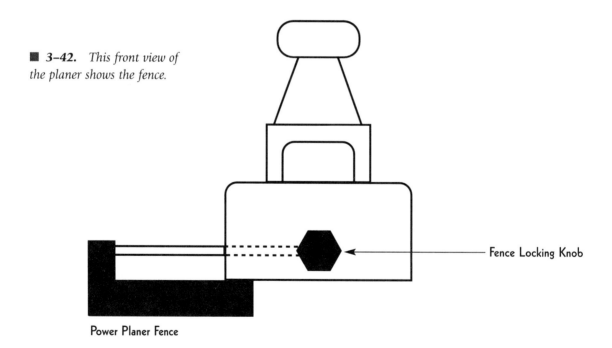

Fence Locking Knob

Power Planer Fence

Front View Power Planer

CHAPTER 4
STATIONARY POWER TOOLS

■ ■ ■ ■ ■ ■ ■ ■ ■ ■ ■ ■ ■ ■

BUYING NEW POWER TOOLS

Some readers may decide to buy one of the power tools discussed in the following pages. Pay close attention to these guidelines when making such a purchase. Purchasing guidelines for specific power tools will be given in the appropriate sections.

1. Purchase the best-quality machine in your price range.
2. Purchase a machine that has been made by a manufacturer you are familiar with.
3. The machine you purchase should be guaranteed by the dealer and the manufacturer.
4. The size and type of motor on the machine should be suitable for your needs. Single-phase 110- and 120-volt motors are useable in most shops.

BUYING USED POWER TOOLS

Some readers may decide to buy a used version of one of the power tools described in the following section. Follow these guidelines when buying a used power tool. Purchasing guidelines for specific power tools will be given in the appropriate sections.

1. Request a demonstration. Listen for any unusual sounds when the saw is running free and when it is cutting.
2. Ask for the manufacturer's instructions that came with the machine.
3. Check the accessories available with the machine.

TABLE SAW

The table saw is probably the most frequently used machine in the woodworker's shop (4–1). It consists of a table with a circular saw blade extending up through it. The saw blade is mounted on a rotating shaft, or *arbor*, and is driven by a motor. The workpiece is moved along the table into the rotating saw blade while supported by an adjustable *fence*, during ripping, or by a *miter gauge*, during crosscutting. The saw's primary use is for straight and square cutting.

A *throat plate*, or *table insert*, surrounds the saw blade (4–2). This removable plate allows access to the saw arbor so that blades can be changed.

■ **4–1.** *A 10-inch, tilting-arbor table saw.*

When the throat plate is in place, the space around the saw blade is reduced so that small cutoffs cannot slide down into the saw.

A *splitter* (4–3) is located directly behind and in line with the saw blade. The splitter helps to keep the saw kerf (the slot cut by the saw) open so that material being cut does not bind on the saw blade, causing the workpiece to be thrown back toward the operator.

■ **4–2.** *This view of the table saw shows its throat plate.*

■ *4–3.* *Splitter and anti-kickback fingers.*

■ *4–4.* *Table-saw guards, which are usually attached to the splitter, protect the operator from cut-off material that can be kicked back.*

Anti-kickback fingers, or *pawls* (4–3), are usually attached to the splitter. These fingers allow the material being cut to move in one direction-toward the rear of the saw. This helps to prevent pieces from being kicked back toward the operator.

Saw *guards* are usually attached to the splitter (4–4). Guards help to protect the operator from being injured by the saw blade and to prevent small pieces of cutoff material from being thrown back toward the operator. The guards and splitters on *tilt-arbor* table saws are designed to tilt with the arbor.

Belt-driven saws are equipped with guards that cover the motor pulley and belt. Properly tensioned belts should deflect about ¼ inch under moderate hand pressure. Loose belts can slip during cutting, reducing saw-blade speed and cutting efficiency. Belt tension can be adjusted by repositioning the motor.

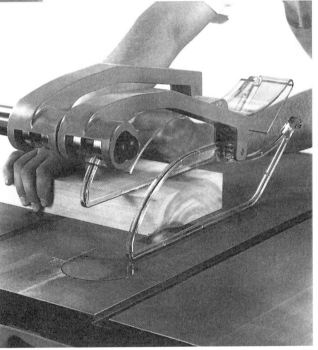

Some of the illustrations in this book may show the saw being used with the guard removed for improved visibility. *Saw guards should be in place whenever the saw is used.*

Two *handwheels* are located under the saw table (4–5). The handwheel mounted on the front of the table saw is used to raise and lower the saw blade. The side-mounted handwheel is used to adjust the angle between the blade and the tabletop. This is called the *tilt wheel*. Each wheel has a locking knob on its hub. The knob is loosened before adjustments are made and then retightened.

Power switches are usually located on the front of the table saw.

■ **4–5.** *Two handwheels located until the table-saw's table are used to raise and lower the blade and adjust the angle between the blade and the tabletop.*

Selecting and Buying a New Table Saw

Before buying a new table saw, refer to "Buying New Power Tools" on page 77. Then read the following guidelines:

1. A tilt-arbor saw that can accommodate a ten-inch-diameter blade is a good choice. Ten-inch table saws should have motors that generate a minimum of 1½ horsepower. If considering a bench model, purchase legs or a table made by the saw manufacturer.

2. The saw's table size should match your needs and work space. Cutting large pieces of material on a small saw can be dangerous. Some manufacturers have table extensions available for their machines. Ask about these accessories.

3. Check basic accessories like blade and belt guards, miter gauges, rip fences, and throat plates. The throat plate should be easy to remove. Throat plates for dado blades should be available.

Check the rip fence for ease of operation by moving and clamping it. It should work smoothly and clamp securely. A micrometer feed knob is a desirable rip-fence feature. This knob allows precision fence adjustment. The rip fence should be parallel to the blade when it is locked.

The miter gauge should be easy to adjust. It should move smoothly. Stops at 90 and 45 degrees are desirable. Stop rods should be available for use with the miter gauge.

4. After checking that the saw is disconnected from the power supply, check the saw arbor. No play or movement should be detected.

Table-Saw Blades

Table-saw blades enable the table saw to perform all of its cutting operations. A sharp, properly selected blade will cut more efficiently and safely than one that is dull or designed for another purpose. Dull blades can overheat during cutting and deform. When this happens, the workpiece tends to bind on the saw blade and be kicked back toward the operator.

There are two general types of blade: *carbide-tipped* and *tool-steel.* Carbide-tipped blades are a better choice because they remain sharp for up to ten times longer than regular steel blades. Saw blades having the largest number of teeth stay sharp longer and produce the smoothest cuts. A typical 10-inch-diameter combination blade has 50 teeth.

Blades with set teeth (4–6, bottom) have teeth that are bent

alternately to the right and left. This causes the blade to make a cut or kerf that is wider than the body of the saw blade.

Hollow-ground blades (4–6, top) produce a very smooth cut because their teeth are not set. Instead, the body of the blade is ground so that the teeth are thicker than it. This helps the saw to produce clearance.

Hollow-ground blades cut most efficiently when they are raised as far above the workpiece

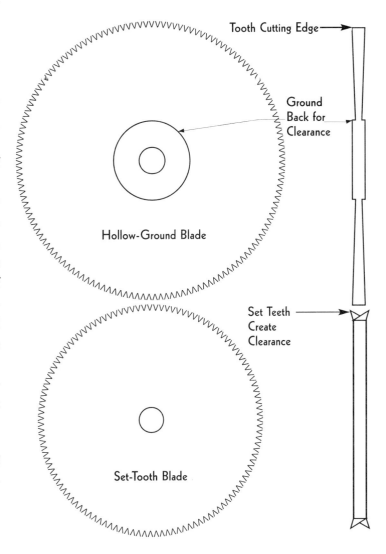

Tooth Cutting Edge

Ground Back for Clearance

Hollow-Ground Blade

Set Teeth Create Clearance

Set-Tooth Blade

■ **4–6.** *Set and hollow-ground saw blades.*

as possible. This makes the use of these blades dangerous, because so much of the blade is exposed. Hollow-ground blades are usually used for trimming cuts because of their tendency to bind when they are used for normal cutting.

Combination blades (4–7) can be used to cut with or across the grain (ripping or crosscutting). Many woodworkers find this all-purpose blade adequate for almost all of their work.

Crosscut blades (4–8) are designed to produce smooth-cut surfaces when cutting across the grain. The typical 10-inch crosscut blade has about 60 teeth.

Rip blades (4–9) are designed to cut smoothly with the grain, without binding. They have chisel-like teeth that produce a smooth-cut surface. The typical 10-inch rip blade has 24 teeth.

Special-purpose blades can be purchased for cutting laminates, miters, and plywood.

■ *4–7. A combination circular-saw blade.*

■ *4–8. A 60-tooth crosscut blade, used to cut across the grain.*

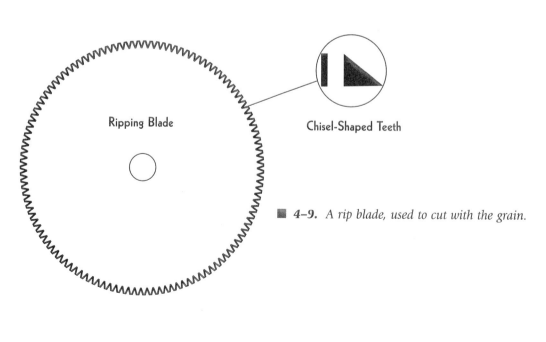

Ripping Blade

Chisel-Shaped Teeth

■ *4–9. A rip blade, used to cut with the grain.*

Safety Techniques

These safety techniques should be followed when using a table saw:

1. Wear approved eye protection and a dust mask.
2. Keep the saw table clear of all debris and make sure all the saw and belt guards are in place.
3. Make sure that the blade is sharp and suitable for the work to be done.
4. Make sure that the blade is securely attached to the saw arbor.
5. Use a throat plate that is appropriate for the work to be done.
6. Check that the blade does not extend more than ¼ inch above the workpiece.
7. Do not stand directly in line with the blade. This will help to prevent injury in the event of kickback.
8. Do not reach over the saw table to support the cut material. A roller stand or an assistant should be used to support the work as it comes off the saw table.
9. Keep the workpiece in contact with the rip fence when making rip cuts.
10. Use two push sticks for ripping. One push stick should be kept on the end of the workpiece between the cutting line and the rip fence. The second should be used to hold the work against the fence.
11. Place workpieces that will be crosscut against the miter gauge. Two hands should be used to hold the work and miter gauge together during cutting.
12. Never attempt "freehand" or unsupported cuts. The work should be supported by the rip fence or the miter gauge.
13. Remove all jewelry and secure loose hair and clothing before using the table saw.
14. Do not cut warped material on the table saw.
15. Do not use the table saw to cut undersized pieces that will bring the hands close to the blade during cutting.
16. Always follow the safety instructions provided by the saw manufacturer.

Crosscutting on the Table Saw

Follow these step-by-step procedures when crosscutting on a table saw:

1. Check the angle formed by the saw blade and table for squareness before using the table saw. This is done by raising the saw blade to its highest point with the handwheel. Use a try square to check this angle (4–10). Use the blade-tilt handwheel to make necessary adjustments.

■ *4–10. A try square is used to check the angle between the tabletop and blade, to ensure that it is at 90 degrees.*

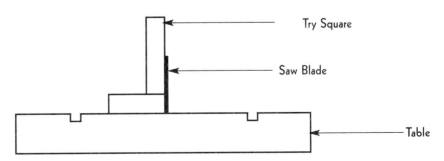

2. Lower the blade so that approximately ¼ inch will project above the surface of the piece being cut.

3. Also check the angle formed by the miter gauge and the saw blade for squareness. This is done by placing the head of a try square against the miter gauge and sliding the gauge into a position that allows the try square blade to be moved against the saw blade (4–11). The miter gauge can be adjusted by loosening the knob on it. The knob must be tightened after the adjustments are made.

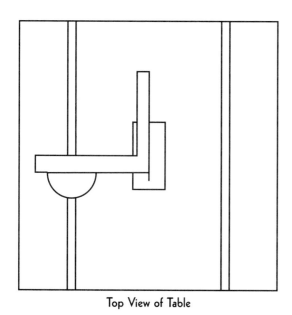

Top View of Table

■ **4–11.** *A try square is also used to check to ensure that the miter gauge is square to the blade.*

CROSSCUTTING SINGLE PIECES TO LENGTH

Follow these step-by-step procedures for crosscutting single pieces to length:

1. Mark the *working edge,* the edge that is square to the working face, with an "X."

2. Mark the *working end,* the end that is square to the working face and working edge, with an "X."

3. Use a try square to lay out the length on the face of the workpiece. Place the try square handle against the working edge when you have drawn the layout line. The layout line is located by measuring from the working end. Extend it to and across the second edge of the piece.

4. Place the working edge of the piece against the face of the miter gauge and move the workpiece so that the layout line is next to the saw blade (4–12). Then make the cut. When this happens, the blade will cut into the scrap area next to the line on the edge.

   This step can be simplified by attaching a wooden *auxiliary fence* to the miter gauge (4–13) and making a saw cut through the wooden fence. This rectangular cut is aligned with the layout line on the workpiece. A test cut ⅛ inch deep is made to verify the alignment.

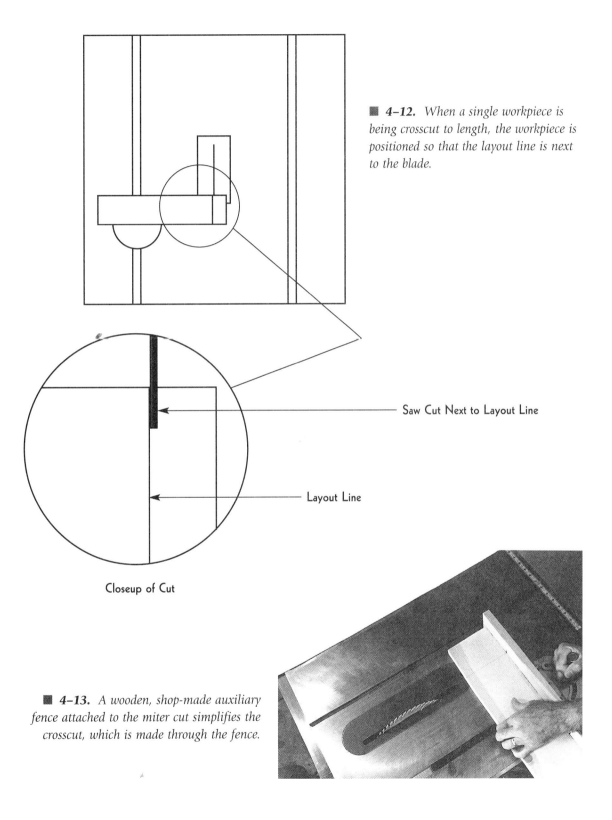

4–12. *When a single workpiece is being crosscut to length, the workpiece is positioned so that the layout line is next to the blade.*

Saw Cut Next to Layout Line

Layout Line

Closeup of Cut

4–13. *A wooden, shop-made auxiliary fence attached to the miter cut simplifies the crosscut, which is made through the fence.*

5. Cut the workpiece. While cutting, hold it firmly against the miter gauge with one hand on the piece and the other on the gauge (4–14). A folded piece of fine sandpaper placed between the workpiece and the miter gauge can be used to help stabilize the piece.

■ **4–14.** *Making the crosscut.*

Extra-wide pieces can be cut by reversing the miter gauge (4–15). A second option consists of fastening a wooden strip to the piece, as shown in 4–16. The strip must be square to the piece's working edge and must fit snugly into the table slot.

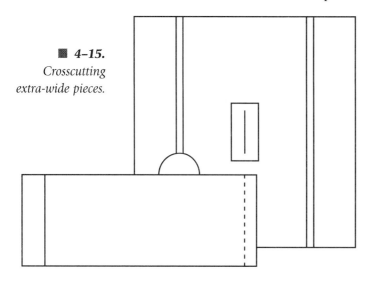

■ **4–15.** *Crosscutting extra-wide pieces.*

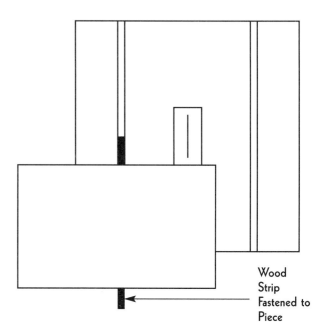

Wood Strip Fastened to Piece

■ **4–16.** *Extra-wide pieces can also be crosscut by fastening a wooden strip to the piece and into the table slot.*

CROSSCUTTING SEVERAL PIECES TO THE SAME LENGTH

Pieces that will be crosscut to the same length can be fastened together and cut as a single piece. Several accessories or user-made items can also be used to cut several pieces to the same length. A clearance block can be fastened to the rip fence or clamped to the saw table to be used as a cutoff stop (4–17). The distance between the saw blade and the clearance block determines the length of the pieces cut. The piece to be crosscut is placed against the miter gauge and slid up to the clearance block. The piece is then crosscut in the normal way. The clearance block, on the rip fence, prevents the cutoff piece

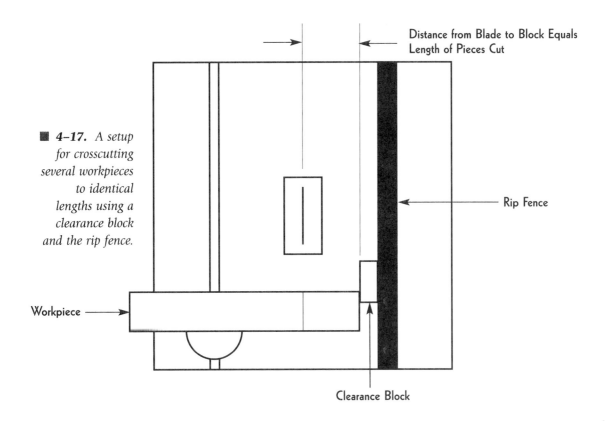

Distance from Blade to Block Equals
Length of Pieces Cut

■ *4–17.* *A setup for crosscutting several workpieces to identical lengths using a clearance block and the rip fence.*

Rip Fence

Workpiece

Clearance Block

from binding between the blade and the rip fence.

A stop block or clamp on the auxiliary fence, which is located on the miter gauge, can also be used as a cutoff stop (4–18). The workpiece is positioned against the stop block for each cut.

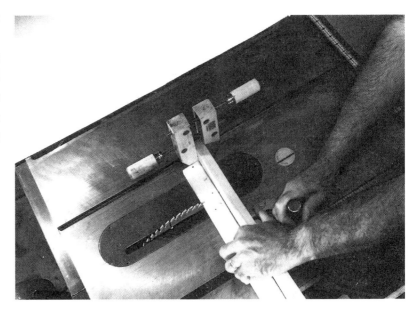

■ *4–18.* *Another option for cross-cutting several workpieces to identical lengths is to use a stop block or clamp on an auxiliary fence.*

Some miter gauges come with stop rods. Stop rods fit into holes on the miter gauge and can be used to control the length of pieces being crosscut (4–19). The distance between the saw blade and the end of the stop rod determines the length of the pieces cut. It is important to check the stop rods to be sure they will clear the saw blade during cutting. This can occur if the miter gauge is placed in the wrong table slot.

DADOES AND RABBETS

Dadoes (U-shaped channels) and rabbets (L-shaped channels) can be made with a series of side-by side-crosscuts until the required material is removed. The use of a dado cutter (also referred to as a dado head) will greatly expedite this process. A standard set of dado cutters consists of two outside cutters, which look like miniature circular saw blades, and a number of inside cutters, or chippers (4–20). These cutters are installed on the saw arbor with the outside cutters on the outside and with the required number of inside cutters sandwiched between them. In effect, this assembly is an extra-thick saw blade that can remove as much as ¾ inch with each pass.

Outside cutters can be used alone for making narrow cuts. *Inside cutters should not be used without the outside cutters in place.* Inside cutters used alone vibrate and can cause a dangerous kickback.

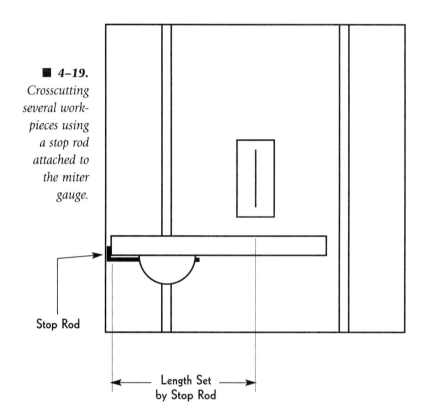

■ *4–19. Crosscutting several work-pieces using a stop rod attached to the miter gauge.*

Stop Rod

Length Set by Stop Rod

■ *4–20. A dado-cutter set consists of two outside cutters, shown at top, and a number of chippers, or inside cutters.*

Follow these step-by-step procedures when cutting dadoes or rabbets:

1. Replace the standard throat plate with a dado throat plate (4–21). Do this whenever dado cutters are being used. Dado throat plates have extra-wide slots to accommodate the extra-wide dado cutters. It is important to replace a dado throat plate with a regular throat plate when reinstalling a saw blade on the arbor.

2. Make the dado or rabbet layout. Do this with a knife, to help limit splitting during cutting.

3. Make the cuts. Crosscutting with the dado cutters is similar to regular crosscutting, except that the cut must be made more slowly. If the dado or rabbet is deep or being

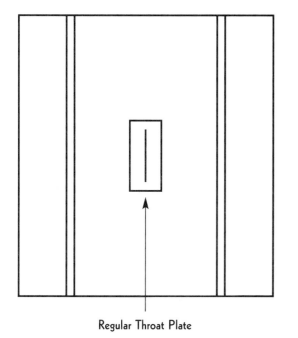

Regular Throat Plate

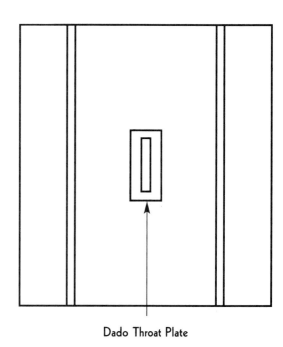

Dado Throat Plate

■ *4–21. When dadoes or rabbets are being cut, the standard throat plate is replaced with a dado throat plate.*

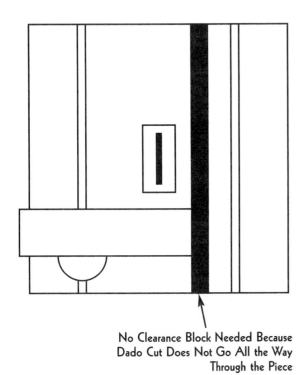

No Clearance Block Needed Because Dado Cut Does Not Go All the Way Through the Piece

■ *4–22. The rip fence can be used as a stop when dado or rabbet cuts are being made.*

cut in a hard wood, like maple, a series of shallow cuts should be made until the required cut depth is reached. Make any trial cuts on scrap material before cutting material intended for use on a project.

The rip fence can be used as a stop for these cuts (4–22). A clearance block is not required because no cutoff pieces are produced.

CUTTING BEVELS AND MITERS

Bevels, which are inclined cuts made across the face of a workpiece, are produced by tilting the

saw blade to the angle required with the blade-tilt wheel. A T-bevel set to the desired angle can be used to check the blade angle (4–23).

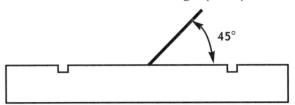

45°

■ *4–23. When bevel or miter cuts are being made, a T-bevel can be used to ensure that the blade is at a 45-degree angle to the tabletop.*

Miters, which are angular cuts made across the face, end, or edge of the workpiece, are produced by loosening the knob on the miter gauge and rotating the miter-gauge head to the new angle. Positioning the workpiece as shown in 4–24 helps to limit the tendency of the piece to slide during cutting. Many miter gauges have positive stops at the common angles such as 45 and 90 degrees.

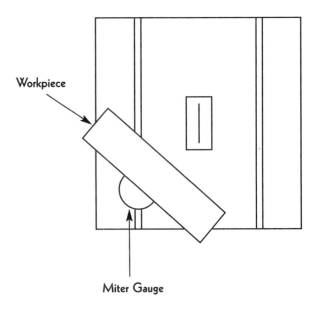

Workpiece

Miter Gauge

■ *4–24. The workpiece is positioned so that it will not slide during cutting.*

Ripping on the Table Saw

Ripping, or cutting with the grain, is done on the table saw using the rip fence. The fence should be parallel to the saw blade or one of the table slots. This can be checked by making a measurement from each end of the rip fence to a table slot. The measurements should be equal. If they are not equal, the fence can usually be adjusted by loosening the bolts holding the two major parts of the fence together and by pushing the fence into alignment with one of the table slots (4–25). The fence must be unlocked while this adjustment is being made. Then the fence is locked and its position is checked again. Once adjusted, the fence should not have to be readjusted unless it has been mishandled.

Straight-edged pieces can be ripped safely on the table saw. The straight edge (working edge) is held against the rip fence during cutting.

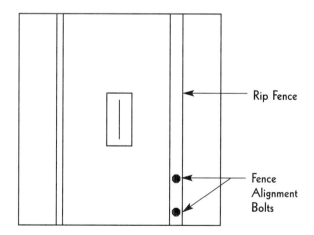

■ **4–25.** *Adjusting the fence usually consists of loosening the bolts that hold the two parts together and aligning the fence with one of the table slots.*

Badly warped or twisted pieces can shift during ripping and should not be cut on the table saw. A piece that does not have a suitable straight edge can be ripped after it has been fastened to an auxiliary piece having one (4–26). The straight edge on the auxiliary piece is held against the rip fence during ripping.

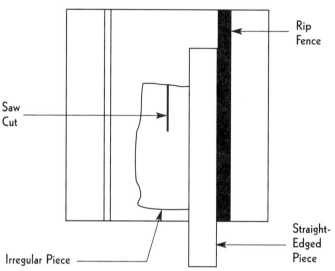

■ **4–26.** *Ripping a workpiece with an irregular edge. The workpiece is attached to a second piece that has a straight edge.*

RIPPING TECHNIQUES

Follow these step-by-step procedures when ripping on the table saw:

1. Adjust the blade so that its teeth are about ¼ inch above the face of the workpiece during cutting.

2. Adjust the fence so that the distance between the blade and the rip fence is equal to the width of the piece required.

When using a saw blade with set teeth, make the measurement from a tooth bent toward the fence (4–27). A test cut ⅛ inch deep should be made to check the distance from the saw kerf to the working edge of the piece.

3. Once the test cut has been made, pull the workpiece from the blade and make the cut.

Use a push stick and featherboard when ripping (4–28).

Extra-long pieces can be ripped in two steps. The first half of the cut is made using the procedures described above. The saw is turned off and the piece is reversed (flipped over, end for end). The working edge is held against the fence while the second half of the cut is completed.

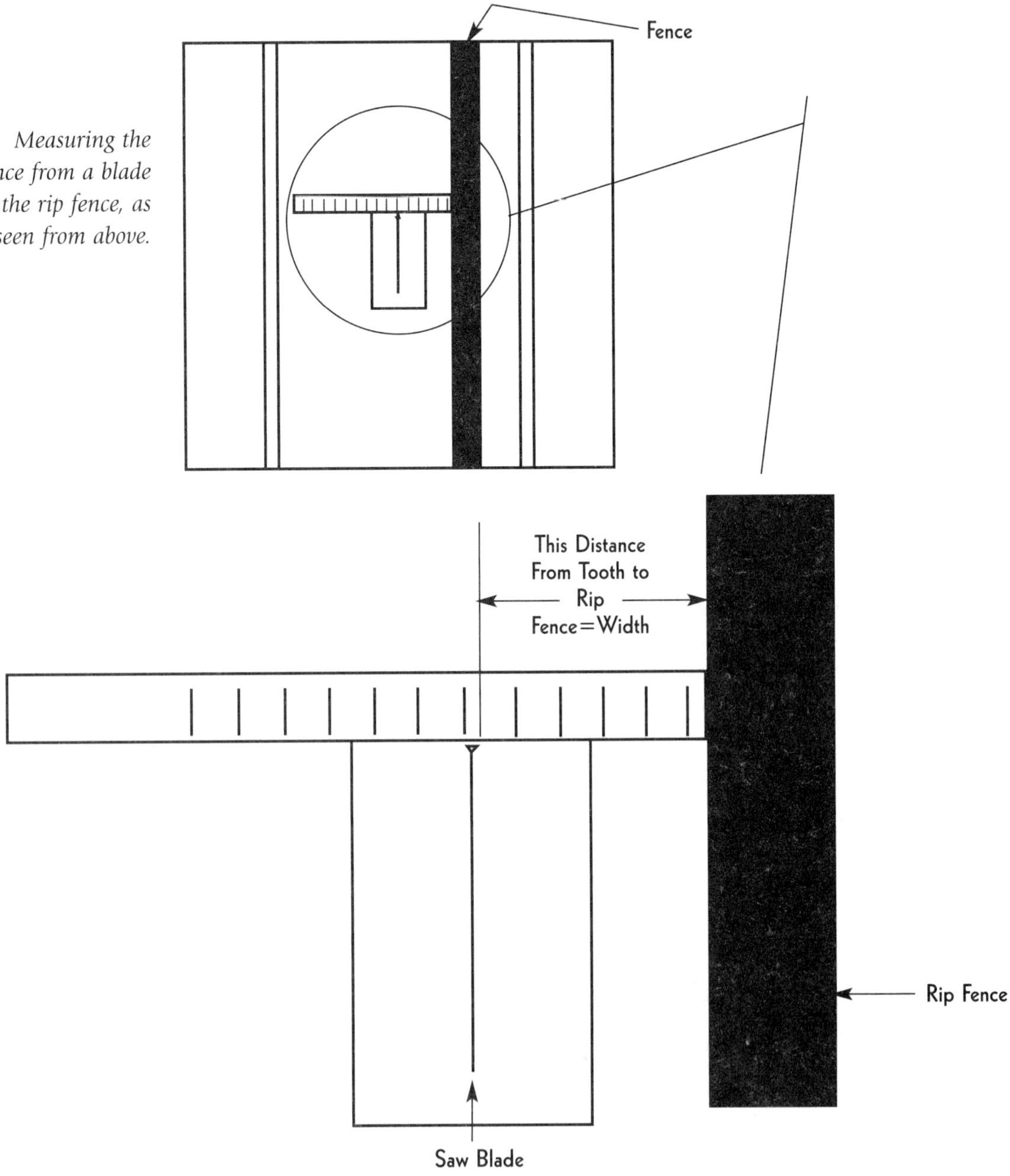

■ **4–27.** *Measuring the distance from a blade tooth to the rip fence, as seen from above.*

Fence

This Distance From Tooth to Rip Fence=Width

Rip Fence

Saw Blade

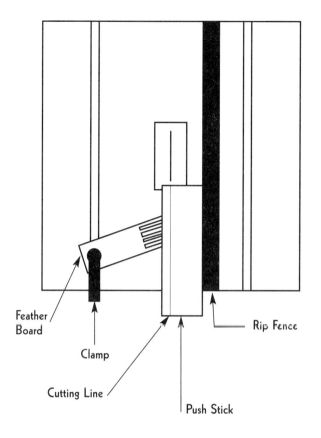

Feather Board

Clamp

Cutting Line

Push Stick

Rip Fence

RESAWING

Resawing is a procedure that is used to rip wide pieces in half by making a series of cuts parallel to the face of the piece. This usually requires the saw guard and splitter to be removed.

Follow these step-by-step procedures when resawing:

1. Adjust the saw blade so that it projects about two inches above the table's surface. Place the working face of the piece against the rip fence and make the first cut (4–29). If the saw appears to be laboring at the two-inch setting, stop the cut and reset the saw to make a shallower cut.

2. Flip the piece over, end for end, place the working face against the rip fence, and make the second cut into the opposite edge. Raise the blade approximately one inch and resaw each cut. Continue this until the piece is cut all the way through from edge to edge.

3. Use a band saw to make the final cut.

■ *4–28.* *Making a rip cut using a push stick and a feather board, as viewed from above*

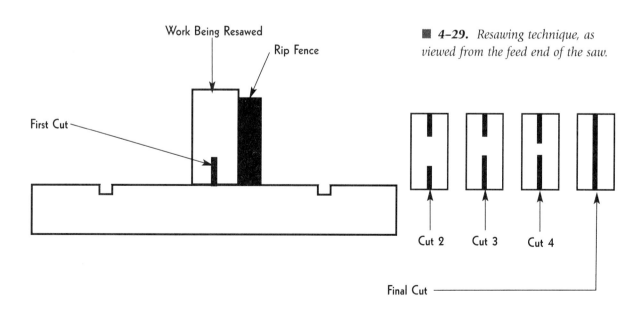

Work Being Resawed

Rip Fence

First Cut

■ *4–29.* *Resawing technique, as viewed from the feed end of the saw.*

Cut 2   Cut 3   Cut 4

Final Cut

BEVELED EDGES

Beveled edges can produced by ripping a piece with the saw blade set at an angle other than 90 degrees. The workpiece and blade should be positioned as shown in 4–30 to reduce the tendency of the piece to bind between the saw blade and the rip fence.

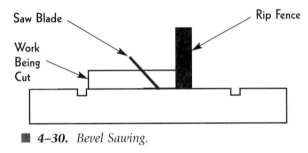

■ *4–30. Bevel Sawing.*

EDGE RABBETS

Edge rabbets can be cut in two steps, using the table saw and the rip fence. The first cut is made into the face of the piece as shown in 4–31a. The second cut is made into the edge as shown in 4–31b. This procedure prevents the cutoff piece from being trapped between the saw blade and the rip fence. A trapped piece can be kicked back toward the operator.

TAPERS

Tapered pieces, pieces with non-parallel edges, can be cut using an adjustable fixture (4–32). The first step is to lay out the taper on the workpiece. Next, place the piece in the fixture and adjust the fixture so that the layout line on the workpiece is parallel to one of the slots in the table of the saw.

Now position the fixture, with the workpiece in place, against the table saw's rip fence. Move the rip fence until the layout line on the workpiece is aligned with the saw blade. At this point,

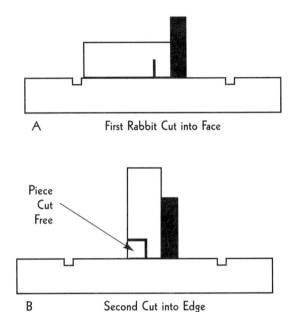

■ *4–31. Cutting edge rabbets. A: A cut being made into the face of the workpiece. B: A second cut being made into the edge of the workpiece.*

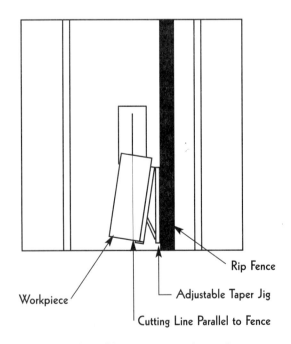

■ *4–32. An adjustable-taper jig can be used to cut tapered pieces, as viewed from above.*

the position of the blade should be checked to ensure that it will not come into contact with the fixture during cutting.

Move the workpiece and taper fixture as a unit along the rip fence while completing the rip cut. Hands should be positioned so that they will not come close to the saw blade during cutting. *If this is not possible, the cut should not be made on the table saw.*

Fixed Taper Fixture

A fixed taper fixture can be made for taper-cutting (4–33). Cut the piece to be tapered to length and width and lay the taper-cut line out on it. Lay out the fixture by placing the workpiece on the taper cutting fixture with the taper-cut line parallel to the table slot. Trace the workpiece onto the fixture and cut out the layout on the band saw. The workpiece must fit snugly into the cutout in the fixture and must be surrounded by the wood on three sides.

Move the workpiece and taper fixture together as a unit against the rip fence and make the cut. It is important for the operator to keep his or her hands positioned so that they will not come

close to the saw blade during cutting. *If this is not possible, the cut should not be made on the table saw.*

RABBET-DADO JOINT

A rabbet-dado joint can be made on the table saw without using any special blades or fixtures (4–34). This joint is a simple lock joint that is often used in drawer or box construction.

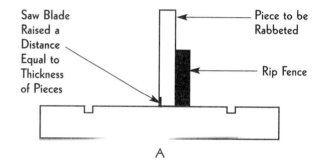

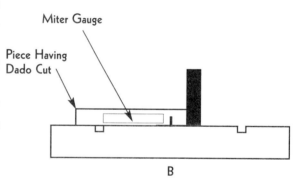

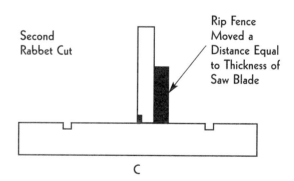

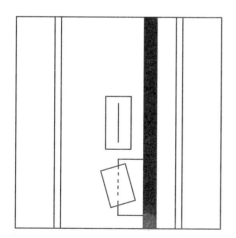

■ *4–33. Setup for fixed-taper jig, as viewed from above.*

■ *4–34. The three steps involved with making a rabbet-dado joint using a standard table-saw blade, as viewed from the feed end of the saw.*

FINGER JOINTS

Finger joints, which are often used in box construction, can be made on the table saw using an auxiliary fence attached to the miter gauge and a fixture. The width of the fingers will equal the thickness of the saw blade.

Making the Fixture

To make the fixture, do the following:

1. Clamp an auxiliary fence to the miter gauge.
2. Raise the saw blade so that it projects above the table a distance equal to the thickness of the pieces to be joined. This can be checked by placing a piece of the material being cut on the saw table next to the blade.
3. Make the first cut through the auxiliary fence. Make a wooden pin that will fit into the saw cut in the fence. The pin should be about one inch long. Insert the pin halfway into the saw cut in the fence.
4. Loosen the clamp holding the auxiliary fence and move the fence to the right a distance equal to the width of the saw cut. Place an extra piece of the pin between the saw blade and the pin, to set this distance.

Fasten the auxiliary fence to the miter gauge with screws.

5. Make the second cut through the auxiliary fence. The distance between the first and second cuts should be equal to the width of the saw cuts (4–35a).

Cutting a Finger Joint

The following procedure is recommended for cutting a finger joint:

1. Make the first cut by placing the first piece of squared-up stock to be joined with its edge against the pin; then cut through it (4–35b).
2. Make the second cut on the stock after placing it *over* the pin. Repeat this process until all of the cuts have been made in the first piece.
3. Make the first cut to the second piece by aligning the edge of the piece with the saw blade, as shown in 4–35c.
4. Move the cut piece to the right until the cut slips over the pin. Make cuts two, three, etc., as described above until all of the required cuts have been made.

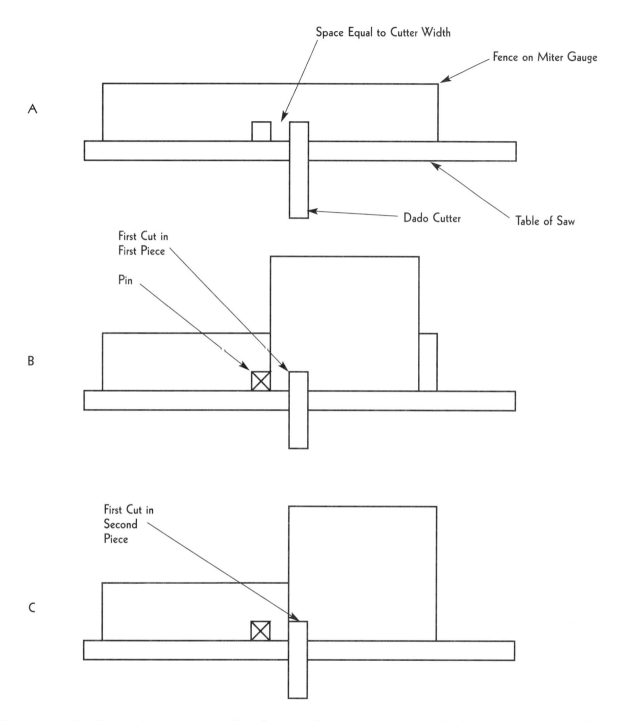

■ **4–35.** *Making finger joints using an auxiliary fence attached to a miter gauge and a fixture. A shows the auxiliary fence with two saw cuts; the distance between the two saw cuts should be equal in width to the saw cuts. B: The first cut is made by placing the first piece of squared-up stock with its edge against the pin. C: The first cut in the second piece of squared-up stock is made by aligning the edge of the piece with the blade. As viewed from the feed end of the saw.*

POWER MITER SAW

The power miter saw (4–36) is a power tool designed to make a variety of cuts that are similar to those made in a miter box. These include cuts that are square to the working face of the piece, but at an angle ranging from 90 to 45 degrees to its working *edge*.

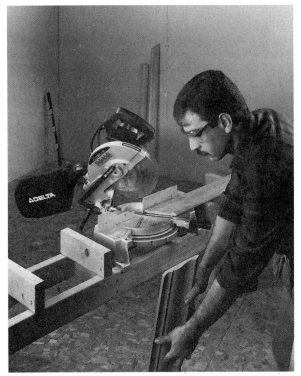

■ *4–37.* *Power miter saw set to make a 45-degree cut.*

■ *4–36.* *Power miter saw set for a 90-degree cut.*

The saw can also be tilted to make cuts ranging from 90 to 45 degrees to the working *face* (4–37). It can also be used make compound miter cuts.

The typical "low-end" saw has an 8¼-inch-diameter saw blade. The maximum cutting width of an 8¼-inch saw blade is 5¼ inches.

It can cut through material up to about 2⅛ inches thick. A 10-inch saw can be used to cut 2 × 6's and 4 × 4's. These saws are light enough to be carried to the job site. Miter saws are especially useful for crosscutting pieces that are too long to cut safely on the table saw (4–38).

■ *4–38.* *Cutting an extra-long piece on the miter saw.*

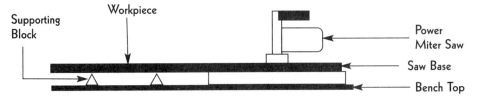

Safety Techniques

These safety techniques should be followed when using a power miter saw:

1. Always follow the safety instructions provided by the manufacturer.
2. Wear approved eye protection and a dust mask.
3. Unplug the saw from its power supply before making any adjustments.
4. Check the saw to be sure that it is locked at the angle desired.
5. Blades should be sharp and securely attached to the saw arbor.
6. Make sure that the working edge of the workpiece is against the saw fence before making a cut.
7. The piece being cut must be long enough for the holding hand to be well away from the saw blade.
8. Only use the saw when the saw guard is in place and operational.
9. Make sure that the power cords are clear of the saw's cutting path.
10. After completing the cuts, return the saw to its starting position. The workpiece can be removed once the blade stops rotating

Cutting with the Power Miter Saw

Follow these step-by-step procedures when cutting with a power miter saw:

1. Make a layout of the cut on the workpiece.
2. Adjust the angle settings as required.
3. Place the working *edge* of the workpiece against the saw fence and align the layout line with the saw blade. This can be done by lowering the saw to the work so that the blade is exposed. Unplug the saw before doing this.
4. Plug the saw in and make the cut while holding the workpiece against the fence.

BAND SAW

Band saws (4–39) are primarily designed for curved cutting. The machine consists of an "endless" blade that travels over two wheels with rubber tires. The rubber tires help to keep the blade from slipping on or cutting into the rims of the wheels. The blade travels through a tiltable table, which is used to support the work as it is cut.

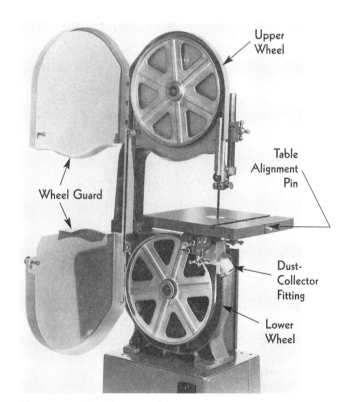

■ 4–39. *A band saw and its components.*

The upper wheel can be raised and lowered to tension the blade. It can be tilted for blade tracking (4–40). Blade supports or thrust bearings located above and below the table are used to keep the saw blade from moving too far back during cutting (4–41).

■ **4–40.** *The tracking knob on a band saw.*

■ **4–41.** *The blade-support system on a band saw.*

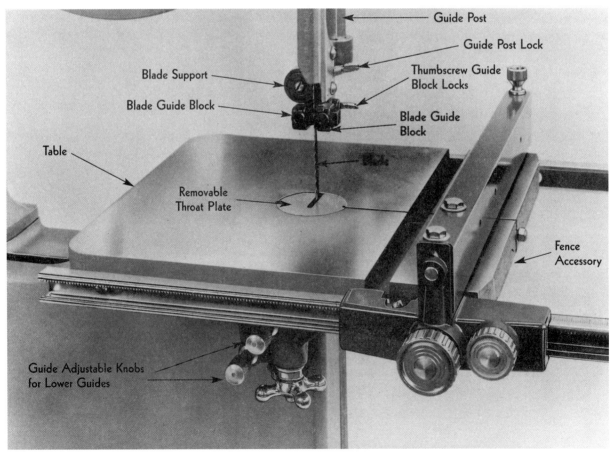

Guide blocks on each side of the blade limit lateral or side-to-side blade movement. The saw blade is adjusted so that the saw teeth remain clear of the guide blocks during cutting and the back edge of the blade does not contact the blade supports until cutting begins.

The upper blade support and guides are mounted on a post that can be raised or lowered to position the blade guides about ⅛ inch above the workpiece. The tiltable saw table has a slot cut into it that allows the saw blade to be installed or removed from the machine. A removable aligning pin is used to keep the table sections on each side of the slot in alignment.

A circular throat plate or table insert surrounds the blade. This plate must be in place when the saw is in use.

The band-saw wheels are enclosed by removable guards or doors that provide protection for the operator and allow access to the wheels. Guards must be in place and doors must be closed whenever the saw is in use.

Guidelines for Buying a New Band Saw

Pay attention to these guidelines when buying a new band saw:

1. Purchase the best machine that you can afford.
2. Select a band saw made by a manufacturer with a reputation for making quality equipment.
3. The saw should come with a dealer and manufacturer warranty.
4. If possible, select a saw with wheels that are at least 14 inches in diameter. This allows 26-inch-wide material to be cut in half on

the saw. A saw of this size should be equipped with a motor that is powerful enough to cut hardwoods up to three or four inches thick.

5. Check the motor to determine its size and type. Single-phase 110–120-volt motors can be connected to a standard power supply system.
6. Check the basic accessories like the saw and belt guards, miter gauges, rip fences, and saw tables for quality and ease of use. Miter gauges should fit snugly into table slots without any side-to-side movement.

Guidelines for Buying a Used Band Saw

Before buying a used band saw, refer to Buying Used Power Tools on page 77. Then read the following guidelines:

1. Make sure that the characteristics of the machine (including the blades and the motor) match your woodworking requirements. *Belt-driven* machines as a general rule are often preferable to *direct-drive* units because many small, direct-drive machines are underpowered. Band saws that have more than two wheels should be avoided. Blades used in these saws don't last as long as those in two-wheel machines.
2. Check the availability and condition of basic accessories like saw and belt guards and the miter gauge, rip fence, throat plate, and motor. The miter gauge should fit snugly into the table slot without any side-to-side movement.
3. Make sure that the blade-tensioning and tracking systems are easy to use. Also check the condition of blade guides and supports.

Blade supports or thrust bearings should turn freely.

4. Test the band saw you are considering buying. The saw blade should not contact the blade support until a cut is made. When the cut is completed, the saw blade should move back to its starting position in front of the blade support. Do not buy a band saw that does not track properly.

Band-Saw Blades

Band-saw blades enable the band saw to perform all its cutting operations. A sharp, properly selected blade will cut more efficiently and safely than one that is dull or worn. Dull blades can overheat during cutting and break. When this happens, the saw blade can whip out of the machine and injure the operator. Worn or cracked blades should be discarded.

Band-saw blades range in width from ⅛ to ¾ inch. A properly tensioned ⅛-inch-wide blade can cut a curve having a ⅛-inch radius. A ¼-inch-wide blade can cut a curve having a 5/8-inch radius. A ½-inch-wide blade can cut a curve having a 2½-inch radius.

Blade pitch is an indication of the number of teeth per inch on a blade. A six-pitch blade has six teeth per inch. This blade is used for cutting thin, hard materials. Blades with a pitch of four have four teeth per inch and are suitable for soft, thick materials. Blades designed for cutting a variety of non-wood materials are available.

Blade length is determined by the size of the band saw's wheels. Check the instructions that come with the band saw to determine blade size.

REPLACING BAND-SAW BLADES

Pay attention to these general instructions for removing band-saw blades. Check the manufacturer's instructions for specific directions.

1. Disconnect the band saw from its power supply.
2. Remove or open the wheel covers.
3. Remove the table-alignment pin and the throat plate.
4. Release the blade tension, using the blade-tensioning knob or lever.
5. Lower the upper wheel until the saw blade becomes slack.
6. Remove the saw blade.
7. Slide the replacement blade through the table slot and hang it over the top wheel. Make sure that the teeth on the portion of the blade going through the table are pointing down.
8. Tension the blade. When the blade is tensioned properly, moderate finger pressure should deflect the blade about ¼ inch.
9. Loosen the blade supports and guides, and move them as far back as possible.
10. Rotate the upper wheel in a clockwise direction. While rotating the wheel, turn the tilt knob until the blade moves to the center of the wheel rim and remains there.
11. Readjust the blade supports so that they are about 1/64 inch behind the back edge of the blade. Adjust the guide blocks so that they are behind the saw teeth.
12. Close the wheel covers. Then reinstall the throat plate and table-aligning pin. Connect the band saw back to its power supply. Make a test cut.

Checking and Aligning Band-Saw Wheels

If a band-saw blade is in good condition and will not remain tracked, check the alignment of the wheels. New band saws sometimes have misaligned wheels. When aligning the wheels, follow these procedures:

1. Disconnect the band saw from its power supply.
2. Remove or open the wheel covers (4–42).

■ **4–42.** *Band-saw wheels must be aligned vertically.*

3. Remove the table-alignment pin and the throat plate.
4. Release the blade tension, using the blade-tensioning knob or lever.
5. Lower the upper wheel until the blade becomes slack.
6. Remove the blade.
7. Remove the table from the band saw.

8. Place a straightedge across the wheels and check their vertical alignment.
9. If the wheels are not in the same vertical plane, one of the wheels must be repositioned. Because saws vary in design, each must be examined to determine how a wheel can be adjusted. On some band saws, washers can be placed behind one of the wheels. In others, the bearing block can be loosened and moved. In any case, the wheels must be brought into alignment.
10. After aligning the wheels, reinstall and tension the saw blade. Test the band saw by turning one of the wheels by hand. If the blade remains tracked, reassemble the machine and make a test cut.

Safety Techniques

These safety techniques should be followed when using a band saw:

1. Wear approved eye protection and a dust mask.
2. Clear the table and make sure the appropriate saw and belt guards are in place.
3. Check the sharpness and condition of the blade.
4. Check the blade guides to make sure that they are not more than ⅛ inch above the surface of the piece to be cut.
5. Make sure that no one is standing near the right side of the saw. If the blade breaks, it can whip out toward the right side of the machine.
6. Keep fingers and hands away from the saw blade. A push stick should be used when necessary.
7. Make sure that the saw comes to a complete

stop before making any attempt to back out of a cut.

8. Properly support any round or irregularly shaped work so that shifting during cutting cannot occur.

9. Do not remove scraps from the work area until the saw comes to a complete stop.

Cutting Curves on the Band Saw

Curved cuts are almost always made on a band saw when one is available. Even small band saws can cut through material up to five or six inches thick. This is because the relatively small area of blade in contact with the material keeps the amount of friction generated low.

Follow these step-by-step procedures when cutting curves on a band saw:

1. Make a layout of the cut on the workpiece (4–43).

2. Reposition the blade guides so that they will be about ⅛ inch above the material during cutting.

3. Turn the saw on and cut excess material away from the layout so that the relief cuts

will not be more than one inch long. The relief cuts allow you to "back out" of the cut without stopping the machine. *The band saw must be fully stopped when backing out of curved cuts or straight cuts longer than one inch in length.*

4. Make the relief cuts at one-inch intervals. Smaller-radius layout lines may require relief cuts that are closer together (4–44).

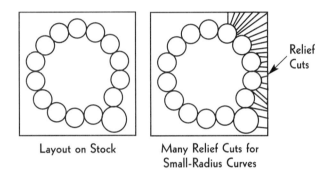

Layout on Stock   Many Relief Cuts for Small-Radius Curves

■ **4–44.** *Relief cuts on a small-radius curve are made closer together.*

5. Cut out the laid-out shape. This cut can be made next to the layout lines to allow extra material for removal during final smoothing and finishing.

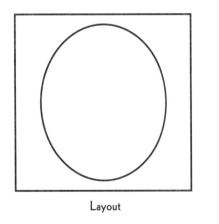

Layout

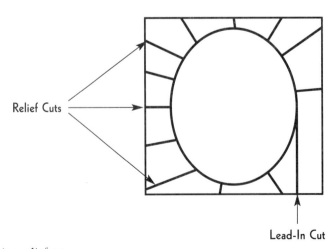

Relief Cuts

Lead-In Cut

■ **4–43.** *A layout of a band-saw cut featuring relief cuts.*

6. Turn the saw off and make sure that it is fully stopped before removing the workpiece.

Straight Cuts on the Band Saw

Straight cuts can be made on the band saw when a wide blade is used.

Crosscutting can be done with a miter gauge when one is available. This cut is made by holding the working edge of the workpiece against the face of the miter gauge during cutting. Excess material should be left for final squaring and smoothing.

Ripping can be done with or without a rip fence. A temporary rip fence can be clamped to the table if necessary (4–45).

Resawing on the band saw allows extra-wide pieces that have been partially ripped on the table saw to be separated (4–46). An extra-wide auxiliary fence is often used for this purpose.

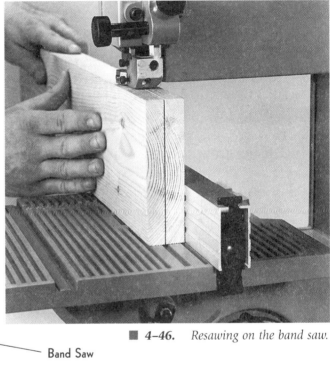

■ **4–46.** *Resawing on the band saw.*

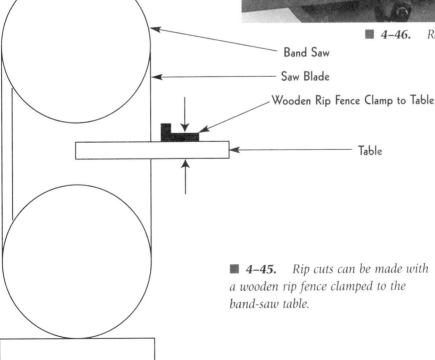

Band Saw

Saw Blade

Wooden Rip Fence Clamp to Table

Table

■ **4–45.** *Rip cuts can be made with a wooden rip fence clamped to the band-saw table.*

Cutting Circles on the Band Saw

Circles can be cut on the band saw by using a simple fixture attached to the saw table (4–47a). Follow these step-by-step procedures:

1. Make the fixture by attaching a piece of ½-inch-thick plywood of appropriate size to the saw table.
2. Cut a slot into the piece of plywood while sliding it into place on the saw table. Drive a nail into the plywood on a line that is at a 90-degree angle to the blade. The distance from the blade to the nail should be equal to the radius of the circle to be cut.
3. Lay out the circle on the workpiece. Cut a notch into the piece as shown in 4–47b. Relief cuts can be made around the circle at one-inch intervals.
4. Drill a hole through the workpiece at the center of the circle layout, using a drill that is equal in size to the nail in the fixture.
5. Place the workpiece over the nail in the fixture. Lower the saw guide until it is about ⅛ inch above the workpiece. Cut out the circle (4–47b).

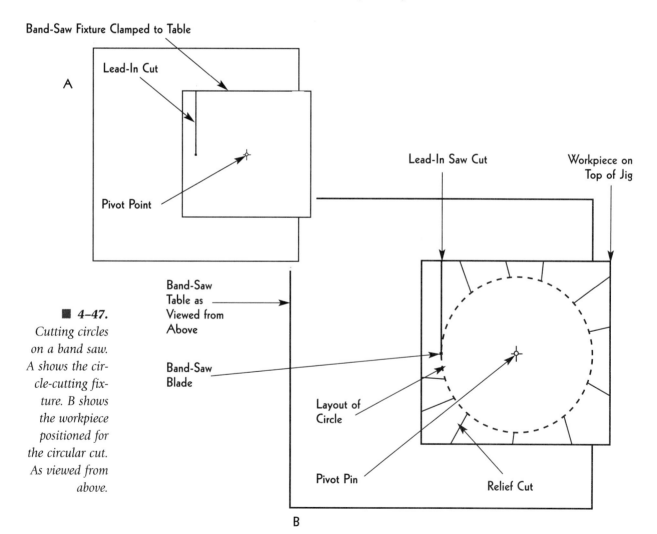

Band-Saw Fixture Clamped to Table

Lead-In Cut

A

Pivot Point

Lead-In Saw Cut

Workpiece on Top of Jig

Band-Saw Table as Viewed from Above

Band-Saw Blade

Layout of Circle

Pivot Pin

Relief Cut

B

■ **4–47.** *Cutting circles on a band saw. A shows the circle-cutting fixture. B shows the workpiece positioned for the circular cut. As viewed from above.*

Compound Sawing

Compound sawing (4–48) can be used to cut out pieces like cabriole legs. After layouts are made on the adjacent surfaces of the workpiece, the first cut is made. The cut pieces are reassembled and taped together, and then the second cut is made. *Relief cuts cannot be used in this procedure.*

■ **4–48.** *Compound-sawing a workpiece. The first cut has already been made.*

Cutting Multiple Pieces

Multiple pieces having an identical shape can be produced by making a series of side-by-side cuts as shown in 4–49 or by stacking and taping pieces together prior to sawing, as shown in 4–50.

■ **4–49.** *Slicing cuts can be used to cut multiple pieces.*

■ **4–50.** *Another way to cut multiple pieces on a band saw is to stack and tape them together and then cut them.*

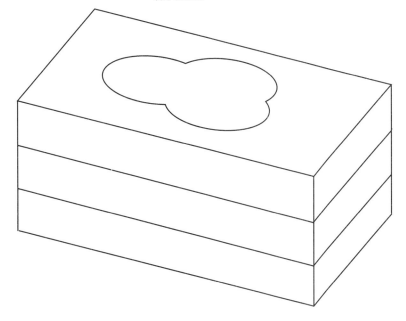

DRILL PRESS

The drill press (4–51) is probably the second most frequently used machine in the woodworker's shop. Its primary purpose is to make holes at right angles to the horizontal surface of the workpiece.

The base and column form the foundation of the drill press. The head is mounted near the top of the column. It consists of a motor and a spin-

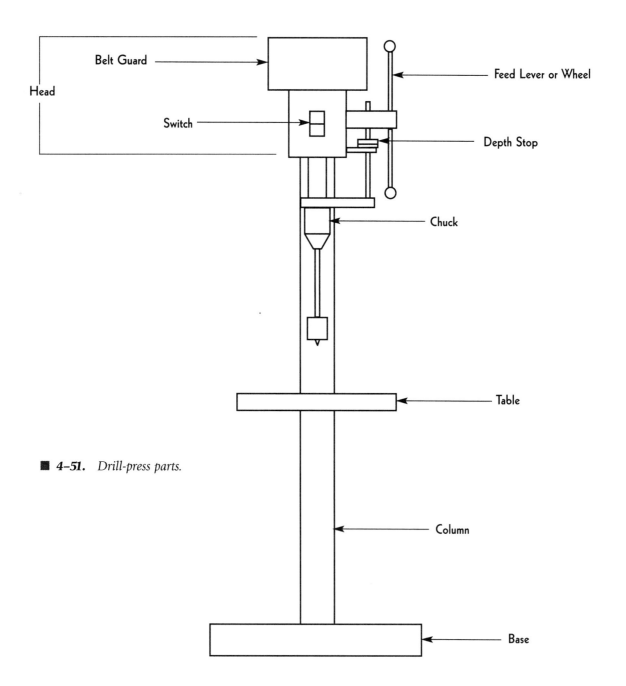

■ *4–51.* *Drill-press parts.*

dle that can be raised and lowered using a feed wheel. A three-jaw chuck attached to the end of the spindle holds the accessories that are used on the drill press.

A *movable table* is mounted on the column between the base and the head. The table supports the work being processed on the drill press. Some machines are equipped with a table that can be tilted. The base of the drill press can be used as a table for extra-large workpieces.

Drill-press capacity is determined by measuring the distance from the center of the chuck to the column. This distance is doubled to indicate the unit's size. For example, a machine that measures 7½ inches from the center of the chuck to the column is classified as a 15-inch drill press.

Guidelines for Buying a New Drill Press

It is useful to remember that the drill press is primarily designed for metalworking. Follow these guidelines when buying a new drill press:

1. Purchase the best machine that you can afford. Floor-mounted machines do not cost much more than bench models, and they do not take up valuable bench space.
2. Select a drill press made by a manufacturer with a reputation for quality.
3. The drill press should come with a dealer and manufacturer warranty.
4. Select a drill press that has a table that can be raised and lowered with a crank or similar device. The table should be sturdy and well supported.
5. Check the size and type of the motor. A ¼-horsepower motor is adequate for most purposes. Most drill presses have stepped motor pulleys that allow spindle speeds to be var-

ied (4–52). A single-spindle-speed machine should be avoided.

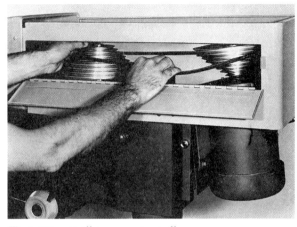

■ *4–52. Drill-press motor pulleys.*

6. Look for a drill press with spindle stops, locks, and travel indicators. These are desirable features. The stop limits spindle travel and can be used to limit hole depth (4–53).

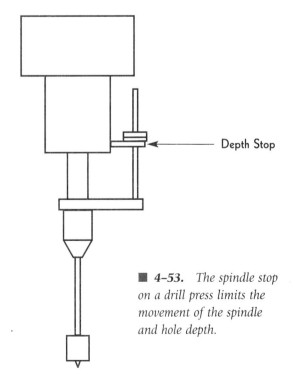

■ *4–53. The spindle stop on a drill press limits the movement of the spindle and hole depth.*

Depth Stop

The lock allows the spindle to be lowered and locked in place. The travel indicator can be used to indicate hole depth.

7. Try to find a drill press with a chuck that has a tapered shank. The tapered shank allows the chuck be removed and replaced easily. A chuck capacity of at least ½ inch is desirable.

Guidelines for Buying a Used Drill Press

Before buying a used drill press, refer to Buying Used Power Tools on page 77. Then read the following guidelines:

1. Check the drill-press spindle for side play. Movement usually indicates worn spindle bearings.
2. Make sure that the locked drill-press table is stable. This can be done by using the chuck to apply pressure to a block of wood placed on the table. Ideally the table should not move when pressure is applied (4–54).

■ **4–54.** *Checking the drill press for movement.*

Safety Techniques

These safety techniques should be followed when using a drill press:

1. Wear approved eye protection and a dust mask.
2. Set the drill press to a speed that is appropriate for the job at hand.
3. Turn off the power supply to the machine before making any adjustments on it.
4. Remove the chuck key from the chuck immediately after using the drill press. If it is left in the chuck, it will be thrown out when the machine is started.
5. Make sure that the belt guards are in place before starting the machine.
6. Properly secure and center the cutting tools in the chuck.
7. Properly secure the workpiece to the table.
8. Lock the table in position before using the machine.
9. Keep feet clear of the drill press base to avoid injury in the event the table falls.

Hole-Making on the Drill Press

Hole-making is the most common operation done on the drill press. Many hole-making devices can be used on this machine. Most of the devices can be used following the procedures outlined below.

BORING HOLES ON THE DRILL PRESS

Follow these step-by-step procedures when boring holes on the drill press:

1. Install the bit to be used in the drill-press chuck. It must be in good condition and it must be centered in the chuck. The drill press shown in 4–55 has an auxiliary wood-

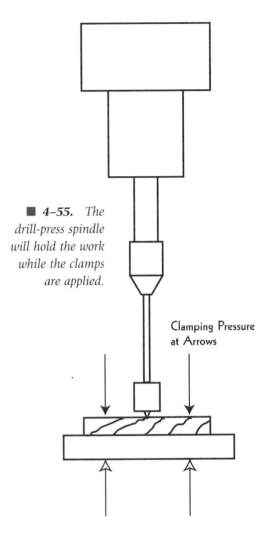

■ *4–55. The drill-press spindle will hold the work while the clamps are applied.*

Clamping Pressure
at Arrows

5. Release the spindle lock, allowing the spindle to return to the top position.

6. Bore the hole using moderate pressure. During the boring process, the bit should be withdrawn from the workpiece periodically so that shavings can be removed from the hole.

If a clean exit hole is required, the piece should be placed on a backup block before the boring begins.

BORING BLIND HOLES

Blind holes are holes that do not go all the way through the workpiece. These holes can be bored to a predetermined depth by setting the depth stop on the drill press (4–56). Lay out the required hole depth on the edge of the work-

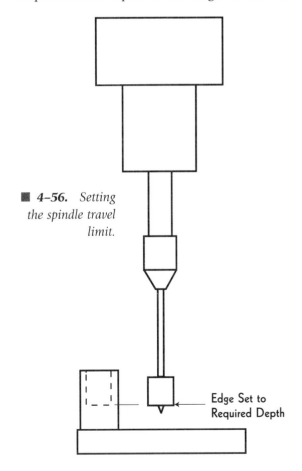

■ *4–56. Setting the spindle travel limit.*

Edge Set to
Required Depth

en table attached to the steel drill-press table.

2. Lay out the center of the hole to be bored on the workpiece. Place the workpiece on the drill-press table and align the layout with the bit in the chuck.

3. Move the bit down until it penetrates the workpiece slightly and lock the drill-press spindle. In the example shown in 4–55, the bit helps to hold the workpiece in position while it is being clamped to the table.

4. Use clamps to secure the workpiece to the drill-press table.

piece and move the bit down to that line. With the spindle held in this position, set the depth stop. Small adjustments can be made by cranking the table up or down. The hole is bored using the procedure described above.

LOCATING AND BORING HOLES IN SEVERAL IDENTICAL PIECES

This job can be accomplished by stacking and fastening the pieces together prior to boring the holes.

If the pieces must be handled individually, positioning strips can be attached to an auxiliary drill-press table. As shown in 4–57, the auxiliary table is being used as a "fixture" that holds and positions the work.

BORING ALIGNED HOLES

This is done by constructing the simple fixture shown in 4–58. Its fence positions the workpiece so that the centerlines of the series of holes are aligned with the center of the boring tool. The workpiece is kept against the fixture fence during boring.

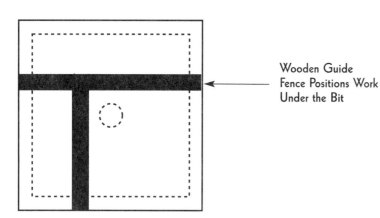

Wooden Guide
Fence Positions Work
Under the Bit

Top View of Drill-Press Table with
Auxiliary Wood Table in Place

■ **4–57.** *Using a positioning strip and an auxiliary drill-press table to locate and bore a hole in several pieces. As view from above.*

■ **4–58.** *Using a fixture to space holes uniformly on a drill press.*

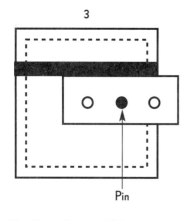

3

Pin

The Space Between Holes
Equals the Distance from the
Removable Pin to the Center of
the Drill-Press Chuck

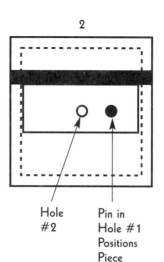

2

Hole
#2

Pin in
Hole #1
Positions
Piece
Hole #2

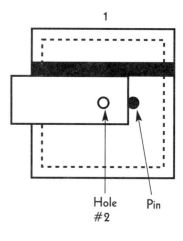

1

Hole
#2

Pin

BORING A SERIES OF EQUALLY SPACED HOLES

Follow these step-by-step procedures to bore a series of equally spaced holes:

1. Lay out the first two holes in the series on the workpiece.
2. Place the workpiece on the fixture shown in 4–58. Bore a hole at the layout of hole one through the workpiece and into the fixture. Insert a dowel through the hole in the workpiece and glue it into the hole in the fixture under it. This dowel holds the workpiece in position on the fixture.
3. Slide the fixture and workpiece to the right until the bit is aligned with the layout of hole two.
4. Clamp the fixture to the drill-press table and bore hole two.
5. Locate each successive hole by lifting the workpiece off the aligning pin and placing the newly bored hole over the pin. Then bore the new hole. Repeat this until all of the holes are bored.

BORING ANGULAR AND POCKET HOLES

Angular holes can be bored, at angles other than 90 degrees, by tilting the drill-press table.

Pocket holes, which are used to fasten table rails to tabletops, can be bored using a shop-made pocket-hole fixture (4–59).

DRUM SANDERS AND ROTARY RASPS

Drum sanders and rotary rasps can be installed and used on the drill press in conjunction with an auxiliary shop-made table (4–60).

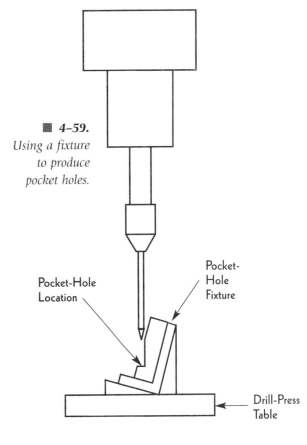

■ **4–59.** *Using a fixture to produce pocket holes.*

Pocket-Hole Location

Pocket-Hole Fixture

Drill-Press Table

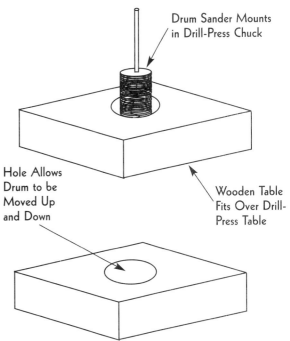

Drum Sander Mounts in Drill-Press Chuck

Wooden Table Fits Over Drill-Press Table

Hole Allows Drum to be Moved Up and Down

■ **4–60.** *Auxiliary drill-press sanding table.*

SCROLL SAW

The scroll saw is often the first machine purchased by the beginning woodworker. This may be the case because the machine is not intimidating and appears to be easy and safe to use. The scroll saw (4–61) is a motorized version of the coping saw. It is designed to make curved cuts in relatively thin materials. Unlike the band saw, which also cuts curves well, it can be used to do piercing. Piercing involves making internal cutouts without lead-in cuts (4–62).

Scroll saws are available in sizes ranging from 15 to 24 inches. A 16-inch scroll saw, for example, measures 16 inches from the blade to the overarm. A two-inch depth of cut is common on scroll saws.

Fixed-arm scroll saws (4–62) have bases that house a crank-like device that causes the lower plunger to reciprocate. The plunger has a chuck attached to its upper end that holds the lower

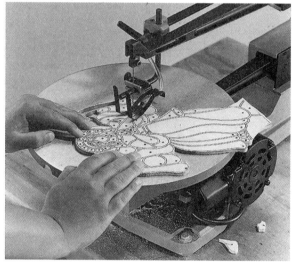

■ *4–62.* *Piercing a workpiece.*

■ *4–61.* *A scroll saw and its components.*

C Frame

Dust Blower

Upper Chuck

Blade

Hold-Down Foot

Removable Throat Plate

Table

end of the saw blade. Stepped pulleys on the motor and the scroll saw allow the speed of the machine to be varied.

A tiltable table with a removable table insert or throat plate is mounted on the base. The table supports the work during cutting.

An overarm is attached to or is an integral part of the base. The overarm holds an adjustable tension sleeve and the upper plunger. The spring in the tension sleeve is compressed during blade installation and keeps the blade rigid during cutting. The upper plunger has a chuck attached to it that engages the upper end of the saw blade.

The guide post houses a blade-support roller and guide disc (4–63). The roller helps to keep the blade from moving too far to the rear of the saw during cutting. The guide disc provides lateral (side-to-side) control. When the blade is properly installed, its downward-pointing teeth are clear of the guide disc.

Some units have a rotatable lower plunger that can hold a rigid blade used for saber-sawing.

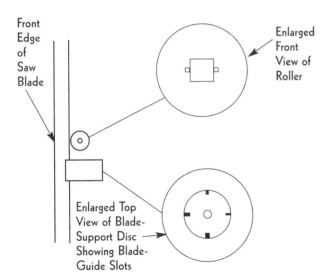

■ **4–63.** *The blade-support roller and guide disc on a scroll saw.*

C-frame scroll saws function in much the same way that coping saws do. The blade is held in a frame that is similar in shape and function to a coping-saw frame. The tensioned blade cuts as the frame is rocked back and forth (4–64). Tension is applied by turning a knob at the top end of the blade.

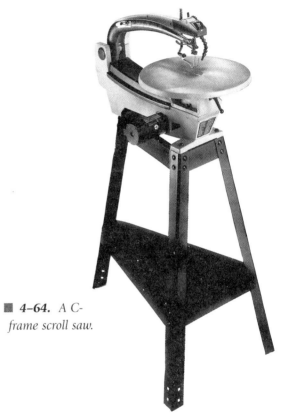

■ **4–64.** *A C-frame scroll saw.*

Buying a New Scroll Saw

Before buying a new scroll saw, refer to Buying New Power Tools on page 77. Then read the following guidelines:

1. A scroll saw with variable-speed capability is desirable. This allows the saw to be used to cut a variety of materials.
2. Select a saw that has a good blade-supporting system. The system should include an

anti-thrust roller and a blade-guide disc with several size slots. This will allow a variety of saw blades to be used.

3. For its increased versatility, select a machine with saber-sawing capability.

4. The selection of a scroll saw with a built-in blower is a good idea. The blower keeps the cutting area clean and visible.

Blades

Blade designed for cutting a variety of materials are available for use on the scroll saw. Narrow blades work best on small-radius curves. Wide blades give good results when used for relatively straight cuts. Hard materials usually require blades having between 15 and 32 teeth per inch. Blades with between 7 and 15 teeth per inch cut faster and are used on softer materials.

INSTALLING A BLADE IN A FIXED-ARM SCROLL SAW

Always read the manufacturer's instructions before installing a saw blade in a fixed-arm scroll saw. Then read and follow these step-by-step general procedures:

1. Turn off the power supply to the machine and move the blade support out of the way.

2. Turn the machine over by hand by turning the motor pulley until the lower plunger is at its highest point.

3. Open the lower chuck and insert the blade into the chuck with the *teeth pointing down.*

4. Use a small square or a square wood block to set the blade square to the table (4–65). Tighten the lower chuck.

5. Release the tension sleeve clamp and move the tension sleeve down until its chuck engages the upper end of the saw blade. Then tighten the upper chuck.

6. Pull the tension sleeve upward, until blade tension is moderate, and clamp the blade.

7. Turn the machine over by hand to make sure that the blade remains properly tensioned.

8. Move the blade support back into position and adjust it as needed.

■ *4–65. A square wood block can be used to set the blade square to the scroll-saw table.*

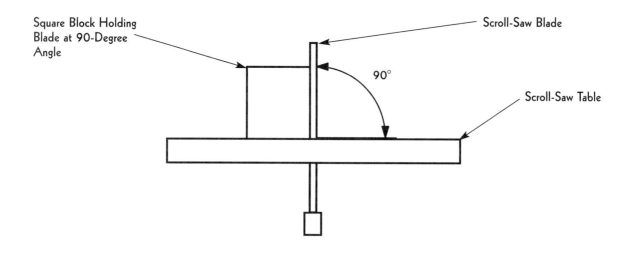

Square Block Holding Blade at 90-Degree Angle

Scroll-Saw Blade

90°

Scroll-Saw Table

Safety Techniques

Follow these safety techniques when using a scroll saw:

1. Wear approved eye protection and a dust mask.
2. Disconnect the power before making any adjustments.
3. Securely install a blade that is in good condition.
4. Make sure that the hold-down is against the workpiece during cutting.
5. Turn the saw over by hand, with the power disconnected, to check its operation before making a cut.
6. Move undersized workpieces into the saw with a push block or stick.

Cutting on the Scroll Saw

Follow these step-by-step procedures when cutting on the scroll saw:

1. Lay out the cuts on the workpiece.
2. Move the hold-down down to the workpiece and tighten the workpiece in place.
3. Turn the saw on and feed the workpiece into the blade slowly. *Tight curves* can be made by halting forward movement while pivoting the workpiece around the moving saw blade. *Blind cuts* require the saw to be stopped before the workpiece is backed away from the blade.

Making Piercing or Internal Cuts on the Scroll Saw

Follow these step-by-step procedures to make piercing cuts:

1. Draw a layout on the workpiece. Remove the blade from the scroll saw.
2. Drill a hole through the workpiece. Then pass the blade through the hole (4–66).

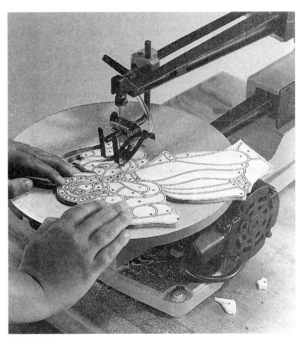

■ **4–66.** *When piercing cuts are made on a scroll saw, a hole is drilled into the workpiece and the blade is inserted into the hole.*

3. Reinstall the blade and readjust the hold-down against the workpiece.
4. Make the required cuts. Remove the blade when cutting is complete.

Saber-Sawing

Saber-sawing is possible on many scroll saws. The relative stiffness of the blades used allows cutting without the need to support the upper end of the blade in a chuck. This allows internal cutting to be done without removing and reinstalling the blade.

Saber-saw blades (4–67) are relatively wide and thick, and they have large teeth. As a result, they cut rapidly and produce a rough-cut surface.

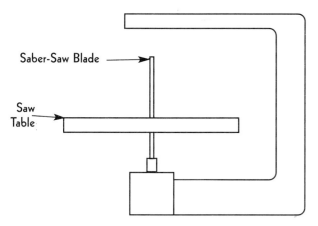

■ **4–67.** *Saber-saw blades can be used to make internal, or piercing, cuts without the need to remove and reinstall the blade.*

Marquetry

Marquetry is a process that is used to make a jig-saw-like assembly of contrasting pieces of wood (4–68). Marquetry is done on the scroll saw by tilting the saw table about five degrees to the left. Two thin pieces of wood, of contrasting color, are taped together in a sandwich-like fashion. The design is laid out and cut using the piercing procedure described earlier (4–69). When the assembly is taken apart, the top cutout will fit snugly into the bottom piece. The fit can be adjusted by changing the table angle slightly.

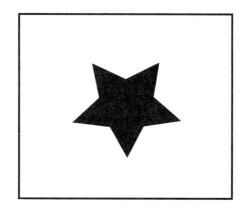

■ **4–68.** *Top and side views showing marquetry layout of a star.*

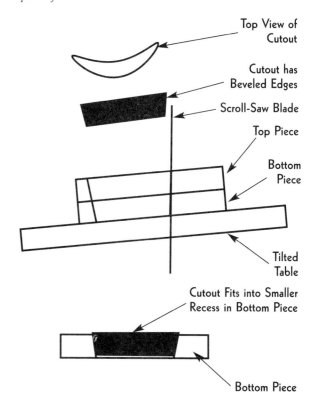

■ **4–69.** *Marquetry cutting technique used to cut out a free-form shape.*

WOOD LATHE

The lathe is popular with many amateur woodworkers. This may be because it is the only woodworking machine that can quickly produce a finished piece. The spinning workpiece responds immediately and dramatically under a cutting tool held in the operator's hands.

The lathe resembles a horizontal drill press (4–70). Workpieces can be mounted between

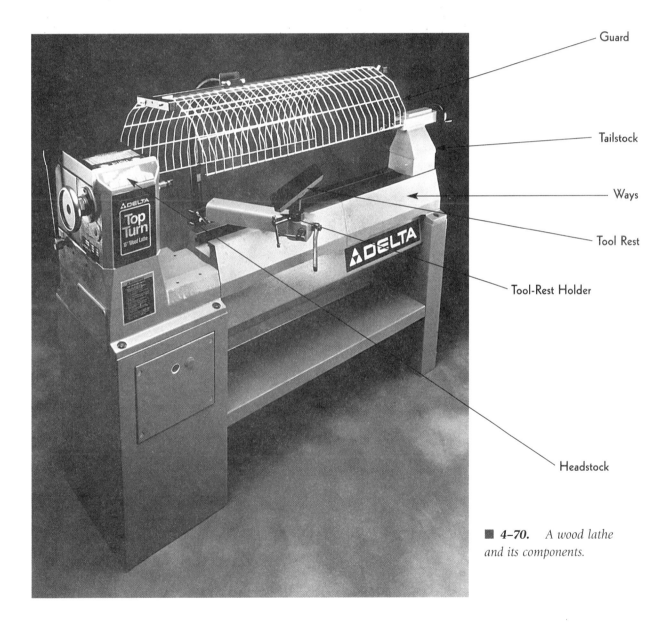

Guard

Tailstock

Ways

Tool Rest

Tool-Rest Holder

Headstock

■ *4–70. A wood lathe and its components.*

centers for *spindle-turning* (4–71) or on a faceplate for *faceplate-turning* (4–72).

The spindle and headstock on a wood lathe are similar to the spindle and headstock of the drill press. The spindle transmits power from the motor to the workpiece as it rotates downward toward the tool rest.

The tool rest is mounted on the ways of the lathe, which correspond to the drill-press column. The tool rest can be moved from side to side, up and down, and set parallel to the workpiece or at an angle to it.

■ *4–72. Faceplate-turning consists of mounting the workpiece to the lathe's faceplate.*

■ *4–71. Spindle-turning consists of mounting the workpiece between the lathe's centers.*

Most of the adjustable parts of the lathe just discussed can be locked in position using a handle or wrench.

Lathe centers (4–73) are used in spindle-turning. *Cross,* or *driving,* centers fit into the headstock spindle and are used to make the workpiece rotate.

The tailstock on a wood lathe is similar to that on the drill-press table. It can be moved toward or away from the headstock. The tailstock has a spindle that can be adjusted by turning the tailstock hand wheel.

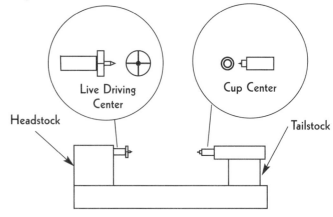

■ *4–73. Lathe centers.*

Cup centers are installed into the tailstock spindle (4–74a). They support the other end of the workpiece during turning between centers. The cup center must be lubricated periodically.

Live tailstock centers rotate with the workpiece and do not require lubrication (4–74b).

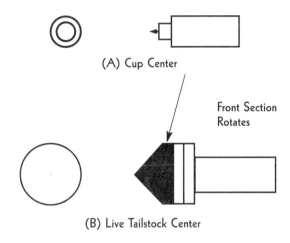

(A) Cup Center

Front Section Rotates

(B) Live Tailstock Center

■ **4–74.** *Top: Cup centers, which are installed in the tailstock spindle, support the other end of the workpiece during turning between centers. Bottom: Live tailstock centers rotate with the workpiece and do not require lubrication.*

Selecting and Buying a Wood Lathe

Before buying a new or used wood lathe, refer to Buying New Power Tools and Buying Used Power Tools on page 77. Then consider finding a lathe with the following features:

1. Larger work requires a lathe that has six inches between the center of its spindle and the ways. This will allow a piece with a 12-inch diameter to be turned. This type of lathe is classified as a 12-inch lathe. A lathe of this size should be long enough to turn a 36-inch-long piece between centers. It should also have a one-horsepower motor.

2. The speed-changing mechanism should be simple and easy to operate.

If space and price constraints dictate the purchase of a smaller lathe, it should have as many of the features of a larger machine as possible. Among the most important features are hollow head- and tailstock spindles and a tailstock handwheel. It should also have at least a ½-horsepower motor.

Safety Techniques

Follow these safety techniques when using a wood lathe. Also remember to follow the safety instructions provided by the manufacturer.

1. Wear a face shield and a dust mask.
2. Make sure that you have removed all jewelry.
3. Secure loose clothing and long hair so that they cannot become entangled in the rotating parts of the machine.
4. Disconnect the power to the lathe whenever making adjustments.
5. After making any adjustments, turn the lathe over with your hands by turning the headstock handwheel. This is to make sure that the workpiece can turn freely.
6. Set the lathe to operate at its lowest speed at the beginning of each job.
7. Use only material that is free of defects like checks and knots.
8. Solid single-wood workpieces are the safest to turn on the lathe. If glued-up assemblies are being used, carefully check them for soundness before and during use.
9. Stop the machine and check it whenever unusual sounds or vibrations develop.
10. Maintain a space of ⅛ inch between the tool rest and the workpiece during turning.

11. Keep the machine clear of tools and other objects that might fall off it during use.

12. Remove the tool rest before attempting any sanding. The lathe should be run at a low speed during sanding.

Cutting and Shaping Techniques

Chisels are used for cutting and shaping pieces on the lathe (4–75). Sharp chisels help to shorten processing time on the lathe. The cutting method is difficult to master and will not be covered in detail here. The tool must be held tangent to the surface of the piece (4–76). Material is removed in the form of shavings. This technique produces a relatively smooth surface. The

■ **4–76.** *When you are using a chisel to shape a workpiece using the cutting technique on the lathe, the tool must be held tangent to the workpiece's surface.*

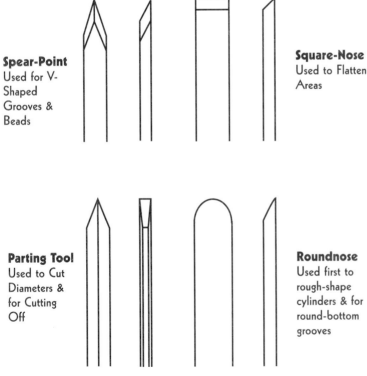

Spear-Point
Used for V-Shaped Grooves & Beads

Square-Nose
Used to Flatten Areas

Parting Tool
Used to Cut Diameters & for Cutting Off

Roundnose
Used first to rough-shape cylinders & for round-bottom grooves

■ **4–75.** *Lathe-turning chisels.*

inexperienced operator will find that the chisels tend to catch on the workpiece during cutting.

Scraping is accomplished by holding the chisel in a horizontal position with its cutting edge aligned with the center of the workpiece (4–77). Many operators prefer chisels with wire edges for scraping. Wire edges are usually left on a tool after grinding. Unlike most tools that have been ground, these chisels do not have their wire edges removed by whetting them on an oilstone.

The scraping method is popular because it is easy to learn and allows the operator good control over the size of the piece being turned. It removes material rapidly while producing a somewhat

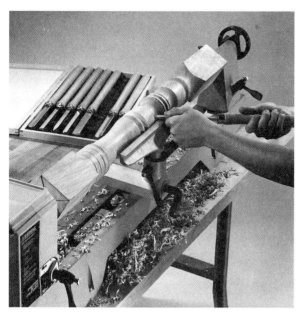

■ **4–77.** *Scraping on a lathe.*

rough surface. As mentioned before, two methods of turning are used: turning between centers (spindle-turning) and faceplate-turning. Each is described below.

TURNING BETWEEN CENTERS (SPINDLE-TURNING)

Follow these step-by-step procedures when turning between centers:

1. Make a full-sized drawing of the workpiece with its diameters indicated (4–78).

2. Cut the workpiece to the dimensions indicated in the drawing, adding one inch to its length and ½ inch to its width and thickness. The squared-up workpiece should have an octagonal cross-section if the material to be turned is hard or more than about 1½ inches square.

3. Mark and locate the centers on each end (4–79). Make saw cuts using a backsaw on the crossed centerlines.

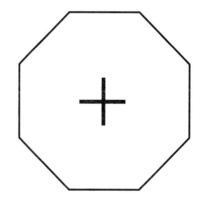

■ **4–79.** *Then locate the centers on each end.*

4. Place the cross driving center in the saw cuts on one end of the workpiece. Tap the center into place with a mallet. Move the driving center and workpiece as a unit while inserting the center into the headstock spindle.

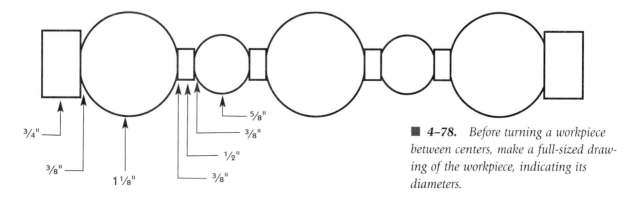

³/₄" ³/₈" 1¹/₈" ³/₈" ½" ³/₈" ⁵/₈"

■ **4–78.** *Before turning a workpiece between centers, make a full-sized drawing of the workpiece, indicating its diameters.*

5. Install a cup or live tailstock center into the tailstock and move the tailstock up along the ways of the lathe to the end of the workpiece.

6. Clamp the tailstock to the ways of the lathe. Move the tailstock spindle into the end of the workpiece by turning the tailstock handwheel. When the center is in place, tighten the tailstock spindle clamp.

7. Move the tool rest into position, parallel to the workpiece and ⅛ inch away from it (4–80). Adjust the tool rest so that the cutting edge of a roundnose chisel, resting on the tool rest, is aligned with the center of the workpiece. Note: During turning, adjust the tool rest periodically so that the cutting edge of the tool in use is aligned with the center of the workpiece.

8. Turn the lathe over by hand to check the clearance between the workpiece and the tool rest. Set the lathe to its slowest speed and turn it on.

9. Place a roundnose chisel on the tool rest, bevel-side down, holding it as shown in 4–81. Move the tool into the rotating workpiece about ¼ inch, and move it from the tailstock end of the workpiece toward the headstock end. This places most of the

■ **4–81.** *The correct hand positioning when roughing-out on a lathe.*

pressure on the headstock bearings rather than on the cup center in the tailstock. If you are right-handed, your left hand should be wrapped around the tool with the heel of the hand against the tool rest. The right hand controls the other end of the tool. This procedure is repeated until a cylinder is formed. The diameter of the cylinder should be equal to the largest diameter on the finished piece.

■ **4–80.** *A roundnose chisel positioned for spindle-turning.*

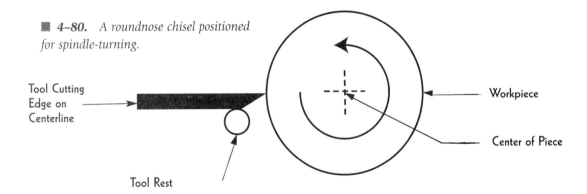

Tool Cutting Edge on Centerline

Tool Rest

Workpiece

Center of Piece

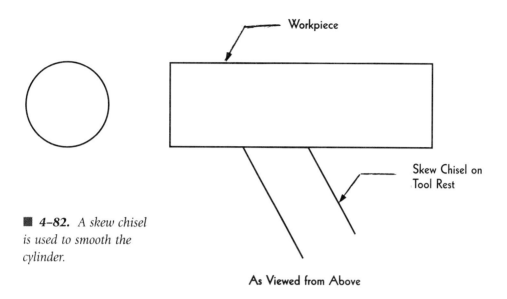

Workpiece

Skew Chisel on
Tool Rest

As Viewed from Above

■ **4–82.** *A skew chisel is used to smooth the cylinder.*

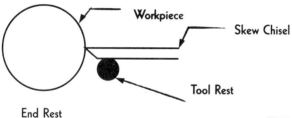

Workpiece

Skew Chisel

Tool Rest

End Rest

10. Straighten and smooth the cylinder with a skew chisel (4–82). In this step, the left hand (of a right-handed operator) holds the front of the tool between the index finger and the thumb. The index finger is kept against the tool rest during cutting. This allows more precise control of the tool during this lighter trimming cut.

11. Locate and mark the diameters shown on the drawing on the workpiece, using a ruler and pencil.

12. Adjust the legs of a pair of outside calipers so that the space between the legs equals the first diameter selected (4–83).

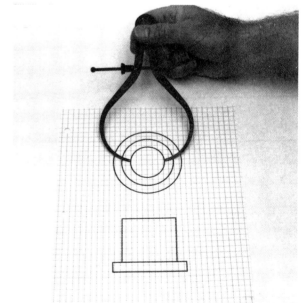

■ **4–83.** *Using calipers to set the drawing diameter.*

13. Use a parting tool to cut a groove into the workpiece at the first diameter line. The parting tool is the only tool that is held with its narrow edge on the tool rest (4–84). All the other tools are held with their broad, flat surfaces down on the tool rest. Check the diameter of the groove periodically with the calipers. Continue cutting until the calipers slip over the cut surface in the groove.

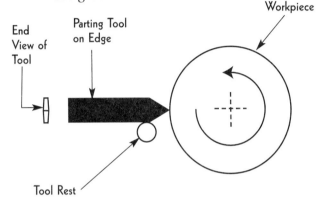

4–84. *The position of the parting tool on the tool rest prior to cutting a groove.*

14. Repeat step 12 for each diameter line. The completed workpiece will have a series of grooves cut to the required diameters, as shown in 4–85. At this point, increase the relatively low spindle speed. This will improve the smoothness of the cuts made.
15. Use the drawing as a guide for shaping each of the elements on the workpiece. Various tools are used to accomplish this. The initial cuts are usually made with a roundnose chisel. The diamond-point chisel is used to widen the grooves made by the parting tool. It is also used to make V-shaped grooves. The skew chisel can be

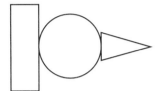

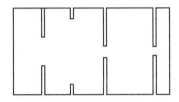 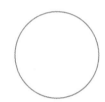

4–85. *Top: The "finished" workpiece as represented in a design drawing. Bottom: The grooves on this workpiece have been cut to the required diameter.*

used for forming convex, rounded bead-like forms.

Practice and experience will help the operator to develop the skills required to fashion various turned elements.
16. Once shaping with tools is finished, begin sanding. Sanding is used to smooth and refine shapes. Strips of cloth-back abrasives are ideal for this purpose (4–86). Initially,

4–86. *Using clothed-back abrasive to sand the turned edge.*

a #80 abrasive can be used. Secondary sanding can be done with a #150 abrasive, and final sanding is done with a #220. A dust mask must be worn during this process.

Once all work is completed, remove the piece from the lathe and cut away the unusable end sections.

FACEPLATE-TURNING (BOWL)

The faceplate-turning process is used in the production of low, wide objects like bowls. Workpieces are mounted on faceplates with screws. Faceplates are screwed onto the lathe's headstock spindle.

Follow these step-by-step procedures when faceplate-turning:

1. Make a full-sized drawing of the piece showing front, top, and sectional views (4–87).

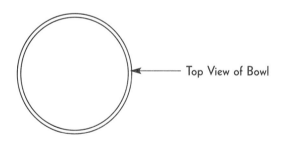

Top View of Bowl

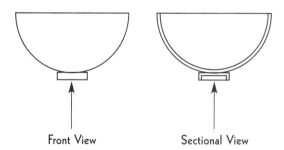

Front View   Sectional View

■ *4–87. Before faceplate-turning, make a full-sized drawing of the piece showing its front, top, and sectional views.*

2. Select a workpiece of a suitable material and square it up. The thickness of the piece should be equal to the height of the bowl plus ¼ inch. The length and width of the piece should be equal to the largest diameter of the bowl plus ½ inch.

3. Cut the block into a cylinder shape on the band saw. The diameter of the cylinder is equal to the largest diameter shown on the drawing plus ½ inch.

4. Center the block on a faceplate and attach it to the faceplate with suitable wood screws (4–88).

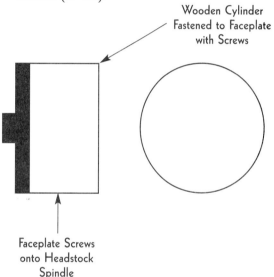

Wooden Cylinder Fastened to Faceplate with Screws

Faceplate Screws onto Headstock Spindle

■ *4–88. The bowl blank attached to the faceplate.*

5. Move the tool rest into position, parallel to the workpiece and ⅛ inch away from it. While turning, adjust the height of the tool rest periodically so that the cutting edge of the tool is aligned with the center of the workpiece.

6. Place a roundnose chisel on the tool rest, bevel side down. Hold it in the roughing-out position. (Refer to 4–81.) Shape the

outside of the piece first. Move the round-nose chisel into the rotating workpiece about ¼ inch and then from the face of the workpiece toward the faceplate (4–89). Repeat this step until the desired shape is developed.

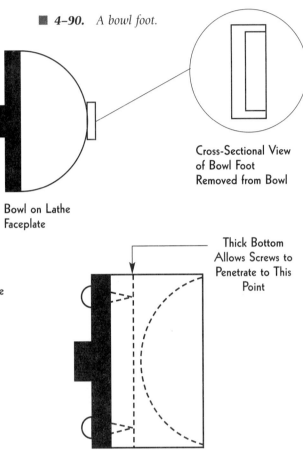

■ *4–90.* *A bowl foot.*

Bowl on Lathe
Faceplate

Cross-Sectional View
of Bowl Foot
Removed from Bowl

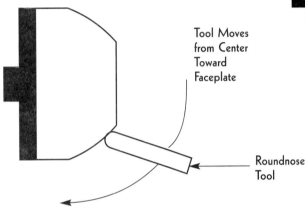

Tool Moves
from Center
Toward
Faceplate

Roundnose
Tool

■ *4–89.* *The roundnose chisel is moved from the face of the workpiece toward the faceplate while being supported by the tool rest.*

Thick Bottom
Allows Screws to
Penetrate to This
Point

Bowl Block Screwed Directly to Faceplate

■ *4–91.* *The bowl bottom is attached to the faceplate with screws.*

7. Cut a recessed foot into the end of the piece. The recess should be as wide as possible and about ¼ of an inch deep (4–90). The workpiece will later be mounted on a chuck block that will be fitted to the foot recess, as described below.

8. Smooth the workpiece using a skew chisel and sandpaper and remove it from the faceplate.

9. If the bowl bottom is thick enough to allow screws to be inserted without interfering when the inside of the piece is hollowed out, reverse the workpiece and attach it to the faceplate with screws (4–91).

10. If the bowl bottom is not thick enough to be attached directly to the faceplate, a chuck block must be prepared and

attached to the faceplate. The chuck block is a wooden cylinder having the same diameter as the faceplate. It is about 1½ inches thick.

Mount the chuck-block workpiece on a faceplate with screws. Form a projection on the chuck block that fits snugly into the foot recess on the workpiece (4–92).

11. Glue the workpiece and chuck block together, placing a piece of heavy brown

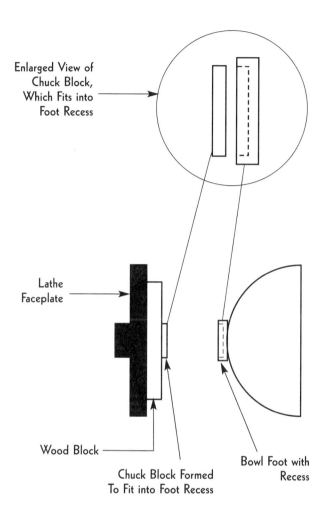

Enlarged View of
Chuck Block,
Which Fits into
Foot Recess

Lathe
Faceplate

Wood Block

Chuck Block Formed
To Fit into Foot Recess

Bowl Foot with
Recess

4–92. *The chuck block on the faceplate is mated to the workpiece foot.*

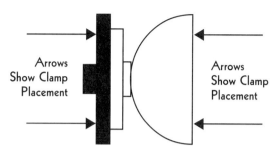

Arrows
Show Clamp
Placement

Arrows
Show Clamp
Placement

Bowl Block Clamped to Chuck Block

4–93. *The clamped workpiece and chuck-block assembly.*

wrapping paper between them. It is important to keep the glue off the sides of the chuck-block projection. Wax can be applied to the sides of the projection before glue is applied. Clamp the assembly and leave it undisturbed until the glue is fully cured (4–93).

12. Mount the faceplate on the lathe and rough out the inside of the bowl with a roundnose chisel. For the initial cuts, set the tool rest parallel to the face of the workpiece. Later in the process, the tool rest is set as close to the surface being cut as possible (4–94).

13. When shaping is complete, sand the inside of the bowl.

14. An attempt should be made to remove the bowl from the chuck block by applying gentle pressure to the workpiece. The paper separator will often split apart when this is done. If separation does not occur, remove the bowl from the chuck block by carefully chiseling away the chuck block while it is held in a vise.

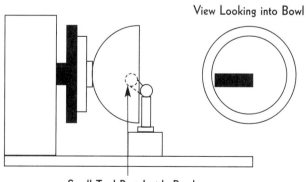

View Looking into Bowl

Small Tool Rest Inside Bowl

4–94. *Position of tool rest when it is used to shape the internal part of the workpiece.*

USING TEMPLATES

A template (pattern piece) can be useful to the lathe operator when several identical turned pieces are required. A template can be prepared by making a copy of the full-sized project drawing and gluing it to a piece of cardboard. The template is cut out as shown in 4–95. Fit the template against the workpiece during turning to verify that the shape is being cut.

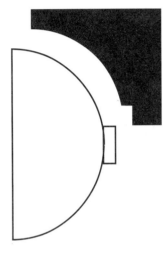

■ **4–95.** *A template is cut out and glued to cardboard. The template is the dark area.*

STATIONARY SANDING MACHINES

The two most common stationary sanding machines are the disc and belt sanders. The two machines are often combined into a single unit that is driven by the same motor (4–96). While the combination machine is less costly than two separate units, both machines run when the power is on.

The *disc sander* (4–97) consists of a disc mounted on a rotating shaft. A tiltable table is used to support the workpiece during sanding.

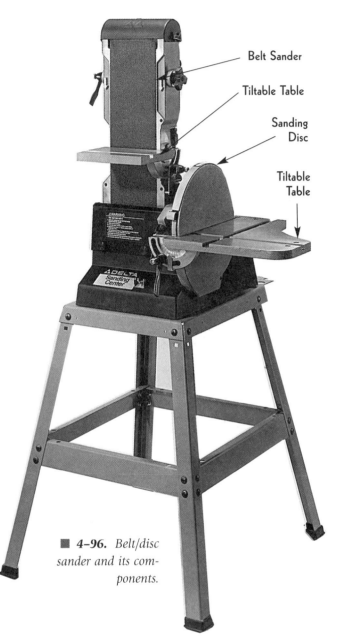

Belt Sander

Tiltable Table

Sanding Disc

Tiltable Table

■ **4–96.** *Belt/disc sander and its components.*

The table is slotted to accept a miter fence. A 12-inch-diameter disc is often used on these machines. This abrasive disc can be adhered to the metal disc with a special adhesive that allows for easy application and removal. Self-adhering discs with a peel-off backing sheet are also available.

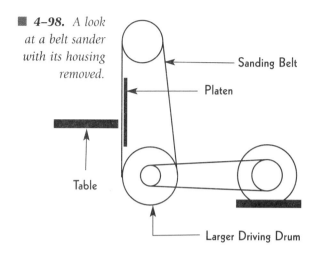

4–98. *A look at a belt sander with its housing removed.*

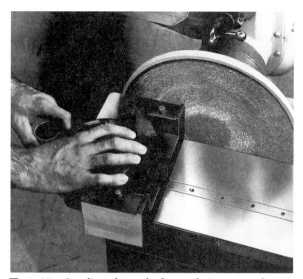

■ **4–97.** *Sanding the end of a workpiece on a disc sander using the miter gauge.*

Disc sanders are often used for squaring the ends of pieces that are six inches or less in width. This is the largest surface that can be sanded safely on a 12-inch disc sander. The machine can also be used for beveling and to create rounded convex surfaces.

The *belt sander* consists of an endless cloth-backed abrasive belt that runs over two cylinders. A metal platen (plate) mounted between the cylinders provides support for the belt during sanding operations.

The large diameter of the *driving drum* helps to provide traction by increasing the area of belt and drum in contact with each other (4–98). The smaller *idler drum* can be moved toward or away from the driving drum to allow the belt to be changed and tensioned. This idler drum can also be tilted so that the belt can be tracked (4–99). A six-inch × 48-inch belt is usually used on combination machines.

A tiltable table is used to support the workpiece during sanding. The table is slotted to

■ **4–99.** *The tensioning and tracking knobs on a belt sander.*

accept a miter fence. Many belt sanders can be set parallel to the machine base or at an angle of up to 90 degrees to the base (4–100).

In addition to performing all the operations of the disc sander, the belt sander can be used to sand much larger surfaces when the drum covers are removed.

■ *4–100. Many belt sanders can be used in vertical or horizontal positions.*

Selecting and Buying a Disc/Belt Sander

Before buying a disc/belt sander, refer to Buying New Power Tools and Buying Used Power Tools on page 77. Then read the following guidelines:

1. Separate belt and disc sanders are a better choice than a combination machine. In most cases, a stand-alone belt sander is the only sander most woodworkers need.
2. Combination units should have a 6 × 48-inch belt and a 12-inch disc.
3. The belt sander should be usable in the vertical or horizontal position.

4. Tables should be adjustable and should have a miter-gauge slot.
5. The machine should be fitted with appropriate guards and dust-collection-hose sleeves.
6. Belt installation should be simple.
7. The belt should stay tracked during sanding.

Safety Techniques

These safety techniques should be followed when using a disc/belt sander. Also observe the manufacturer's safety instructions.

1. Wear approved eye protection and a dust mask.
2. Shut off the power before making any adjustments on the machine.
3. Limit sanding to the portion of the disc that is traveling down toward the table. This will direct dust downward and will keep the work against the table.
4. Make sure both tables are clear before turning the machine on. Vibration can cause loose objects to fall from the tables when the sander is running.
5. Check the belt tracking and disc adherence before beginning sanding operations.
6. Keep hands and fingers at a safe distance from the belt and disc surfaces.
7. Do not sand small pieces. They cannot be held safely.

Squaring Ends on a Disc Sander

Follow these step-by-step procedures when squaring ends on a disc sander:

1. Check the miter gauge for squareness to the surface of the disc. Place the gauge in the

table slot and put a square against it, as shown in 4–101. Make adjustments as required.

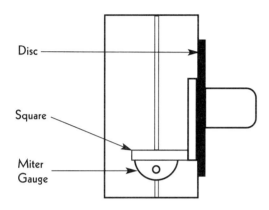

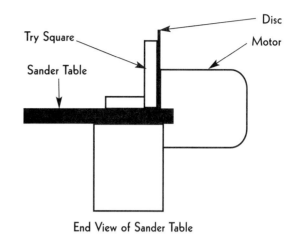

4–102. *Checking that the table is square to the sanding disc.*

4–101. *When squaring ends on a disc sander, the first step consists of using a square to check that the miter gauge is square to the sanding disc.*

2. Check the table for squareness to the disc (4–102). Loosen the table clamp and adjust the table if necessary.
3. Turn the machine on. Place the workpiece against the miter gauge and move it into the left quadrant of the sanding disc. Move the workpiece and the miter gauge back and forth about ½ inch during sanding to reduce surface scoring.
4. Check the work periodically with a try square until the end is square.

Chamfers and Bevels

Chamfers and bevels are produced in a similar manner, with the table tilted to the desired chamfer or bevel angle.

The belt sander can also be used to end-sand chamfers and bevels. This is done using a miter

gauge in much the same way it is used on the disc sander (4–103).

The belt sander's relatively large sanding area, 6 × 14 inches, also allows face-sanding to be done. Pieces being face-sanded must be thick enough to be held safely in the operator's fingers.

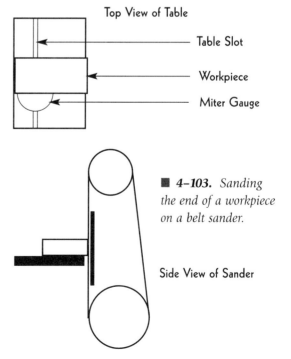

4–103. *Sanding the end of a workpiece on a belt sander.*

CHAPTER 5
STEP-BY-STEP PROJECT-MAKING

■ ■ ■ ■ ■ ■ ■ ■ ■ ■ ■ ■ ■

The purpose of this chapter is to provide the novice woodworker with a rational, well-thought-out approach to project-making. Most experienced woodworkers follow an informal series of steps similar to those discussed here. To suit his or her own needs, the reader should pick and choose from among the information presented.

The first step in making any project is to create or find a project design. This process is discussed in detail in Chapter 1. A dimensioned or full-sized drawing might be required for a complex piece, while a rough sketch on graph paper might work for a simpler piece.

PROJECT-MAKING PROCEDURES

Follow these step-by-step procedures when making a project. Each of these steps is discussed more fully in the following pages. They will be based on the example of a step-stool project.

1. Make a cutting list from the project drawing (Table 5–1).
2. Obtain the materials necessary to make the project.
3. Rough-cut the material, using the cutting list as a guide.
4. Produce working ends and edges on each piece.
5. Square-up all rectangular pieces.
6. Complete all joinery.
7. Complete all surface decorations like marquetry, carving, etc.
8. Do the initial sanding.
9. Make a trial assembly of the parts.
10. Permanently assemble the parts.
11. Sand the project and apply a finish.

Cutting List for Step Stool

Part	Number Required	Finishing Dimensions (Thickness × Width × Length)	Material
Top	1	¾ × 6 × 12"	Pine
Side	2	¾ × 10 × 10¼" *	Pine
Step	1	¾ × 5 × 10½"	Pine
Rail (Front)		¾ × 1½ × 10½"	Pine
Rail (Rear)		¾ × 1½ × 10½"	Pine
Dowels		⅜ × 1½"	Birch

Non-wood materials

Hardware:

| Steel Wood Screws (Flat Head) | 4 | 2" #10 | |

| Finishing Materials: Primer Enamel | ½ pint ½ pint | | |

Miscellaneous

*These sides will be made up of two pieces joined edge to edge from material used for other parts.

Table 5–1. *A cutting list for a step stool. Finished sizes of the project parts are used, to avoid confusion. When the parts are laid out, extra material is added for cutting and squaring.*

Step One: Making the Cutting List from the Project Drawing

The cutting list shown in Table 5–1 can be used as a guide for obtaining stock. It contains finished sizes of the project parts to avoid confusion. When the parts are laid out, extra material will be added for cutting and squaring. The cutting list was made for a step stool.

The *part* column in the cutting list names the part: side, top, etc. The *number required* column refers to the number of identical parts needed, such as the two sides. The *finished dimensions* column lists the dimensions of the pieces using the conventional woodworking sequence: thickness, width, and length.

The *material* column lists the material used to make the part. The *non-wood material* space is used to list non-wood items. There are also *hardware* and *finishing materials columns*. The *miscellaneous* box can be used can be used for notes.

Step Two: Obtaining the Necessary Materials

Follow these guidelines for obtaining the necessary materials from the lumberyard. They are based on the assumption that the woodworker will be building many step stools.

1. Develop a list of specifications to ensure that the material being purchased will be of the necessary quality.
2. Determine whether a charge will be made for delivery. Will the driver deliver the material into the shop, or is the price for sidewalk delivery?
3. Ideally, the material being purchased should be free of natural defects like knots and seasoning defects like warping. Straight-grained material is the easiest to work with.

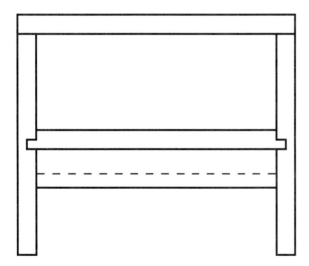
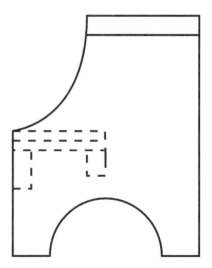

■ *5–1. Front and side views of the step stool.*

Step Three: Rough-Cutting the Material

The next step is to rough-cut the material using the cutting list as a reference. If the project is to be made with hand tools or portable power tools, add ½ inch to the length and width dimensions in the cutting list. This leaves an inch of space between parts on the layout made on the material (5–2).

For this step-stool project, 1 × 8 material is a good choice. The one-inch thickness is actually ¾ inch, and the eight-inch width is actually 7½ inches. That is because the one-and eight-inch dimensions are *nominal* sizes. A board of this width will accommodate all of the pieces on the list except the sides. Each of the sides will be made by joining two pieces together edge to edge.

Follow these step-by-step procedures to rough-cut the material:

1. Make a trial layout of the pieces on the material to be used. Lay the largest pieces out first. Place smaller pieces in the spaces left around the larger pieces.
2. Place the layouts against the edges of the workpieces because these edges are usually straight and square.
3. Where possible, align pieces of the same *length* vertically, edge to edge. This facilitates crosscutting.

4. Align pieces of the same *width* horizontally, end to end, to facilitate ripping.
5. If hand tools are being used, cut the six-foot-long board into six pieces using a crosscut saw. Leave each piece with about ½ inch of extra material on each end.
6. Rip three of the pieces to rough width, using a rip saw.

The pieces in 5–3 can be produced from a piece measuring ¾ × 7½ × 72 inches. This piece is referred to as a 1 × 8 × 6.

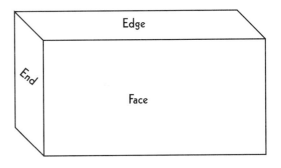

■ **5–3.** *Workpiece surfaces.*

■ **5–2.** *The project parts roughly laid out on the stock.*

Step Four: Producing Working Ends and Edges

All rectangular or square workpieces have six surfaces: two faces, two edges, and two ends (5–3). Workpiece dimensions refer to these six surfaces. Thickness is defined as the distance between faces. Width is defined as the distance between edges. Length is defined as the distance between ends.

A working surface is a reference surface. Measurements with test tools such as try squares are made from and against this surface.

A *working face* should be smooth and flat. The material being used is checked for flatness with a straightedge such as a ruler. If the material is cupped, the concave face is selected and marked as the working face (5–4).

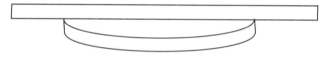

■ *5–4. Checking the flatness of stock with a ruler.*

A *working edge* should be smooth, straight, and at a 90-degree angle to the working face.

A *working end* should be smooth, straight, and at a 90-degree angle to the working face and edge.

A hand plane can be used to smooth, straighten, and square the working edge. Place the workpiece in a suitable bench vise and plane with the grain, using a plane that is set for a very light cut (5–5). The objective is to remove as little material as possible. Selecting the "best" edge helps to reduce the amount of material removed during this process. The "best" edge is the one that is closest to being smooth straight and square.

During planing, the surface should be

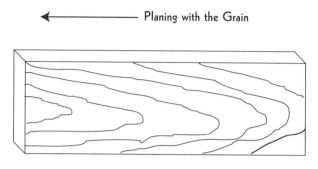

— Planing with the Grain

■ *5–5. Plane with the grain when you are smoothing, straightening, and squaring the working edge of stock.*

checked frequently with a try square and a straightedge (5–6). Remove the workpiece from the vise to measure it. Place the try-square handle against the working face because the working edge must be square to the working face. Mark the completed edge with an "X" to designate it as the working edge.

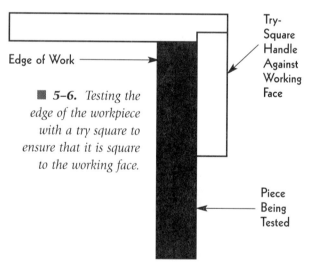

Edge of Work

Try-Square Handle Against Working Face

Piece Being Tested

■ *5–6. Testing the edge of the workpiece with a try square to ensure that it is square to the working face.*

A *portable power planer* can be substituted for the hand plane. The workpiece is handled in much the same way it is for hand-planing.

A *table saw* fitted with a smooth-cutting blade can also be used for edge-squaring. The working face is placed down on the table while a small amount of material is ripped away.

A *joiner* can be used for edge-squaring when available. When using a joiner, smooth the workpiece's working end straight and square to the working face and the working edge.

SMOOTHENING, STRAIGHTENING, AND SQUARING THE ENDS

The ends can be smoothed, straightened, and made square to the working face and the working edge with a hand plane. If the end is less than four inches long, a block plane should be used.

When using a hand plane to work on the ends, place the workpiece in a bench vise with about one inch extending above the vise jaws. Planing across the whole end from edge to edge should be avoided because it can cause the second edge to split. Splitting can be avoided by planing in from each edge toward the middle (5–7). An alternative method is to place a piece

of scrap against the second edge of the piece during planing (5–8). The completed end is marked as the working end.

The *table saw* can also be used to square ends. The working edge of the workpiece is placed against the miter gauge with the working face down against the table. A small amount of material is cut away. The workpiece can be stabilized, for this light cut, by placing a piece of folded sandpaper between the piece and the miter gauge.

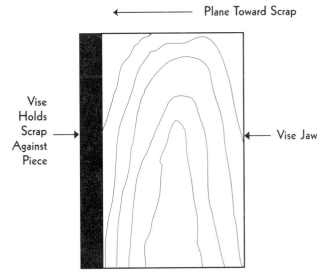

Planing End Grain Toward Scrap Piece Prevents Splitting Edge

■ *5–8. Planing an end using a scrap piece against the edge to prevent splitting.*

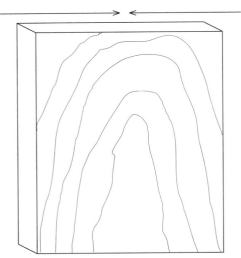

Plane Toward Center from Each Edge to Avoid Splitting Edge

■ *5–7. When planing the ends of the workpiece, plane toward the center, to avoid splitting.*

At this stage in the squaring process, the workpiece has three working, or reference, surfaces. These working surfaces are generally left undisturbed from this point on. Almost all cutting or shaping will be done on the other three surfaces of the piece.

Step Five: Squaring Up All Rectangular Pieces

Most project parts are square or rectangular in shape. The process of reducing workpieces to finished dimensions with all adjacent surfaces square to each other is known as squaring up stock.

SQUARING UP STOCK WITH HAND TOOLS

If you are using hand tools, follow these step-by-step procedures for squaring up stock:

1. Lay the required length out on the workpiece by measuring from its working end. Carry the layout line all the way around the workpiece, using a try square.

2. Lay a cutting line out approximately ⅛ inch from the layout line. Using a try square, carry the line all the way around the workpiece.

3. Cut off the excess material using a backsaw and a bench hook (5–9).

4. Plane the end of the piece until the length layout line is reached. *Do not cut any of the line away during planing or the piece will be undersized.*

5. Lay out the required width by measuring from the working edge in two places. This will help to ensure that the line is parallel to the working edge. Carry the line all the way around the workpiece, using a try square and a ruler.

6. Again lay out a cutting line approximately ⅛ inch from the layout line. Also carry this line all the way around the workpiece using a try square and a ruler.

7. Place the workpiece in the vise in a vertical position and rip off the excess material (5–10).

8. Plane the piece to the width layout line with a hand plane. *Do not cut away any of the line during planing or the piece will be undersized.*

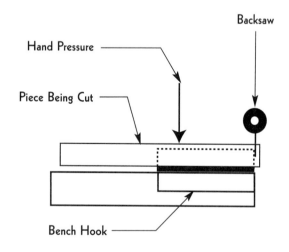

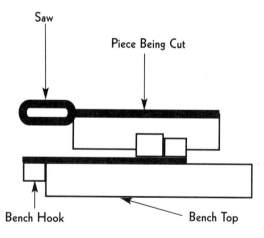

■ *5–9. Using a backsaw and bench hook to cut off excess material.*

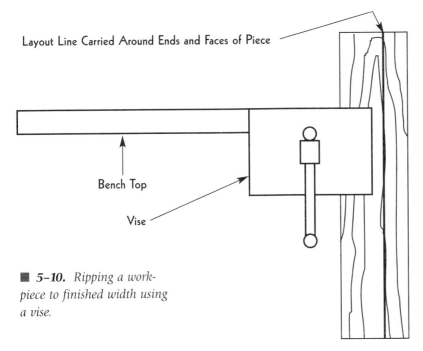

Layout Line Carried Around Ends and Faces of Piece

Bench Top

Vise

■ *5–10. Ripping a work-piece to finished width using a vise.*

SQUARING UP STOCK WITH A TABLE SAW

Stock can also be squared up using a table saw. After laying out the finished length and width, crosscut the pieces to length and rip them to width.

If duplicate pieces are required, cut all of the pieces to length using the same setup on the saw. When the crosscutting is complete, rip all the pieces to width using the same setup on the saw.

Step Six: Completing the Joinery

Joints are two or more pieces of wood that have been coupled together. The two main objectives of making joinery are to establish the position or location of each piece with respect to the others and to create joints that are strong and durable.

The strength of the joint depends on the amount of contact surface area it has. A joint with two square inches of surface glued together is twice as strong as a similar joint with one square inch of contact surface area.

In the days before strong modern synthetic adhesives were available, complex joints having large contact surfaces were essential. Today complex joints like dovetails are often used for their visual impact as much as for the added strength they provide.

Establishing the location of pieces being joined is important. Although a butt joint may be easy to make, it does not provide for the positive positioning of the pieces being joined. Adding two dowels to a butt joint helps to ensure the correct position of the pieces with respect to each other (5–11). Joints that provide positive positioning of the pieces simplify trial assemblies and clamping.

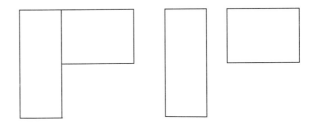

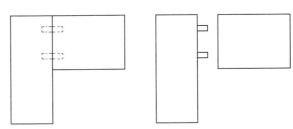

■ *5–11. A butt joint with and without dowels.*

GENERAL JOINT-MAKING GUIDELINES

Follow these general guidelines when making joints:

1. Use common working or reference surfaces when making the layouts.
2. Whenever possible, superimpose the pieces of the joint instead of measuring them. For example, one piece of a lap joint can be placed on top of the other to locate a layout line.
3. Joints made with hand tools should have layout lines made with a knife. Knife lines help to limit splitting during chiseling and sawing.
4. Make the female elements first in joints having male and female components. For example, tenons can be trimmed to fit mortises much more easily than vice versa (5–12).
5. Gang duplicate pieces together and lay them out as a unit whenever possible (5–13).

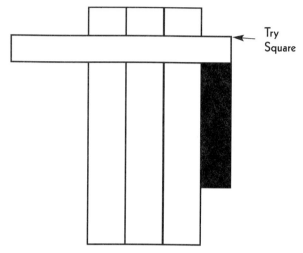

Three Identical Pieces "Ganged" for Layout

■ *5–13.* *"Ganging up" duplicate pieces to lay them out together.*

TYPES OF JOINT

The most common types of joint used in woodworking include butt, dowel, bevel, lap, rabbet, dado, mortise-and-tenon, and dovetail joints.

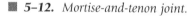

■ *5–12.* *Mortise-and-tenon joint.*

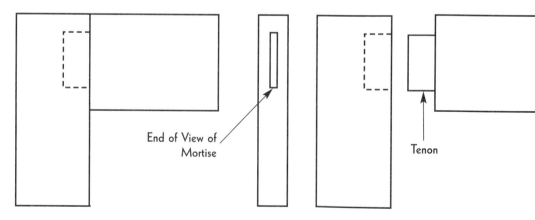

End of View of Mortise

Assembled Mortise-and-Tenon Joint

Tenon

Unassembled Mortise-and-Tenon Joint

These joints are described in order of complexity, the simpler joints described first and the most complex last.

Butt Joints

The typical butt joint consists of pieces that meet at right angles, with the end of one component placed against the face of the second (5–14). Butt-joint design does not provide for the positive location of the pieces with respect to each other. In addition, even the best glues don't adhere to end grain well. As a result, most butt joints are reinforced in some way. The reinforced joints shown in 5–15 are glued before fastenings are applied.

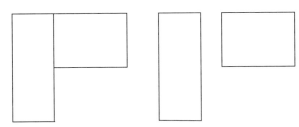

■ **5–14.** *A simple butt joint.*

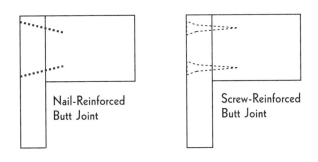

Nail-Reinforced Butt Joint

Screw-Reinforced Butt Joint

■ **5–15.** *Butt joints reinforced with nails and screws.*

Nailed Butt Joints

Follow these step-by-step procedures when making nailed butt joints:

1. Square up the pieces to be joined.
2. Lay out the joint on the face of the first piece (5–16). This layout consists of two lines drawn with a try square. The distance between the lines is equal to the thickness of the second piece.

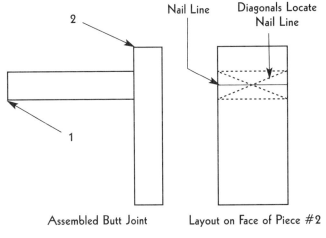

Assembled Butt Joint   Layout on Face of Piece #2

■ **5–16.** *Butt-joint layout.*

3. Drill a hole through the first piece at the center of the layout. A nail with its head removed can be used in the drill for this operation.
4. Insert a nail into the drilled hole and align and move the two pieces together. Drive the nail partway into the second piece and separate the pieces.

5. Place the second piece in a bench vise with its end flush with the vise jaws (5–17). Apply glue to the end.

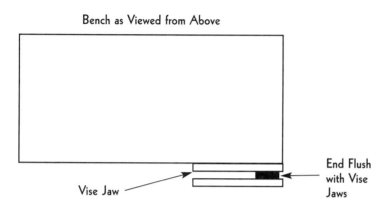

Bench as Viewed from Above

Vise Jaw

End Flush with Vise Jaws

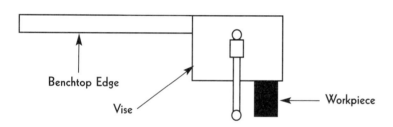

Benchtop Edge

Vise

Workpiece

■ *5–17.* *The second butt-joint piece is placed in a bench vise, its ends flush with the vise jaws.*

6. Place the first piece on the end of the piece in the vise. Position the pieces by inserting the nail protruding out of the first piece into the nail hole in the end of the second piece in the vise. Drive the nail home with a hammer.

7. Remove the assembly from the vise and check the position of the pieces against the layout. Make adjustments if necessary and return the piece to the vise.

8. Drive two more nails into the assembly

(5–18). The angled nail holds the pieces together more securely than straight nails would.

Screw-Reinforced Butt Joints

Follow these step-by-step procedures when making screw-reinforced butt joints:

1. Square up the pieces to be joined.

2. Lay out the joint on the face of the first piece. This layout consists of two lines drawn with a try square. The distance between the lines is equal to the thickness of the second piece. (Refer to 5–16.)

3. Locate and drill screw holes with a drill that is equal to the *root diameter* of the screws. (See Fasteners on pages 173 to 179.)

4. Place the first piece in a vise and align it with the end of the second piece, which should be clamped to the benchtop (5–19). Drill holes into the end of the

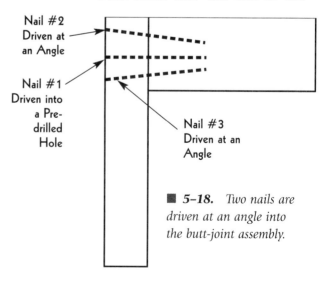

Nail #2 Driven at an Angle

Nail #1 Driven into a Predrilled Hole

Nail #3 Driven at an Angle

■ *5–18.* *Two nails are driven at an angle into the butt-joint assembly.*

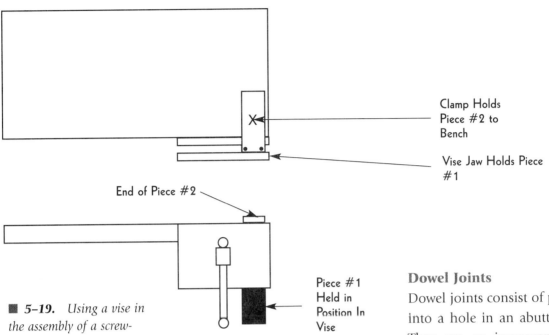

Clamp Holds
Piece #2 to
Bench

Vise Jaw Holds Piece
#1

End of Piece #2

Piece #1
Held in
Position In
Vise

■ **5–19.** *Using a vise in the assembly of a screw-reinforced butt joint.*

second piece using, the first piece as a guide. These holes should be equal to the root diameter of the screws.

5. Unclamp and remove the second piece. Countersink the holes in the first piece as required, using a drill equal to the *shank diameter* of the screws to be used. (See Fasteners on pages 173 to 179.)

6. Apply glue to the end of the second piece and clamp it to the benchtop against the first piece in the vise.

7. Drive the screws into both pieces.

The holding power of the screws in end grain can be greatly increased by driving the screws into a dowel inserted into the edge of the second piece.

Dowel Joints

Dowel joints consist of pins fitted into a hole in an abutting piece. They are an improvement over butt joints. The dowels locate the pieces being joined with respect to each other (5–20).

The diameter of the dowels used should be from one-half to one-third the thickness of the thinnest piece they are used to join. If two ¾-inch-thick pieces are to be joined, a ¼- or ⅜-inch dowel is used.

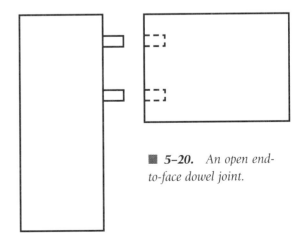

■ **5–20.** *An open end-to-face dowel joint.*

The bottom of dowel holes should be at least ⅜ inch away from the nearest surface (5–21).

Manufactured dowel pins are between 1¼ and 1½ inches long. Therefore, the holes bored for the pins should be about ⅝ to ¾ inch deep.

In smaller assemblies, dowel holes should be located approximately one-half to one inch in from each edge.

⅜" Minimum Distance

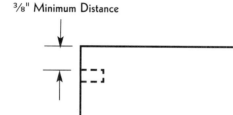

■ **5–21.** *Dowel holes should be at least ⅜ inch away from the edge.*

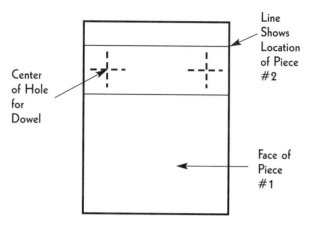

■ **5–22.** *Locating the centers of through dowel holes.*

4. Bore one hole through the first piece into the second piece.
5. Insert a dowel into the first hole to stabilize the assembly. Bore the second hole through the first piece into the second piece.
6. Remove the assembly from the vise, apply the glue, and clamp the pieces together until the glue sets. After the glue sets, trim any protruding dowel flush to the face of the piece.

Blind End-to-Face Dowel Joints
In a blind dowel joint, the dowels are hidden. Follow these step-by-step procedures when making one:
1. Square up the pieces to be joined.
2. Lay out the joint on the face of the first piece. The layout consists of two lines drawn with a try square. The distance between the lines is equal to the thickness of the second piece. (Refer to 5-16.) (These lines will be used to align the pieces when they are placed in the vise and on the benchtop.)
3. Lay out the dowel-hole centers on the end of the second piece (5–23).
4. Bore one of the holes into the end and insert a dowel center into the hole (5–24).

End-to-Face Dowel Joints
Follow these step-by-step procedures when you are making end-to-face dowel joints:
1. Square up the pieces to be joined.
2. Lay out the joint on the face of the first piece. The layout consists of two lines drawn with a try square. The distance between the lines is equal to the thickness of the second piece. (Refer to 5–16.) (These lines will be used to align the pieces when they are placed in the vise and on the benchtop.) Carry the layout lines around to the opposite face of the piece using a try square. Locate the centers of the holes on the layout (5–22).
3. Arrange the pieces as shown in 5–19, with the first piece in the vise and the second clamped to the benchtop.

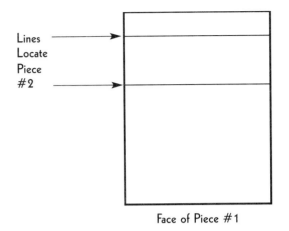

Lines Locate Piece #2

Face of Piece #1

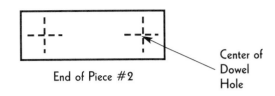

End of Piece #2

Center of Dowel Hole

■ **5–23.** *The layout of the dowel-hole centers on the end of the second piece.*

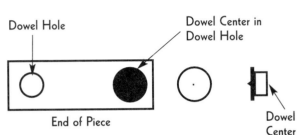

Dowel Hole

Dowel Center in Dowel Hole

Dowel Center

End of Piece

■ **5–24.** *Dowel center and one hole in the end of the workpiece.*

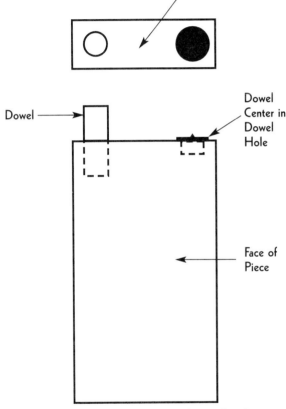

End

Dowel

Dowel Center in Dowel Hole

Face of Piece

■ **5–25.** *The workpiece end with one dowel center and one dowel in place.*

5. Place the pieces in the vise and on the benchtop, as shown in 5–19, and push them together. The dowel center will dent the piece in the vise, thus locating the dowel hole's center.

6. Bore a blind hole of the appropriate diameter and depth at the point indicated by the dowel center.

7. Insert a dowel pin into the matching hole in the end of the second piece, and place a dowel center in the second hole in the end of these piece (5–25).

8. Bore a blind hole of the appropriate diame-

ter and depth at the location indicated by the dowel center.

At this point, the joint can be glued, assembled, and clamped.

Edge-to-Edge Dowel Joints

Edge-to-edge dowel joints are commonly used to join together relatively narrow pieces to make large assemblies like tabletops. Even when extra-wide material is available, it is often ripped into pieces that are two or three inches wide, and then reassembled using edge-to-edge dowel joinery. This is done to limit the warping of extra-wide pieces. The narrow pieces are alternated so that as each piece warps, a relatively flat overall surface is maintained (5–26).

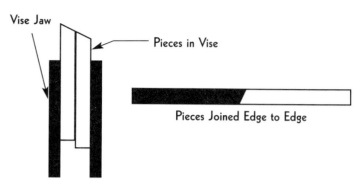

■ **5–27.** *Mating edges planed together for a perfect fit.*

■ **5–26.** *Four narrow pieces will warp less than one wide piece.*

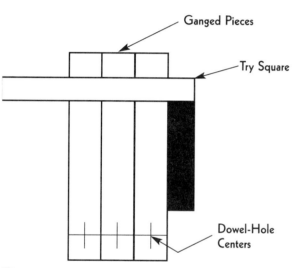

■ **5–28.** *Laying out an edge-to-edge dowel joint on several ganged pieces.*

Follow these step-by-step procedures when making an edge-to-edge dowel joint:

1. Square up the pieces but leave them oversized in length. This will allow the glued-up assembly to be trimmed to final size. If the pieces are being squared up with hand tools, plane the edges of mating pieces at the same time, with the pieces in the vise face to face (5–27). This will ensure a perfect fit even if the edges are not perfectly square.

2. Lay the joint out by locating the dowel centers on the edges of the ganged pieces. Ganging the pieces improves accuracy and speeds up the layout process (5–28). Space the dowels at six-inch intervals, starting two inches in from each end.

3. Bore the holes on a drill press or with hand tools. A doweling jig can be used if one is available (5–29).

   An alternate method utilizes the holes bored in the first piece to locate holes in the second piece with dowel centers. (Refer to Making Blind End-to-Face Dowel Joints on pages 146 and 147.)

4. After making a trial assembly, apply the glue and place the pieces in clamps until the glue sets.

■ **5–29.** *A doweling jig can be used to bore holes in the edge of a workpiece.*

Apply the glue to the glue block. Insert the screws into the holes and draw the two pieces together with the screws.

Check that the pieces are square to each other, adjust them if necessary, and allow the glue to set.

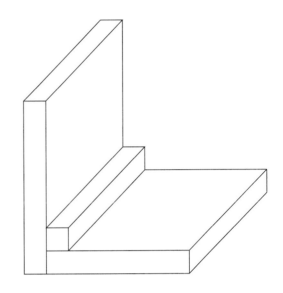

Reinforcing Butt Joints with a Glue Block

Glue blocks can be used in the reinforcement and assembly of end-to-face butt joints (5–30). This joint can be useful in situations where a glue block is not objectionable, clamping is difficult, or clamps are not available.

Position the block about 1/16 from the end of the first piece. The 1/16-inch space left between the glue block and the end of the piece will allow the pieces to be drawn together with screws. Apply the glue and screw the block into place on the first piece.

Move the second piece into position against the first piece. Drill holes, equal to the root diameter of the screws, through the glue block and into the second piece. Redrill the holes in the glue block with a screw-shank-sized drill.

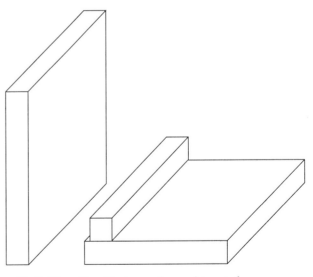

■ **5–30.** *Glue blocks can be used to reinforce a corner butt joint.*

Beveled or Miter Joints

The typical miter joint is formed at the intersection of two pieces meeting end to end (5–31). The angle at the end of each piece is equal to one-half the angle formed by the two pieces. The most common miter joint is the right-angle

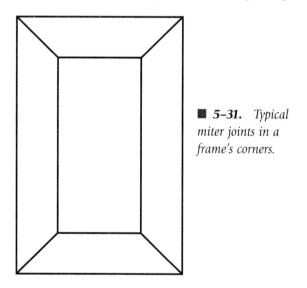

■ *5–31. Typical miter joints in a frame's corners.*

miter. The pieces form a 90-degree angle. Each piece is cut to a 45-degree angle. Miter joints tend to be weak because the end grain forming the joint does not glue well. As a result, most miter joints are reinforced in some way.

Two of the more common methods of reinforcement are slip feathers (5–32) and dowels (5–33).

Making a Miter Joint

All miter joints begin with a layout. The joint can be cut using a miter box, a power miter saw, or a table saw. (See Stationary Power Tools on pages 77 to 135 for information on the power miter saw and the table saw.)

A miter box is a three-sided box having a series of saw cuts at 45 and 90 degrees. These cuts are used to guide a backsaw during cutting (5–34). The workpiece is placed in the miter box, which has been secured to the workbench. The edge of the workpiece is placed against the

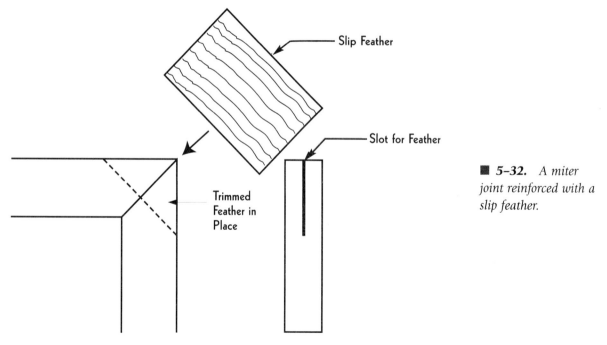

Slip Feather

Slot for Feather

Trimmed
Feather in
Place

■ *5–32. A miter joint reinforced with a slip feather.*

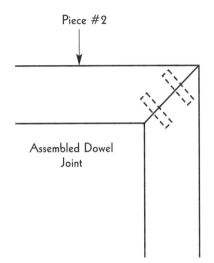

Piece #2

Assembled Dowel Joint

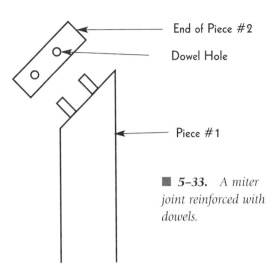

End of Piece #2

Dowel Hole

Piece #1

■ *5–33.* *A miter joint reinforced with dowels.*

■ *5–34.* *A miter box and a backsaw can be used to cut miters.*

far side of the miter box. The layout line is aligned with the saw blade and clamped in place, and the saw cut is made.

Resawing a Miter Joint

After all the pieces have been cut, a trial assembly is made. If an adjustment is required, the pieces are placed in a miter vise and resawed.

This operation produces ends that are parallel to each other because they were cut simultaneously (5–35). If a miter vise is not available, a miter clamp can be used to hold the pieces (5–36). Glue is applied to the miter joint, and it

■ *5–35.* *Resawing miter-joint pieces.*

■ *5–36.* *Miter clamps can be used to hold miter-joint pieces.*

is clamped in a miter vise or miter clamp until the glue sets.

Slip-Feather-Reinforced Miter Joints

Slip-feather-reinforced miter joints are among the simplest to make. The slip feather is a piece of veneer or resawed wood (5–37). Follow these step-by-step procedures when making slip-feather-reinforced miter joints:

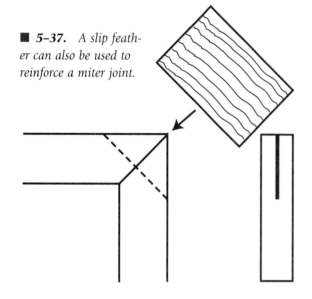

■ *5–37. A slip feather can also be used to reinforce a miter joint.*

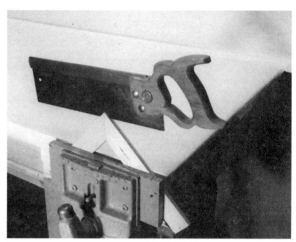

■ *5–38. Cutting a slot for a slip feather using a backsaw.*

1. Make a miter joint is made as described above.
2. After the glue sets, place the assembly in a bench vise and make a saw cut through the joint (5–38).
3. Cut a suitable piece of veneer with glue and insert it into the cut. The grain on the slip feather should be at 90 degrees to the joint line.
4. Clamp the assembly by applying pressure from face to face on the workpiece (5–39). Additional slip feathers can be added to strengthen or decorate the joint.

■ *5–39. Clamping a slip feather in a miter joint.*

Dowel-Reinforced Miter Joints

Dowel-reinforced miter joints (5–40) are made in much the same way dowel-reinforced butt joints are made. After cutting the miters and laying out the holes for the dowels, bore the two holes into the face of one of the miters. Dowel centers should be used to locate the matching holes. Assemble and glue the pieces in a miter vise or clamp to complete the job.

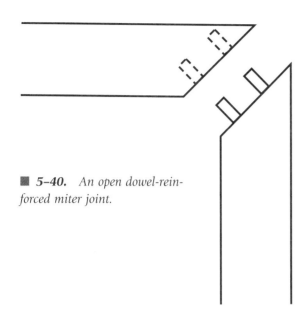

■ **5–40.** *An open dowel-reinforced miter joint.*

Making a Picture Frame

Miters are commonly used in the construction of items like picture frames. In items of this type, the opposite sides of the frame must be equal in length.

When making picture frames, the dimensions of the object to be framed must be considered in determining the length of the frame parts. Length measurements are made along the area shown in 5–41, which represents a rabbet that will hold the framed object.

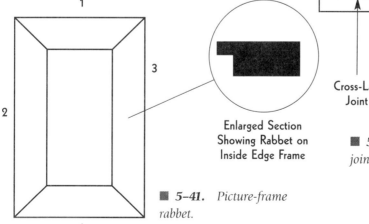

Enlarged Section
Showing Rabbet on
Inside Edge Frame

■ **5–41.** *Picture-frame rabbet.*

Frame assembly usually involves three steps:

1. Gluing together parts 1 and 2 (shown in 5–41).
2. Gluing together parts 3 and 4 (shown in 5–41).
3. After the glue sets, the two L-shaped parts are assembled. They are resawn in a miter vise or clamp before they are glued and clamped together. Resawing creates matching surfaces that are parallel.

Lap Joints

Lap joints are strong and relatively easy to design and make. The most common form of lap joint consists of two pieces overlapping at right angles to each other. Each piece is reduced to half of its original thickness in the area of the overlap. Several basic versions of the joint are shown in 5–42. Below are instructions for making a middle lap joint.

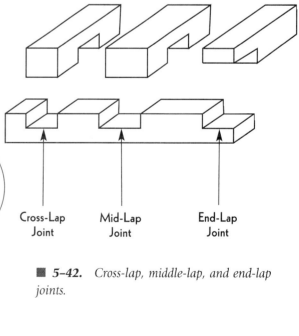

Cross-Lap Joint   Mid-Lap Joint   End-Lap Joint

■ **5–42.** *Cross-lap, middle-lap, and end-lap joints.*

Middle Lap Joint

Follow these step-by-step procedures when making a middle lap joint:

1. Lay out the middle-lap part of the joint on squared-up material (5–43).

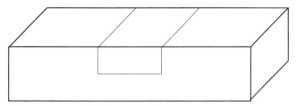

■ *5–43.   Middle-lap joint layout.*

2. Trace the layout with a utility knife.
3. Make a series of cuts into the workpiece with a back or dovetail saw, spacing the cuts about ½ inch apart (5–44). They should stop about ¹⁄₁₆ inch short of the layout line.

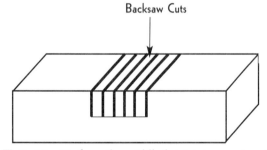

■ *5–44.   To form the middle-lap joints, a series of cuts are made to the workpiece with a backsaw.*

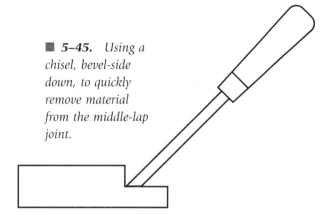

■ *5–45.   Using a chisel, bevel-side down, to quickly remove material from the middle-lap joint.*

4. Chisel away the material between the cuts, using the chisel bevel-side down (5–45).
5. Final-trim to the layout line. Place the chisel on a guide strip, bevel-side up, during the chiseling (5–46). The guide strip should be half the thickness of the workpiece. If the joint is being made on ¾-inch-thick material, a piece of ⅜-inch-thick plywood can be used as a guide strip.
6. Lay out the end-lap half of the joint using the completed middle lap (5–47).
7. Using steps one through five above, complete the end-lap part of the joint layout. This sequence allows the male half of the joint-the end lap-to be trimmed to fit the female middle lap.

■ *5–46.   Using a chisel, bevel-side up, with a guide strip for final trimming.*

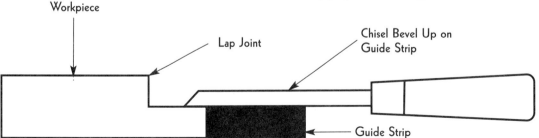

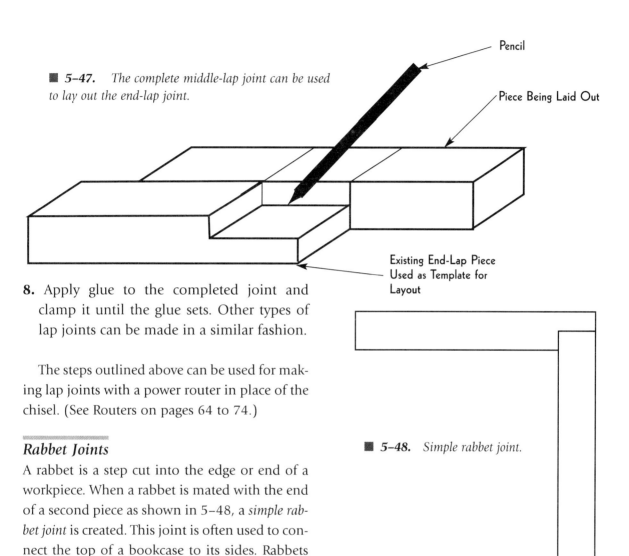

■ **5–47.** *The complete middle-lap joint can be used to lay out the end-lap joint.*

Pencil

Piece Being Laid Out

Existing End-Lap Piece
Used as Template for
Layout

■ **5–48.** *Simple rabbet joint.*

8. Apply glue to the completed joint and clamp it until the glue sets. Other types of lap joints can be made in a similar fashion.

The steps outlined above can be used for making lap joints with a power router in place of the chisel. (See Routers on pages 64 to 74.)

Rabbet Joints

A rabbet is a step cut into the edge or end of a workpiece. When a rabbet is mated with the end of a second piece as shown in 5–48, a *simple rabbet joint* is created. This joint is often used to connect the top of a bookcase to its sides. Rabbets can also be inserted into dadoes, forming a *rabbet-dado joint*. This joint is often used in drawer construction.

The cutaway portion of a rabbet is usually equal to half the thickness of the material it is cut into. However, it can be as much as two-thirds the thickness of the material if necessary.

The rabbet helps to locate or position the pieces being joined. It adds surface area for gluing and hides the end grain of the second piece.

A rabbet can be cut using the table saw or a router.

Dado Joints

A dado is a recess cut across the grain. A recess cut with the grain is called a *groove,* as in tongue-and-groove joint. The maximum depth of a dado is usually equal to one-half the thickness of the piece it is cut into.

A *simple dado joint* can be made by making a dado wide enough to receive a second piece at a 90-degree angle. Joints of this type are often

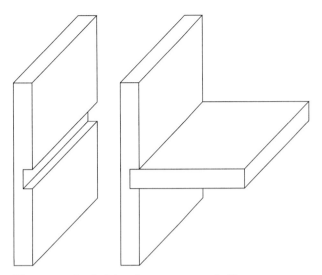

■ *5–49.* *Dado joint that supports a shelf.*

■ *5–51.* *Dado joint that supports a shelf.*

used to locate and support shelves in a cabinet or bookcase (5–49).

Blind dadoes are cut partway across a surface (5–50). They can be cut using a router or a table saw. If a table saw is being used, the workpieces is placed against the miter gauge during cutting. To speed up the process, a set of dado cutters is often used in place of a regular saw blade (5–51).

The rabbet and dado can be combined to make a *rabbet-dado* joint. This joint can be cut on the table saw using a standard blade. (Refer to Table Saws on pages 78 to 97.)

Mortise-and-Tenon Joints

The mortise-and-tenon (M & T) joint consists of rectangular tongue or tenon that fits into a matching rectangular recess in a second piece (5–52). This relatively complex joint provides excellent strength and locates pieces with accuracy.

Mortise-and-tenon joints were widely used before the development of dependable synthetic adhesives. A mortise-and-tenon assembly can be secured with pins (usually dowels), eliminating the need for glue.

Variations of the mortise-and-tenon joint, such as one which features a *stub tenon*, are still widely used in frame-and-panel construction (5–53). The mortise-and-tenon joints shown in

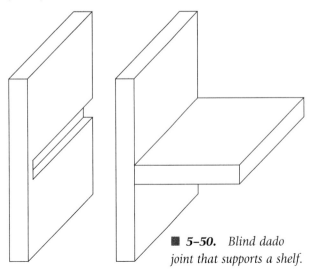

■ *5–50.* *Blind dado joint that supports a shelf.*

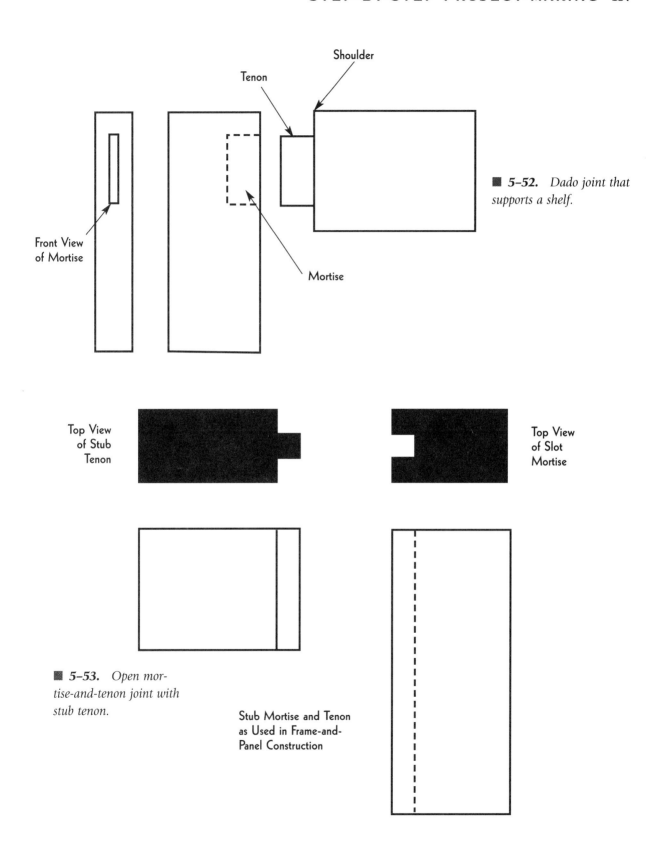

Shoulder

Tenon

■ *5–52.* *Dado joint that supports a shelf.*

Front View
of Mortise

Mortise

Top View
of Stub
Tenon

Top View
of Slot
Mortise

■ *5–53.* *Open mortise-and-tenon joint with stub tenon.*

Stub Mortise and Tenon
as Used in Frame-and-
Panel Construction

(5–54) are among the more common forms of the joint.

The tenons should be one-third to one-half as *thick* as the piece they are part of. Tenon *width* is determined by shoulder size. Shoulders should be uniform in width all around the base of the tenon. Tenon *length* should be no more than two-thirds the width of the piece that the tenon is to fit into.

Mortise size is determined by tenon size.

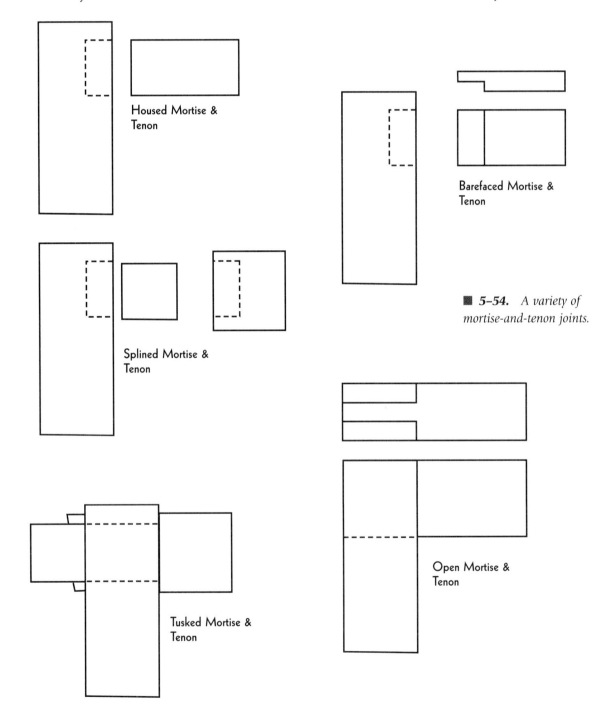

Housed Mortise & Tenon

Splined Mortise & Tenon

Tusked Mortise & Tenon

Barefaced Mortise & Tenon

■ *5–54. A variety of mortise-and-tenon joints.*

Open Mortise & Tenon

Mortises and tenons are usually centered on workpiece surfaces. A minimum of 3/16 inch of material is left behind mortises, and at least ½ inch of material is left above them (5–55).

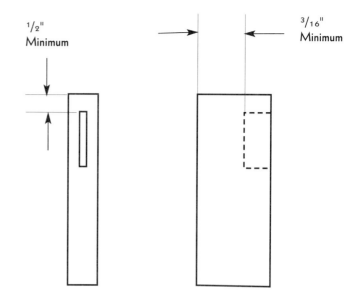

■ **5–55.** *A minimum of 3/16 inch is needed behind the mortises, and at least ½ inch is needed above them.*

Blind Mortise-and-Tenon Joint

Follow these step-by-step procedures for making a blind mortise-and-tenon joint:

1. Lay out the mortises and tenons on squared-up material.

2. Make the mortises first, so that the tenons can be cut to fit them. Bore a series of blind holes along the centerline of the mortise layout using a bit that is equal in diameter to the width of the mortise (5–56).

■ **5–56.** *Blind holes bored into a mortise layout.*

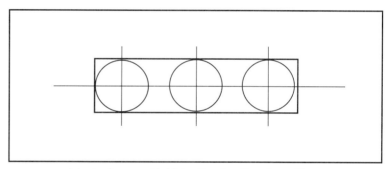

Mortise Layout with Holes Bored as Seen from Above

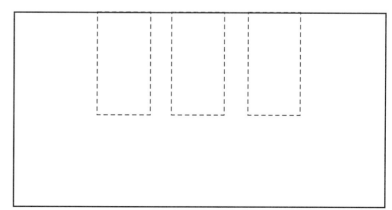

Side View Showing Hidden Outline of Blind Bored holes

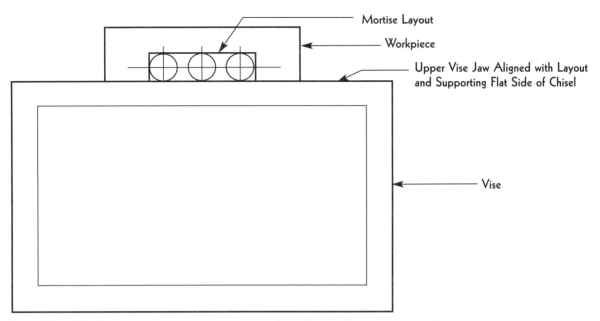

■ *5–57.* *Chiseling out the remaining material to form the mortises in a mortise layout.*

3. Chisel out the remaining material, using vise liner blocks as chisel guides (5–57).

4. Cut the mortises. A router can be used to do this, in which case a router bit with a diameter equal to the width of the mortise is used. The resulting mortise will have rounded ends that will have to be squared using hand tools (5–58).

A drill press can also be used to cut the mortise. Many drill-press manufacturers produce a mortising attachment for their drill presses. This device is mounted onto the drill-press spindle and allows a hollow chisel, with a bit rotating inside it, to cut a square hole. A series of these holes are cut next to each other to produce a mortise.

5. Next, make the tenons. This can be done using hand tools. Cut the cheeks and shoulders with a dovetail or backsaw (5–59). Make these cuts about 1/16 inch away from the layout line, leaving material for final trimming with a chisel.

When cutting the shoulders, use a guide block clamped to the workpiece (5–60). A miter box can be used for this operation if available.

6. Trim the tenons with a chisel until they fit the mortise. Small amounts of material can be removed by scraping the tenon with the chisel. Tenons can also be cut on the table saw or with a router. (Refer to Table Saws on pages 78 to 97 and Routers on pages 64 to 74.)

7. Make a trial assembly of the parts.

■ *5–58.* *A router-cut mortise with rounded ends.*

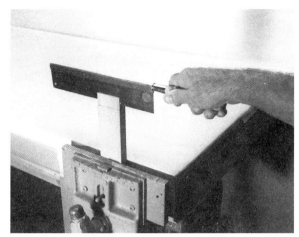

■ **5–59.** *Making tenon cheek cuts with a dovetail saw.*

8. Coat the completed joint with glue, and assembly and clamp it until the glue sets.

Other versions of the mortise-and-tenon joint can be made using the general procedures outlined above.

Dovetail Joints

Dovetail joints an excellent example of self-locking joints. The design of the joint provides strength and locates the pieces being joined with respect to each other. The material from which it is made determines the strength of the joint. Dovetail joints made of a hard, dense wood such as oak are relatively strong and durable. Joints

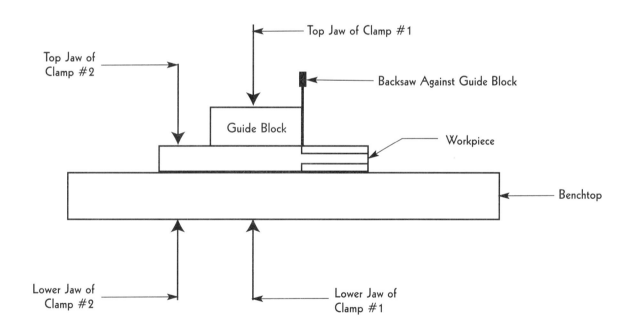

■ **5–60.** *Using a guide block clamped to the workpiece to making tenon shoulder cuts.*

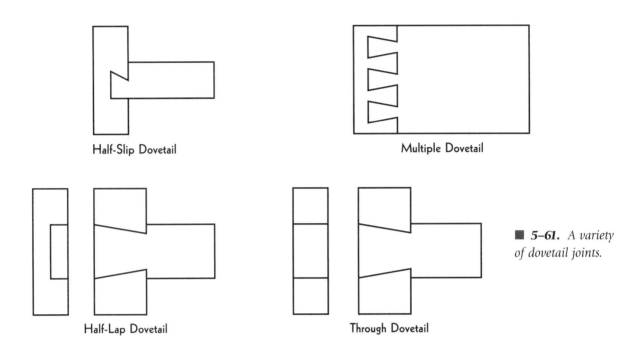

Half-Slip Dovetail

Multiple Dovetail

Half-Lap Dovetail

Through Dovetail

■ *5–61. A variety of dovetail joints.*

made of a softwood such as pine are less strong and durable. All dovetail joints have male components, pins, which fit into female components, sockets, or tails. Several types of dovetail joint are shown in 5–61.

The slopes on pins and tails on many joints are usually made with a ratio of one to six or one to seven (5–62). If the slope is too great, such as one to four, the corner of the tail will tend to break off under pressure.

Single Through Dovetail Joint

Follow these step-by-step procedures to make a single through dovetail joint:

1. Divide the end of the first piece, which is for the socket, or tail, into three equal parts. The slanted lines on the end of the piece shown in 5–63 are made using a T-bevel set to a

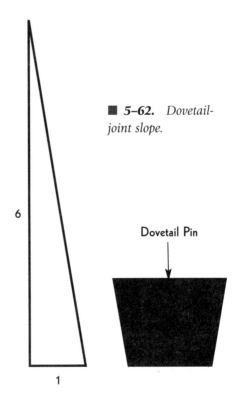

■ *5–62. Dovetail-joint slope.*

6

1

Dovetail Pin

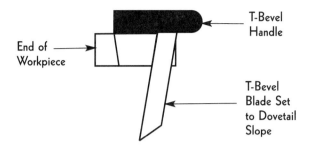

■ **5-63.** *Laying out a dovetail joint with a T-bevel.*

one-in-seven slope. Cutting the socket first allows it to be used to locate and lay out the pin.

2. Make cuts next to the layout lines with a dovetail or backsaw, leaving about ¹⁄₁₆ inch material for trimming with a chisel.
3. Chisel out the material between the saw cuts (5-64). Do the final trimming with the piece mounted in a bench vise (5-65).
4. Place the socket on the first piece on top of the second piece and use it to lay out the pin on the second piece (5-66). Complete the layout with a try square.

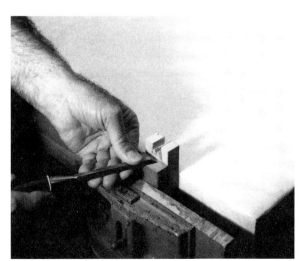

■ **5-64.** *Chiseling out the material between the saw cuts to form a through dovetail joint.*

5. Cut out the pin and trim it to fit the socket. Make a trial assembly. Then apply glue to the joint and clamp it until the glue sets.

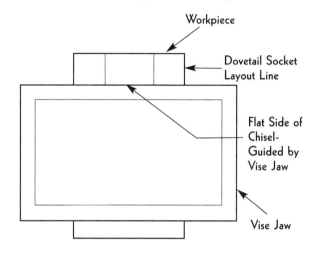

■ **5-65.** *Trimming the socket while it is in a vise.*

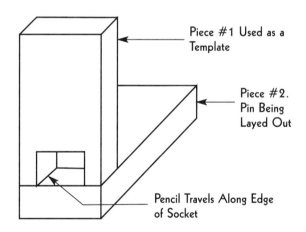

■ **5-66.** *Laying out the pin on the second piece, using the socket on the first piece.*

Multiple Dovetail Joints

Multiple dovetail joints are often cut using a router and a dovetail fixture (5–67). The fixture is used to hold the pieces to be joined at right angles to each other. A template, positioned on the pieces, guides the router. A dovetail bit in the router cuts sockets and tails on the pieces as it follows the template. The fit of the joint is adjusted by raising or lowering the router bit.

5–67. *Dovetail router fixture.*

Step Seven: Completing Surface Decorations

Techniques such as inlaying, marquetry, carving, and laminating can be used to decorate wood surfaces.

INLAYING

Inlaying involves filling a recess, cut into a surface, with thin pieces of wood of contrasting colors. The piece shown in 5–68 was made by making four shallow saw cuts on the table saw using the rip fence as a guide. Strips of contrasting

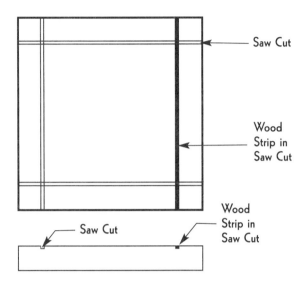

5–68. *Inlaying technique on a table saw.*

wood were glued into the saw cuts. When the glue had set, the surface was sanded flat.

The circular inlay decorations shown in 5–69 were produced by boring several shallow, blind

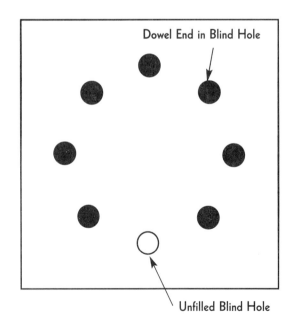

5–69. *Circular dowel inlays.*

holes in the surface and then filling the holes with dowels of contrasting colors.

To make the star-shaped inlay shown in 5–70, follow these step-by-step procedures:

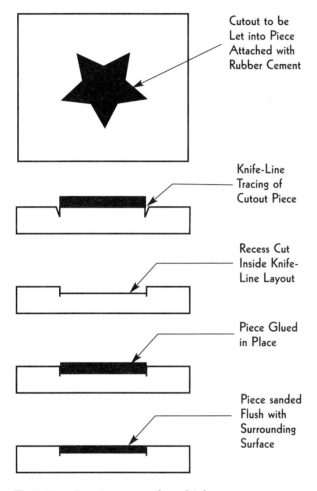

Cutout to be Let into Piece Attached with Rubber Cement

Knife-Line Tracing of Cutout Piece

Recess Cut Inside Knife-Line Layout

Piece Glued in Place

Piece sanded Flush with Surrounding Surface

■ *5–70. Creating a star-shaped inlay.*

1. Make a full-sized template of the inlay shape.

2. Use the template to lay out the shape on the thin inlay material. Standard commercial veneers ½₈ inch thick can be used for inlaying.

3. Cut the shape out using a sharp knife or a scroll saw.

4. With rubber cement, attach the inlay piece to the surface of the piece to be inlayed.

5. Make an outline of the piece with a thin-bladed knife.

6. Separate the pieces and rout or chisel out the material inside the knife cuts. The depth of recess should allow the inlay to project slightly above the surrounding surface.

7. Glue the inlay into place and sand it flush to the surrounding surface after the glue sets.

MARQUETRY

In marquetry, a thin sheet of wood consisting of many pieces assembled in jigsaw-puzzle fashion is used to cover and decorate the surface. A relatively large surface is usually involved. Commercially made marquetry designs are available for use in this process. One popular example is the checkerboard pattern.

The marquetry piece is often glued to a thin sheet of paper that is removed after the marquetry has been applied to the surface to be decorated.

LAMINATION

Lamination consists of gluing layers of wood together to form a plywood-like assembly. If contrasting colored layers of wood are used, patterns emerge as the laminated piece is shaped. The oval box lid shown in 5–71 consists of three laminated layers. The middle layer is lighter than the top or bottom layer; it appears in the illustration as a light oval ring. This pattern emerged as the surface of the box lid was being rounded on a belt sander.

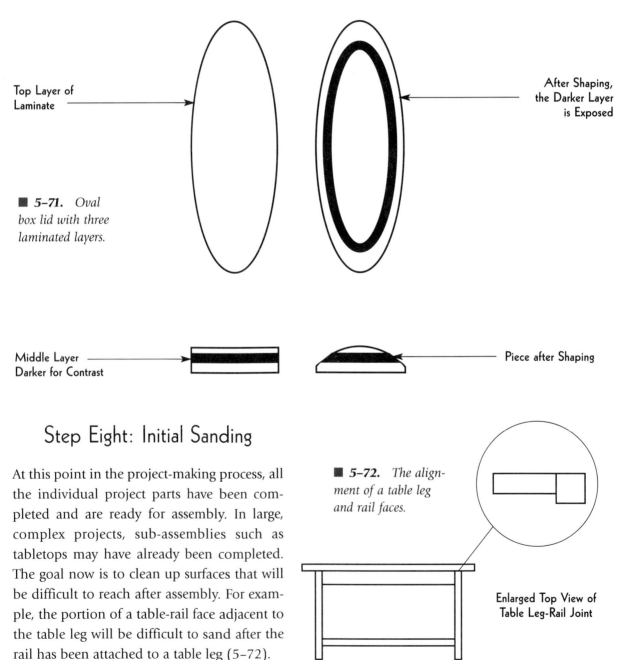

Top Layer of Laminate

After Shaping, the Darker Layer is Exposed

■ *5–71.* *Oval box lid with three laminated layers.*

Middle Layer Darker for Contrast

Piece after Shaping

Step Eight: Initial Sanding

At this point in the project-making process, all the individual project parts have been completed and are ready for assembly. In large, complex projects, sub-assemblies such as tabletops may have already been completed. The goal now is to clean up surfaces that will be difficult to reach after assembly. For example, the portion of a table-rail face adjacent to the table leg will be difficult to sand after the rail has been attached to a table leg (5–72).

■ *5–72.* *The alignment of a table leg and rail faces.*

Enlarged Top View of Table Leg-Rail Joint

Surfaces that are to have glue applied should not be sanded, because excessive sanding can shred the surface and interfere with glue adhesion.

PRESANDING PROCEDURES

Follow these presanding procedures:
1. Try to remove pencil marks with a regular pencil eraser.
2. Try to remove other blemishes and stains with solvents like paint thinner before starting to sand.
3. Remove glue residue on sub-assemblies by scraping it off.

SANDING TECHNIQUE

For this initial sanding, sand the pieces with the grain, using suitable power equipment. Begin with #80-grit abrasive and end with #120 grit. Remove tool marks and other blemishes using the #80 abrasive. Once all of the blemishes and tool marks have been removed, use the finer abrasives to remove the abrasive scratches. Stubborn areas may require hand-sanding.

able open assembly time, as discussed below. In order for glue to cure properly, pieces must be assembled and clamped during this open assembly time period. If the assembly takes too long, the woodworker may be faced with the difficult job of removing the glue and starting over.

CLAMPING TOOLS

Many types of clamping tools can be used to hold pieces together.

The *bench vise* is used to hold work securely while it is being processed. It can also be used to clamp small assemblies while glue cures. The typical bench vise has 4x10-inch jaws that can hold pieces that are up to 12 inches in width.

Many vises have a *dog* attached to the movable jaw. This dog can be pulled up so that it projects above the vise jaws. In the "up" position, the dog and a bench stop can be used to hold extra-wide workpieces (5–73).

Hardwood blocks are usually attached to the inside of the vise jaws to keep them from marring work held in the vise.

Step Nine: Making a Trial Assembly

The principal reason for a trial assembly is to resolve clamping problems that may slow down the final assembly. Once glue has been applied, there is not much time to make adjustments. Each type of glue has an allow-

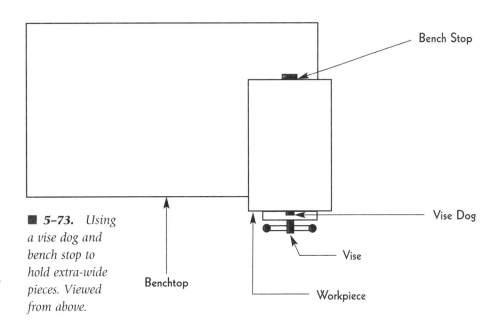

■ *5–73. Using a vise dog and bench stop to hold extra-wide pieces. Viewed from above.*

Bench Stop

Vise Dog

Vise

Benchtop

Workpiece

C-clamps are made of steel and are primarily designed for use in metalworking (5–74). However, their relatively low cost and ease of use make these clamps popular with woodworkers. Workpieces must be protected from being damaged by the metal clamp jaws. This can be done by placing wooden blocks between the clamp jaws and the workpiece.

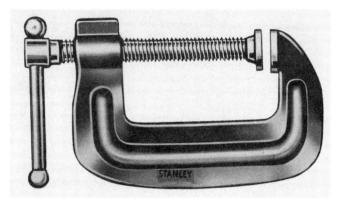

■ *5–74. C-clamp.*

C-clamp size is indicated in inches. A four-inch clamp can be used with pieces that are up to four inches thick.

Hand-screw clamps (5–75) are wooden parallel clamps. They provide a large contact surface area, and their wooden construction helps to

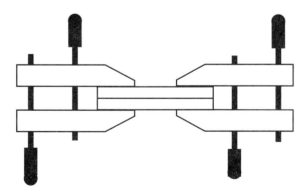

■ *5–75. Hand-screw clamps in use.*

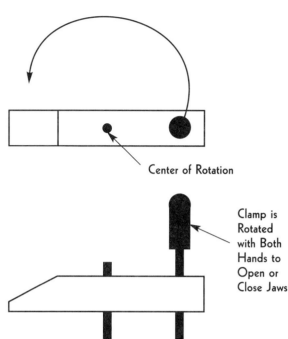

Center of Rotation

Clamp is Rotated with Both Hands to Open or Close Jaws

■ *5–76. Adjusting a hand-screw clamp. The outside handle pivots around the inside handle*

prevent damage to workpieces. A variety of sizes are available, with maximum jaw openings ranging from two to fourteen inches.

Maximum holding pressure for hand-screw clamps is obtained when the clamp jaws are parallel to each other. The clamps are opened by pivoting the outside clamp handle around the inside handle (5–76).They should be opened the distance it takes for the jaws to fit over the assembly being clamped. Then the outside handle is used for final tightening.

Bar and pipe clamps are used for clamping large assemblies such as tabletops (5–77). Bar clamps

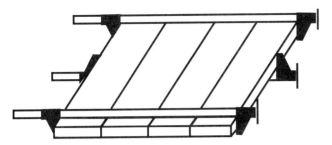

■ *5–77.* *Bar clamps can be used to clamp a large assembly.*

are available in lengths ranging from two to six feet. They have three principal parts: a rigid bar, a sliding jaw, and a screw-driven jaw. The sliding jaw is used for large adjustments. The screw-driven jaw is used for final tightening.

Pipe-fixture clamps (5–78) are an inexpensive alternative to bar clamps. The screw-driven jaw fits onto the threaded end of a piece of common one-inch iron pipe. The sliding jaw fits over the pipe and is used for large adjustments. Pipe clamps are less rigid than bar clamps of similar length.

Assemblies must be protected from being marred by the metal jaws of bar and pipe clamps. This can be accomplished by using wooden strips, or cauls, between the clamp jaws and the material being clamped. These strips also help to distribute clamp pressure in a more uniform way. (Refer to 5–77.)

Stiffening blocks help to counteract the tendency of wide assemblies, such as tabletops, to flex under clamping pressure. These blocks are applied before the bar clamps are fully tightened. The blocks can be protected from seeping glue by placing a piece of plastic wrap or newspaper between the block and the glue joint. If this is not done, the blocks may adhere to the assembly being glued. Alternating the clamps, as shown in 5–77, also helps to keep assemblies flat.

Box-shaped assemblies, such as those used in cabinet carcass construction, can be clamped with bar clamps (5–79). Rapid-action bar clamps can be placed and tightened with one

■ *5–78.* *Pipe clamp.*

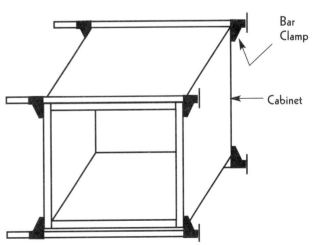

■ *5–79.* *Using bar clamps on a cabinet.*

hand (5–80). This allows the other hand to be used to steady the assembly as clamps are applied. This type of clamp can also be used for prying assemblies apart by reversing the tightening component. Plastic pads on the clamp reduce its tendency to mar the workpiece.

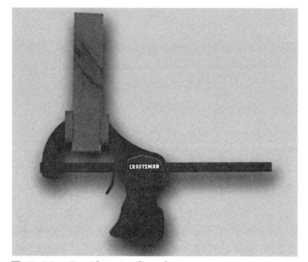

■ *5–80.* *Rapid-action bar clamp.*

Strap, or *web, clamps* are used to clamp assemblies such as hexagonal frames (5–81). Pulling the loose end of the strap tightens the strap clamp until the clamp is in contact with the object being clamped. Final pressure is applied by rotating the clamp spindle with a screwdriver or wrench. A ratchet on the spindle keeps the strap in tension as it is tightened. The ratchet pawl is lifted to release tension on the strap.

The strap should be protected from seeping glue by placing a piece of plastic wrap between the strap and the glue joint.

Spring clamps (5–82) are used to apply pressure to small assemblies.

■ *5–82.* *Spring clamps.*

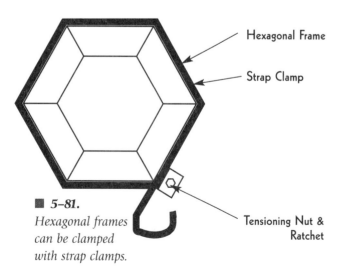

Hexagonal Frame

Strap Clamp

■ *5–81.*
Hexagonal frames can be clamped with strap clamps.

Tensioning Nut & Ratchet

Step Ten: Permanently Assembling the Project

Once a trial assembly has been completed, the project is ready for final assembly. Most projects require the use of glue in this process.

GLUE SELECTION AND USE

The woodworker can select from many types and brands of glue. Among the factors affecting glue selection are the following:

1. Ease of application and setting time.
2. Open assembly time period.
3. The type of wood being glued.
4. Environmental conditions to which the glue joint will be exposed.
5. Shelf life.
6. Health and environmental considerations.

Ease of Application and Setting Time

A glue that comes ready to use out of a squeeze bottle is probably the first choice of most amateur woodworkers. Other forms of application include brushing and rolling glue on. Glues that allow 30 minutes of open assembly time are useable on most projects. Complex projects, with many joints, can usually be broken down into sub-assemblies that can be glued and clamped within 30 minutes.

The wood to be glued must be relatively dry. Air- and kiln-dried wood can usually be glued successfully

Glues such as *polyvinyl resin* (white glue) or *aliphatic resin* (yellow carpenter's glue) allow clamps to be removed in about 35 minutes. Complete curing of the glue requires 24 hours.

Open Assembly Time

Open assembly time is the time available for applying the glue and assembling and clamping components. If this time limit is exceeded, the glue may not develop its full strength. One applied, glue is difficult to remove. It is important to have a trial assembly to help ensure that the job can be completed in the open assembly time for the glue being used.

Type of Wood Being Glued

Oily woods such as teak and rosewood can be difficult to glue. Wiping the surface of these woods with lacquer thinner can sometimes improve glue adhesion.

Soft, permeable woods such as pine, basswood, chestnut, and alder are relatively easy to glue. Harder woods usually adhere better when viscous, thick glues are applied and when clamping pressure is relatively high.

Environmental Conditions

Exposure to moisture is the most common concern of the woodworker. Many glues are moisture-resistant, but very few are waterproof. Moisture-resistant glues will tolerate moist locations for extended periods, but cannot tolerate immersion in water. Most glues, with the exception of the polyvinyl resins (white glues), are heat-resistant.

Shelf Life

Many glue labels do not list shelf life. The condition of the glue often gives an indication of its usability. Glues that have become very thick and lumpy should not be used. Glues and finishing materials should be dated by the buyer at the time of purchase. Whenever glue quality is questionable, it should be tested on scrap material.

Label directions should be followed closely when using any glue.

Health Considerations

Health hazards should be considered when selecting a glue for use. Some glues contain toxic materials that can irritate skin or cause other problems. Latex gloves can help to protect the skin from irritants.

A suitable dust mask should be worn when handling glues that contain finely powered materials.

Commonly Used Glues

Glue Type	Uses	Open Assembly Time/ Curing Time	Advantages	Disadvantages
Polyvinyl Resin	Soft, Porous Woods and Other Materials	30 Minutes 24 Hours	No Mixing Fast-Drying Nontoxic Strong Bond Cleaned Up with Water	Not Water-Resistant Not Heat-Resistant Not Tacky
Aliphatic Resin	All Non-Oily Woods and Wood Products	30 Minutes 24 Hours	Water—and Heat-Resistant No Mixing Fast-drying Nontoxic Strong Bond Tacky Cleaned Up with Water	Not Waterproof
Polyurethane	Wood Foam Concrete Metal	2 Hours 24 Hours	Waterproof Can Be Used on Many Materials	Skin and Eye Irritant Difficult to Clean Up
Plastic Resin	All Non-Oily Woods	24 Hours	Waterproof Viscosity Can Be Varied Light-Color Glue Line	Skin and Eye Irritant Pieces Must Fit Well Long Clamping Time
Resorcinol	All Woods	24 Hours	Waterproof: Can Be Used in Underwater Applications	Skin and Eye Irritant Very Dark Glue Line

Table 5–2. *A description of some of the more commonly used glues.*

FASTENERS

Nails and *screws* are used in the assembly process to hold parts together. Sometimes they are used alone, and at other times they are used to hold pieces together as glue cures. They are also used to attach hinges, drawer slides, and other hardware to workpieces.

Nails

Nails are the simplest and oldest type of fastener. They owe their holding power to their ability to displace wood fibers. The displaced fibers press against the surface of the nail and help to hold it in place (5–83). Nails have more holding power when driven into edges or faces than when driven into ends. The larger and rougher the surface of the nail, the better it holds.

Nails are most often used in carpentry and trim work. Some woodworkers use finishing

Nail in End Grain Does Not Displace Fibers & Has Limited Holding Power

Nail Driven into Face Displaces Fibers & Has Good Holding Power

■ *5–83. Nails in face and end grain.*

nails in the assembly of cabinets that are to be finished with an opaque finish such as paint.

The two main types of nails are *finishing* and *common nails.* Finishing nails have smaller heads than common nails (5–84).

Common Nail
Larger Head & Thickness Provide Greater Holding Power

Finishing Nail
Smaller Head Allows Nail to be Set and Hidden

Smaller Thickness Allows Driving into Thin Materials Without Splitting

■ *5–84. Common nails (top) and finishing nails.*

Nails are available in lengths ranging from one and one-half to six inches. Nail length is also indicated in terms of *penny size*, abbreviated "d." Nails that are 1½, 2½, and 3½ inches long are also known as 4d, 8d, and 16d nails.

Nails less than two inches in length are sized in fractions of an inch and wire-gauge size. The more common *wire nail* lengths are ½, ¾, ⅞, and 1 inch. Wire-gauge sizes include #17, 18, 19, and

20. A 1½ #18 wire nail is one that is 1½ inches long and made from wire that will fit into a # 18 wire gauge. An 1½ inch #18 *brad* is exactly like the wire nail except that it has a small head (5–85).

Nail length can be calculated by multiplying the thickness of the wood the nail is going through by three (5–86). The length of a nail that is to be driven through a piece of wood ¾ inch thick is: ¾ × 3=9⁄4 or 2¼ inches.

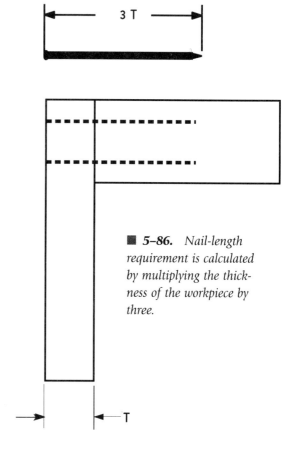

■ *5–86. Nail-length requirement is calculated by multiplying the thickness of the workpiece by three.*

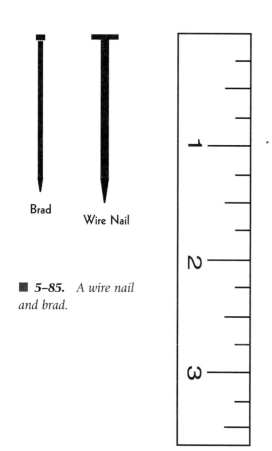

Brad
Wire Nail

■ *5–85. A wire nail and brad.*

Driving a Nail

Driving a nail properly requires a hammer that is suitable for the nail being driven. Small nails can be driven with a light (10-ounce) hammer. Larger nails may require a heavier (16-ounce) hammer.

The nail is held in position with one hand, while the hammer is used to tap the nail head lightly. Once the nail is self-supporting, the hand holding the nail is removed.

The hammer should be held with the hand close to the end of the handle. The handle should be kept at a 90-degree angle to the nail during driving (5–87). This will help to prevent the nail from bending.

■ *5–87.* *Correct hammer position when driving a nail.*

■ *5–89.* *Drawing a nail using a claw hammer and block.*

Finishing nail heads can be hidden by driving them below the surface of the wood with a nail set (5–88). The nail hole can be filled to hide the nail head.

Driving nails close to the end of a piece can result in splitting. This can be avoided by drilling a hole through the piece prior to nailing. A nail, with its head removed, can be used as a drill bit.

Blunting the point of the nail can help to reduce the tendency of the nail to split the wood.

Finishing nails can be removed by driving the nail through the piece until it emerges on the opposite face, where it can be pulled out with a pair of pliers.

Wood Screws

Wood screws have two main advantages over nails: They hold better and they can be removed and replaced easily. Screws are especially useful in situations where the use of clamps is impractical. Screw power can be used to hold pieces together while the glue sets. Counterbored screws are almost invisible (5–90).

■ *5–88.* *Nail set.*

Removing Nails

Nails can be pulled out or drawn using the claws of the hammer. Long nails should be drawn in two steps. First the nail is pulled out about an inch; then a block is placed under the hammer to complete the removal (5–89).

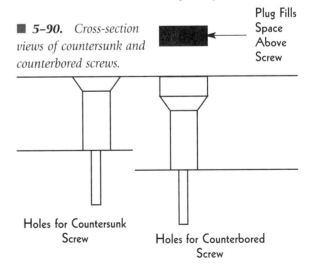

■ *5–90.* *Cross-section views of countersunk and counterbored screws.*

Plug Fills Space Above Screw

Holes for Countersunk Screw

Holes for Counterbored Screw

Screws are packaged in boxes of one hundred. Boxes are labeled with the following information: screw length in inches, head type, number, material the screw is made of, and finish.

Screw *length* is measured from the top of the head to the point. The most common *head types* are the flat, round, and oval heads. Screw *number* refers to the diameter of the screw shank by wire gauge number (Table 5–3). A number-five screw has a shank diameter of ¼ inch, while a number-ten screw has a shank diameter of 3/16 inch.

Phillips screws must be driven with a special Phillips screwdriver. These screws are often driven with a power screwdriver.

Screws are usually made of steel, although brass and stainless-steel screws are available at extra cost. Among the more common screw finishes available are *blued, cadmium,* and *zinc.* All of these finishes are rust-resistant.

Screw Selection

Screw selection is usually determined by the dimensions of the pieces being joined together. Ideally, the head and shank should be in the first piece, and the threaded section in the second piece (5–91).

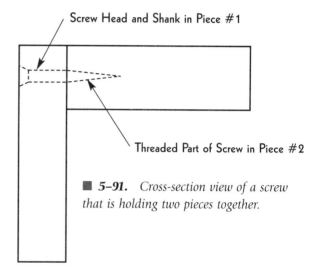

Screw Head and Shank in Piece #1

Threaded Part of Screw in Piece #2

■ **5–91.** *Cross-section view of a screw that is holding two pieces together.*

*Screw Number	Clearance Hole Shank Diameter (Inches)	Pilot Hole Thread Root Diameter (Inches)
4	7/64	1/16
5	1/8	3/32
6	9/64	3/32
7	5/32	7/62
8	11/64	1/8
9	3/16	1/8
10	3/16	1/8
11	13/64	9/64
12	7/32	9/64

*Screw Number = Head Diameter in Sixteenths x 2 Minus 2

Table 5–3. *Screw-hole chart.*

Screw length is determined by tripling the thickness of the first piece being joined. The length of a screw that is to be driven through a piece of wood ¾ inch thick is found by multiplying the thickness of the wood by 3. Therefore, ¾ × 3 = 9/4, or 2¼ inches. So in this example, a 2¼-inch screw would be required.

Screw diameter or number is determined by considering screw length, wood hardness, and screw material. Higher-number, larger-diameter screws are used when the wood is hard and the screw is long or made of a soft material such as brass. In general, screws numbered six through ten are among the most commonly used.

Calculating the Shank Diameter or Number of a Screw

To calculate the shank diameter or number of the screw, do the following:

1. Determine the diameter of the screw in sixteenths of an inch by measuring it.
2. Double the numerator, which is the top number of the fraction. Disregard the denominator, the bottom number.
3. Subtract two from the numerator. The resulting number is the screw number. For example, when the numerator of a 6/16-inch screwhead diameter is doubled, the result is 12/16. Two is then subtracted from the numerator, 12, leaving the number 10. So a number-ten screw is the screw that should be used.

Increasing Screw-Holding Power

Screws hold better in face or edge grain than in end grain. Inserting a dowel in a hole drilled in line with and at right angles to the screw greatly increases screw-holding power in end grain. This is because the screw is anchored by the dowel (5–92).

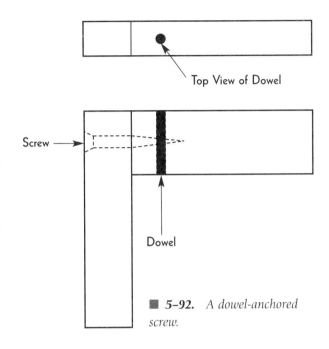

Top View of Dowel

Screw →

Dowel

■ **5–92.** *A dowel-anchored screw.*

Fastening with Wood Screws

Follow these procedures when fastening wood screws:

1. Place the pieces to be joined in position and clamp them.
2. Drill a hole through the first piece and into the second piece. The drill bit used should have a diameter equal to the root diameter of the screw to be used. (Refer to Table 5–3 for drill-bit size.) Softwoods such as sugar pine do not require a root-diameter hole.
3. Separate the pieces and redrill the hole in the first piece with a bit that has a diameter equal to the shank diameter of the screw to be used. (Refer to Table 5–3 for drill-bit size.)
4. If a flat-head screw is to be used, countersink this hole (5–93).

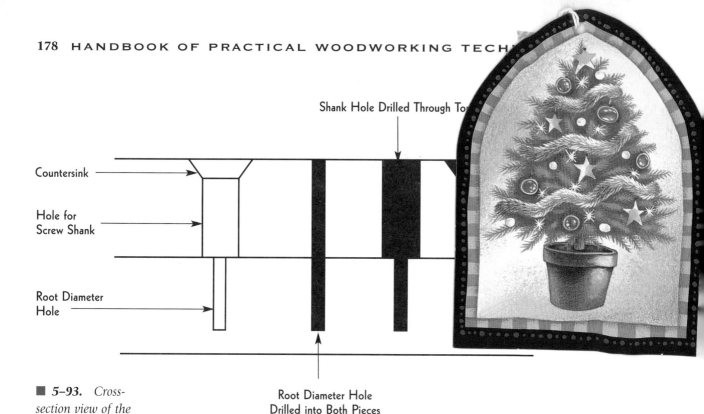

Shank Hole Drilled Through To

Countersink

Hole for
Screw Shank

Root Diameter
Hole

Root Diameter Hole
Drilled into Both Pieces
First

■ *5–93.* *Cross-section view of the holes for a counter-sunk screw.*

5. If the screw is to be counterbored, enlarge the top of the shank hole by counterboring. Place a suitable wooden plug in the counterbored hole over the screw head.

Combination bits are available for each screw length and diameter, and will drill all of the required holes in one operation (5–94).

Sheetrock, Deck, and Bugle-Head Screws
Sheetrock, deck, and bugle-head screws (5–95) are wood screws that are designed to be driven with special Phillips power drivers or portable electric drills with variable-speed capabilities. These flat-head screws are made of a type of steel that allows power driving without damage to the screw head. They are designed for use in soft-woods such as redwood and fir and do not usu-ally require predilled holes or countersinking. This greatly reduces installation time.

The shank diameters of these screws are

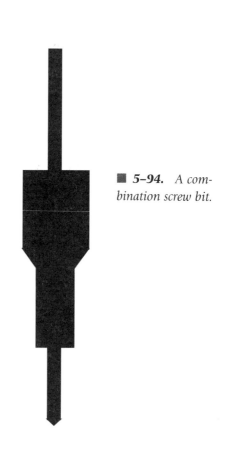

■ *5–94.* *A combination screw bit.*

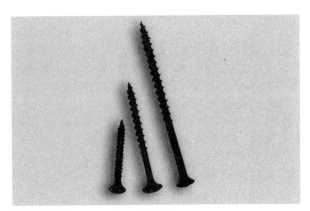

■ **5–95.** *Sheetrock and deck screws.*

smaller than the thread diameters. This allows the pieces being joined to be pulled together as the screws are tightened.

These screws range in number from six to ten, but these numbers are not the same as regular wood-screw numbers. They range in length from 1 to 4½ inches.

Sheetrock, deck, and bugle-head screws are available with coarse or fine threads. Coarse screws have between eight and ten threads per inch, while fine screws have between 16 and 24 threads.

Step Eleven: Sanding and Finishing the Project

After glue is applied, the project parts are assembled and clamped or fastened together. Remove any glue seepage using a moistened cloth. Remove the clamps after the glue has set. At this point, the piece is ready for final sanding and finishing. This is covered in Chapter 7.

CHAPTER 6

FURNITURE & CARCASS CONSTRUCTION

■■■■■■■■■■■■■■

This chapter contains information on furniture and carcass construction. This involves fine woodworking, which consists of working with a variety of woods to tolerances of plus or minus 1/16 inch.

LEG-RAIL DESIGN AND CONSTRUCTION

Legs and rails are used in the construction of furniture such as tables and chairs. Legs are used to support and raise pieces to the height required. For maximum strength, they are usually made of solid wood. Rails help to stiffen legs and provide support for horizontal surfaces such as tabletops and chair seats (6–1). Rails can be made of solid wood or well-constructed laminates.

Leg joints are put under considerable stress whenever a table is pushed or a leg is kicked. The legs act as levers that are working against the joints that connect the legs to the rest of the piece (6–2). Reinforcing the connecting joint

■ 6–1. *Table legs support and raise pieces to the required height. Table rails stiffen legs and provide support for horizontal surfaces.*

Apron Rail

Stretcher

can help the leg resist this pressure. This is often done by installing corner plates, or corner blocks, to the legs and the nearby rails (6–3).

Secondary rails, or stretchers, are sometimes used to help limit leg leverage (6–4). Chair stretchers are often connected to chair legs with dowels.

The leg-rail joints used today include the reinforced butt joint (refer to 6–3), the stub mortise-and-tenon joint (6–5), the dovetailed mortise-

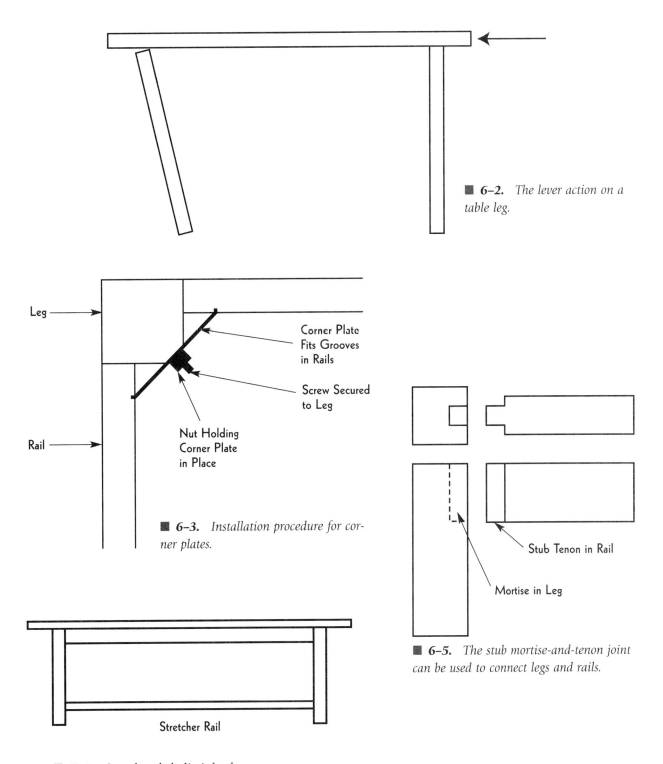

■ **6–2.** *The lever action on a table leg.*

Leg

Corner Plate
Fits Grooves
in Rails

Screw Secured
to Leg

Nut Holding
Corner Plate
in Place

Rail

■ **6–3.** *Installation procedure for corner plates.*

Stub Tenon in Rail

Mortise in Leg

■ **6–5.** *The stub mortise-and-tenon joint can be used to connect legs and rails.*

Stretcher Rail

■ **6–4.** *Stretchers help limit leg leverage.*

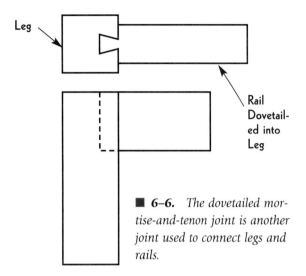

6-6. *The dovetailed mortise-and-tenon joint is another joint used to connect legs and rails.*

Leg

Rail Dovetailed into Leg

Contemporary pieces often have joints that are part of shaped sculptural components. These joints must be made with care to avoid producing weak, short-grain areas near the joints (6–8). This type of short grain fractures easily. Many woodworkers complete this joinery while the pieces are in rectangular, squared-up form. Extra material is left around the joints for removal during shaping after the pieces have been assembled.

and-tenon joint (6–6), and the dowel joint (6–7). Complex leg-rail joints were used more frequently in the days before synthetic glues were developed.

Corner plates or blocks are often used to reinforce the simpler joints that are widely used today. The plates or blocks are easy to install and allow easy leg removal. This makes shipping the table much easier.

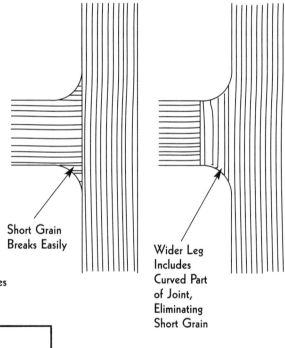

Short Grain Breaks Easily

Wider Leg Includes Curved Part of Joint, Eliminating Short Grain

6-8. *Shaped components should be carefully made, so that short grain is not near the joints.*

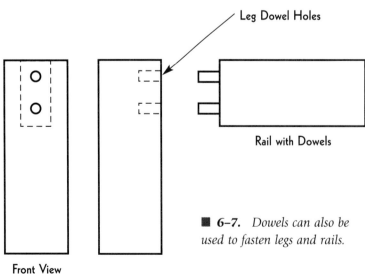

Leg Dowel Holes

Rail with Dowels

Front View of Leg

6-7. *Dowels can also be used to fasten legs and rails.*

TABLE AND CABINET TOPS

Large, solid-wood assemblies for table and cabinet tops are usually made using dowel or plate joinery. Even when extra-wide material is available, it is often ripped into pieces that are two or three inches wide and are then rejoined, edge to edge, with dowels. This is done to help limit warping.

The ripped pieces are alternated so that as each piece warps, a relatively flat overall surface will be maintained (6–9). The edges of these tops can be shaped with a router.

■ **6–9.** *Warping is reduced when narrow, alternate pieces are used instead of one wide piece.*

Among the other materials used in the fabrication of table and cabinet tops are: plywood (veneer- and lumber-core) and various kinds of manufactured particle—and fiberboard. These materials are often covered with wood veneers or plastic laminates.

A variety of edge treatments are available for use with non-solid wood tops and other components. Among these are wood framing (6–10), wood or plastic edge banding (6–11), wood molding (6–12), or tongue-and-groove edging (6–13).

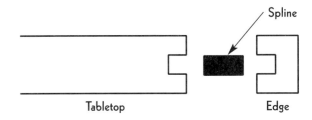

■ **6–10.** *Splined tabletop edge.*

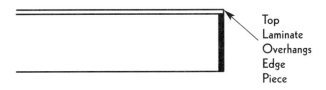

■ **6–11.** *Veneer or plastic-laminate tabletop edging.*

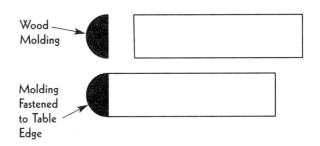

■ **6–12.** *Tabletop wood-molding edge.*

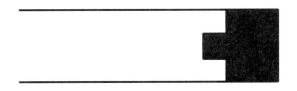

■ **6–13.** *Tabletop tongue-and-groove edging.*

Fastening Tops to Cabinets or Rails

Solid-wood tops must be attached to cabinets or rails using methods that allow the tops to expand and contract across the grain. Among the fastenings that allow expansion and contraction are: stepped blocks (6–14), S-shaped metal rail fasteners (6–15), and angle plates with oval holes (6–16).

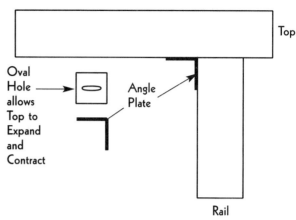

6–16. *Angle-plate tabletop fastener.*

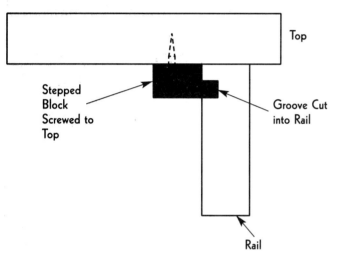

6–14. *Stepped-block tabletop fastener.*

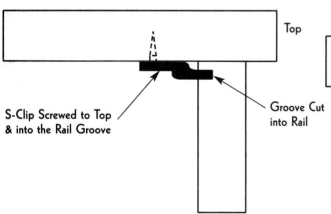

6–15. *S-shaped metal-clip tabletop fastener.*

Non-solid wood tops can be attached with fasteners that do not allow movement. These include corner blocks (6–17), screws in pocket holes (6–18), and dowels (also 6–18).

Screws can also be driven through the tops and into the rails. The screw heads can be hidden with plugs. These plugs will be visible, but may be acceptable when used as part of the decorative surface treatment.

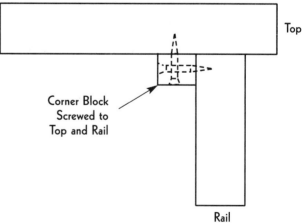

6–17. *Corner-block tabletop fastener.*

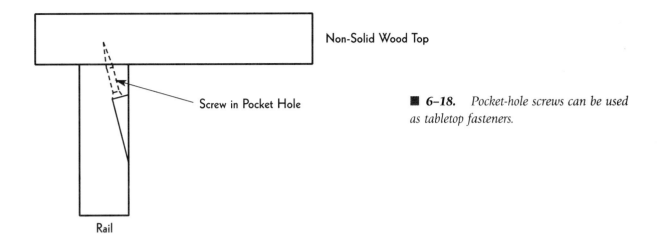

Non-Solid Wood Top

Screw in Pocket Hole

Rail

■ **6–18.** *Pocket-hole screws can be used as tabletop fasteners.*

Table Inserts

Table inserts, or drop leaves, can be used to increase the size of a tabletop that is being used in a tight space. This type of tabletop consists of two pieces mounted on telescoping rails (6–19a). When the table is unlocked, it is pulled open to accommodate one or more leaves. The leaves are held in place by dowels that fit into matching holes in the table edges.

The drop leaves are permanently attached to the table with hinges. When additional space is necessary, the leaves are swung up and locked into place (6–19b).

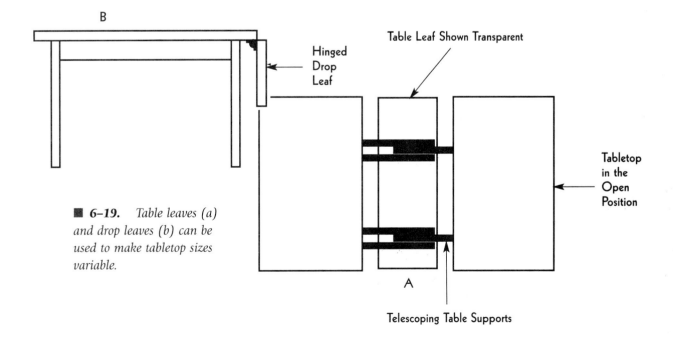

B

Hinged Drop Leaf

Table Leaf Shown Transparent

Tabletop in the Open Position

■ **6–19.** *Table leaves (a) and drop leaves (b) can be used to make tabletop sizes variable.*

A

Telescoping Table Supports

CARCASS CONSTRUCTION

Cabinets are basically well-constructed boxes. The boxes usually have at least one open end to allow access to the interior. Doors or drawers are usually fitted into or onto the open end of the carcass. This is known as carcass construction.

Because one or more sides of the carcass are open, the box tends to deform when pressure is applied to it (6–20). The carcass can be strengthened in a variety of ways. A back can be added. Horizontal dividers for drawers can be attached. A base or plinth can be fastened to the carcass bottom (6–21). The opening can be framed. Posts, which serve as door supports and legs, can be attached to the front of the carcass (6–22).

The materials used in carcass construction include solid wood, plywood, and various types of fiberboard. Most of the materials, except solid wood, are covered with a material such as veneer or plastic laminate. Wood veneers are applied so that the grain pattern simulates that of solid wood (6–23).

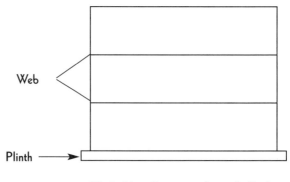

■ **6–21.** *Carcass webs and plinth.*

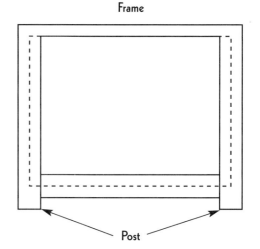

■ **6–22.** *Carcass frame and post.*

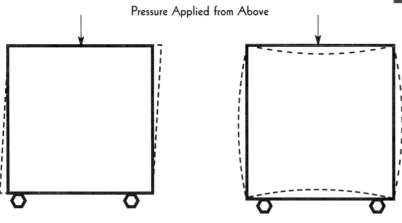

■ **6–20.** *A carcass tends to deform when pressure is applied to it.*

Grain Direction Around Cabinet

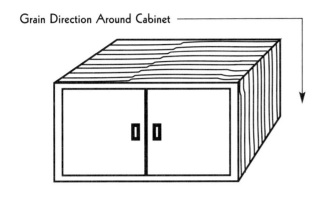

■ **6–23.** *The grain direction on the top and sides of the cabinet.*

Plywood is relatively strong and dimensionally stable. It has the added advantage of being relatively light in weight.

Fiberboards such as medium-density fiberboard (MDF) are popular because of their dimensional stability and relatively low cost. However, all fiberboards are much heavier than plywood.

The joinery used to fasten together carcass pieces includes the butt joint (6–24a), the rabbet-dado joint (6–24b), the glue-block-rein-

forced butt joint (6–24c), the rabbet joint (6–24d), and the tongue-and-groove joint (6–24e). The joint selected should be suitable for the material used in the carcass.

If the top is to be covered after assembly with a plastic laminate, for example, flat-head wood screws can be used to fasten the pieces together. Through dowels can be used in solid-wood construction if they add an acceptable decorative element to the piece.

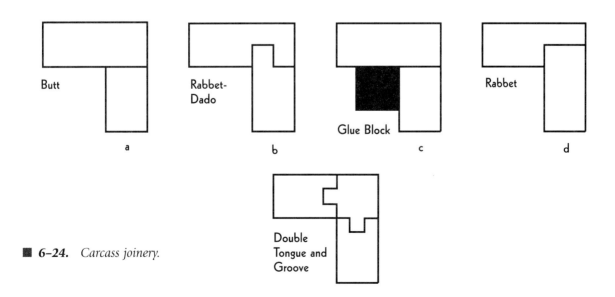

Butt   a

Rabbet-Dado   b

Glue Block   c

Rabbet   d

Double Tongue and Groove

■ **6–24.** *Carcass joinery.*

Two-piece knockdown (KD) fittings are often used to hold non-wood carcass components together (6–25). A knockdown fitting consists of two parts: a cylindrical cam and a bolt. The cam is placed into a ⅝-inch hole in the face of the first piece. The bolt is screwed into the edge of the second piece. When the pieces are assembled, the cam engages the head of the bolt. As the cam is rotated, it draws the bolt in, pulling the two pieces together.

These fittings are popular in commercial work because they allow furniture to be shipped in unassembled or knockdown form. This greatly reducing shipping costs. The use of these fittings also allows the unassembled pieces to be finished prior to assembly.

The *tops* of the simplest carcasses make up one of the four sides of the basic carcass. More complex pieces often have a separate top that is fastened to the basic carcass. Separate tops can be

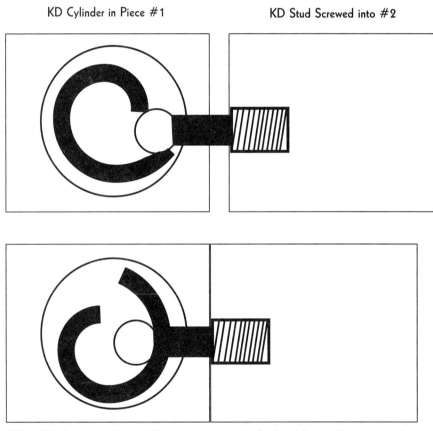

KD Cylinder in Piece #1   KD Stud Screwed into #2

When KD Cylinder is Rotated Counterclockwise, the Stud and Piece #2 are Moved to
the Left, Pulling the Pieces Together

■ **6–25.** *Fastening procedure for two-piece knockdown fittings.*

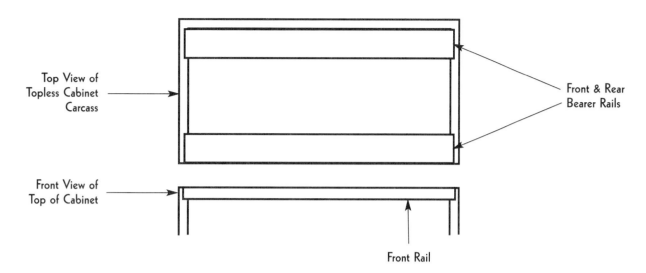

■ **6–26.** *Front and rear bearer rails for the carcass top.*

fastened to carcass tops or to top rails (6–26). If solid wood is not being used in the carcass, all of the exposed edges must be covered with a material such as veneer, plastic laminate, or solid-wood edging.

Carcass *bottoms* are similar in construction to the tops. If a separate base is to be added, open or framed construction may be used in constructing the carcass.

Carcass *backs* can be used to strengthen and square the carcass. Backs are usually made of ¼-inch plywood or hardboard. A back that fits into a rabbeted recess strengthens the carcass more than one that is nailed onto the back edges of the piece. In addition, a nailed-on back is visible from the side of the piece (6–27).

■ **6–27.** *Carcass back.*

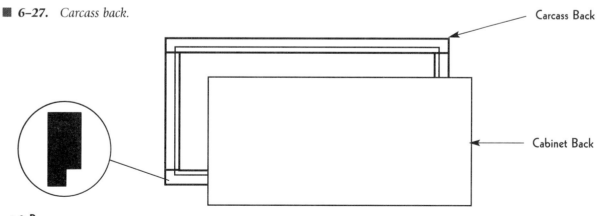

Frame-and-panel construction (6–28) was developed in the days before materials like plywood were commonly available. The relatively thick cabinet frame is used to keep the panel flat and to allow it to expand and contract within the frame. Frame-and-panel pieces are lighter than pieces constructed of solid wood.

Typically, carcass sides are fabricated as separate units and then joined to carcass tops and bottoms. This type of construction is used in the construction of period pieces, e.g., Early American pieces (6–29).

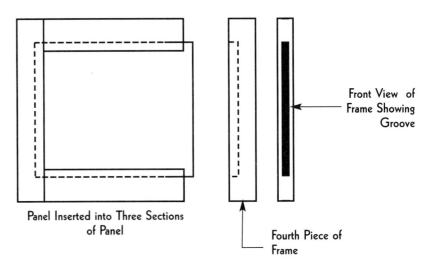

Panel Inserted into Three Sections of Panel

Front View of Frame Showing Groove

Fourth Piece of Frame

■ **6–28.** *Frame-and-panel construction.*

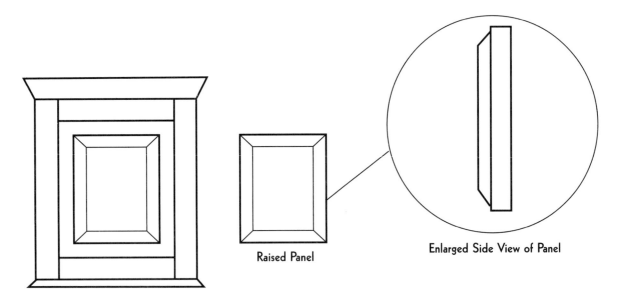

Raised Panel

Enlarged Side View of Panel

■ **6–29.** *Early American piece with raised panel.*

In *modern construction*, frames are sometimes used under flush panels of materials such as plywood (6–30).

Horizontal dividers are often installed in cabinets to support drawers. The dividers can be made of solid material or they can be open frames (6–31). The dividers can be fastened using dowels or other suitable joinery.

Vertical dividers can be constructed and attached in much the same way horizontal dividers are. Solid vertical dividers are more commonly used because their surfaces are usually visible.

Carcass *bases* are often added to carcasses for stylistic reasons. Bases or plinths raise the carcass so that doors can swing freely and lower drawers

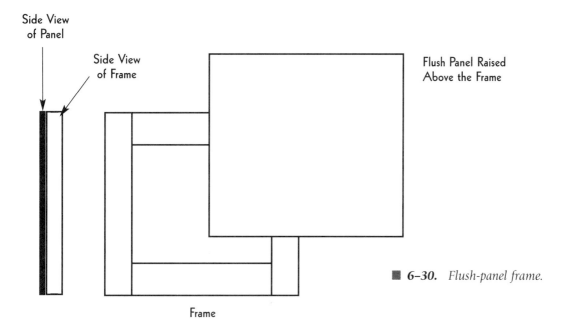

Side View of Panel

Side View of Frame

Flush Panel Raised Above the Frame

Frame

■ *6–30. Flush-panel frame.*

■ *6–31. Horizontal dividers are often used in cabinets to support drawers.*

Horizontal Cabinet Dividers

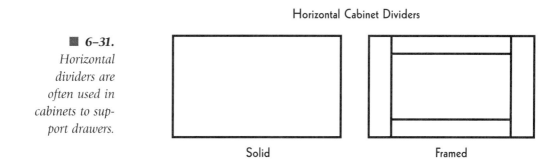

Solid

Framed

can be reached more easily. They also stiffen and strengthen the carcass. Separate bases-open structures that match the footprint of the carcass they are to support (6–32) are not generally used in the simplest contemporary pieces (6–33).

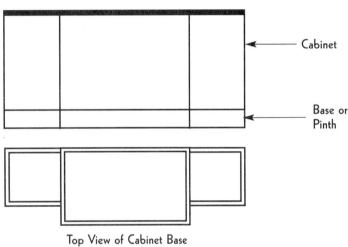

Top View of Cabinet Base

■ **6-32.** *Base or plinth frame.*

■ **6-33.** *This contemporary cabinet has an integral base.*

DOORS

Cabinet doors can be of solid construction, utilizing materials such as veneered plywood or fiberboard, or they can be built up using frame-and-panel construction (6–34). Doors can be mounted using a variety of mounting systems, including sliding and hinging systems.

Sliding doors are not generally used in fine-furniture construction; they do not completely close off the interior of the cabinet and they are not aligned

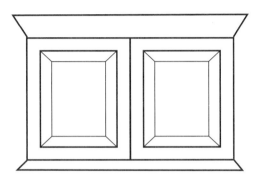

■ **6-34.** *Frame-and-panel doors.*

(6–35). This system only allows access to half the cabinet interior at a time.

Tambour doors are flexible sliding doors that operate like the top of a rolltop desk. These doors can travel horizontally or vertically. They are made up of a series of strips that have been glued to a backing material such as canvas. Carcass parts must be square to each other or tambour doors will not operate smoothly.

The doors fit into a pair of router-cut grooves (6–36). These tracks are cut slightly wider than the thickness of the door. The track curves are widened, by hand, to allow the tambour to travel around the curves more easily. After the curves have been widened, a considerable amount of trimming and fitting is carried out until the doors move smoothly.

The principal advantage of the tambour door system is that the door is completely hidden and out of the way when open. Tambour door material can be obtained from woodworking suppliers.

Overlay doors completely cover the front of the cabinet. *Flush doors* fit into some or all of the opening.

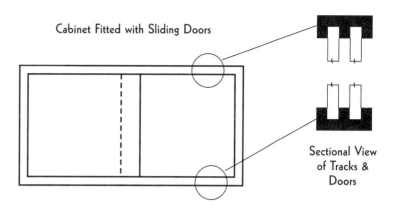

Cabinet Fitted with Sliding Doors

Sectional View of Tracks & Doors

■ **6–35.** *Sliding doors only allow access to half of the cabinet interior at a time.*

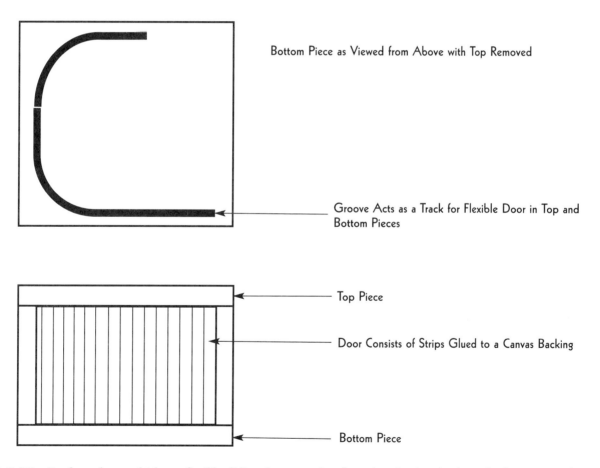

Bottom Piece as Viewed from Above with Top Removed

Groove Acts as a Track for Flexible Door in Top and Bottom Pieces

Top Piece

Door Consists of Strips Glued to a Canvas Backing

Bottom Piece

■ **6–36.** *Tambour doors, which are flexible sliding doors, consist of a series of strips glued to a backing material.*

Edge Treatment and Installation Techniques

Door edges or stiles that are attached to hinges must be capable of supporting the weight of the door. This usually requires that the hinge stile be made of solid wood.

Edges that meet at a pair of doors are treated in a variety of ways (6–37). These include butted edges, rabbeted edges, and closing strips.

The four edges on a full-overlay door are covered by the door. This requires placing slightly oversized doors over the carcass opening and then trimming the doors to fit.

Partially flush doors fit under carcass tops. These doors are fitted by placing the tops of the doors against the undersides of the projecting carcass tops. Then the sides and bottoms of the doors are trimmed to fit over the carcass opening (6–38).

Cabinet Door Edge Meetings

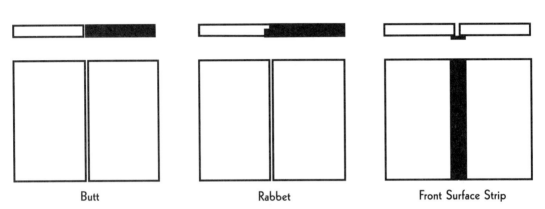

Butt   Rabbet   Front Surface Strip

■ **6–37.** *Edge treatments for meeting cabinet doors.*

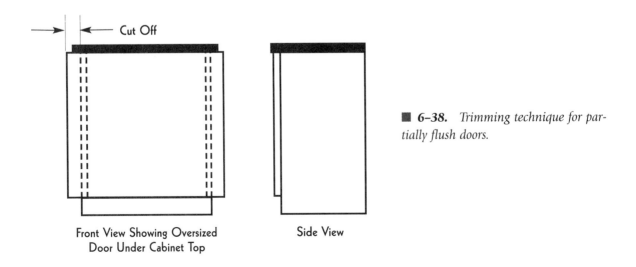

Cut Off

Front View Showing Oversized Door Under Cabinet Top   Side View

■ **6–38.** *Trimming technique for partially flush doors.*

Fitting Flush Doors into Carcass Openings

Flush doors, which fit into the carcass opening, are the most challenging to install. This is because the edges of the doors are framed by the carcass. Door and carcass edges that are not parallel are highly visible. If possible, the doors should be fabricated and fitted as a single unit. After fitting, the door is cut in half to form two doors.

Follow these step-by-step procedures when fitting flush doors into carcass openings:

1. Fit the tops and bottoms of the doors into the carcass opening first. These surfaces are usually parallel and can be trimmed easily. About ⅛ inch clearance should be left between the doors and the carcass.
2. Place the partially trimmed door unit over the carcass. Trace the inside edge of the carcass on the back of the door unit from the inside of the carcass (6–39).
3. Once the door unit is fitted to the opening, cut it in half to create two doors of equal width.

Hinges

Hinging is the most common method of mounting doors. Hinged doors allow full access to the interior of the cabinet.

A variety of hinges is available for use with doors. These include butt, pivot, hidden, and European-style hinges, as well as hinges that do not use mortises. Many hinges have built-in springs that make them self-closing.

Hinge size is determined by leaf length as measured from one edge of the leaf to the other along the barrel of the hinge.

■ **6–39.** *Technique for fitting flush doors into a cabinet.*

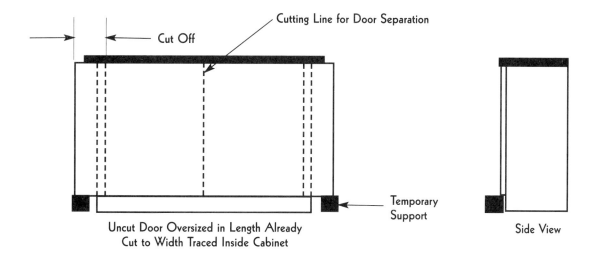

Cutting Line for Door Separation

Cut Off

Temporary Support

Uncut Door Oversized in Length Already
Cut to Width Traced Inside Cabinet

Side View

BUTT HINGES

Butt hinges are available in a variety of sizes and widths. Piano hinges, the larger of the two butt hinges shown in 6-40, can be cut to the required length using a hacksaw. The use of a continuous hinge such as the piano hinge helps to stiffen or stabilize the edge of the surface it is attached to.

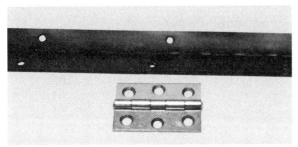

■ **6–40.** *Trimming technique for partially flush doors.*

Butt hinges are installed by cutting out a recess, or gain, for each of the hinge leaves. The hinge leaf is used as a template or pattern for the gain. The hinge leaves must fit into the gains tightly so that the hinges cannot shift position. Gain depth is equal to one-half the distance from the outside of one hinge leaf to the outside of the second hinge leaf when the leaves are parallel (6–41).

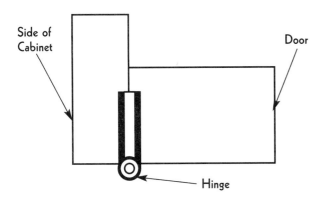

■ **6–41.** *Installing a butt hinge.*

Follow these step-by-step procedures when installing butt hinges. All types of butt hinges are installed in this manner:

1. Place the reversed hinge on the edge of the door in the desired location. The hinge barrel should be against the edge of the door stile (6–42).

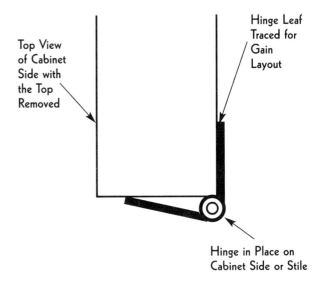

■ **6–42.** *Laying out a hinge gain on a cabinet side.*

2. Trace the hinge leaf with a utility knife. Deeper knife cuts will be made after the hinge is removed.
3. Chisel the gain out to the required depth. A router can be used for this purpose on larger hinges.
4. Repeat steps 1 to 3 for each of the hinges to be installed.
5. Attach the hinges to the door using the screws provided.
6. Open the hinges and place the door into the carcass opening. Use shims at the bottom of the door to maintain clearance (6–43).
7. Trace the hinge leaves, using a pencil, onto the carcass (6–44).

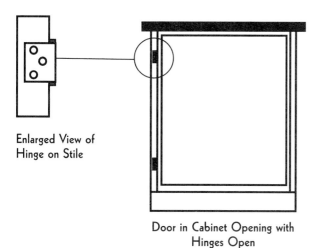

Enlarged View of
Hinge on Stile

Door in Cabinet Opening with
Hinges Open

■ **6–43.** *Positioning of door in cabinet opening.*

MORTISELESS HINGES

Mortiseless hinges (6–45) are mounted directly on the surface and do not require gains to be cut. The door and carcass are separated by a space equal to the thickness of the hinge. These hinges are often used for folding doors and screens.

8. Remove the door and hinge. Carry the hinge layout around to the inside of the cabinet, using a try square and pencil. Outline the pencil-line layout with a utility knife and chisel the gain out.

9. After all of the gains have been located and cut, mount the doors on the cabinet with screws.

■ **6–45.** *A Mortiseless hinge.*

■ **6–44.** *Laying out a hinge gain on a cabinet side.*

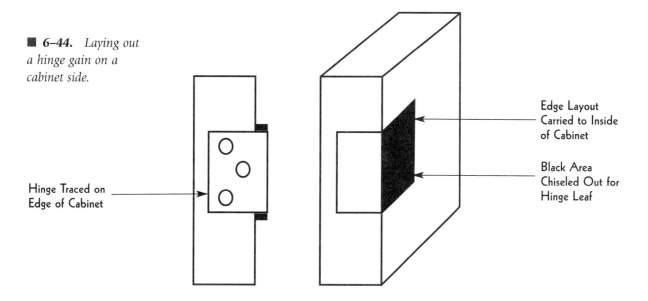

Hinge Traced on
Edge of Cabinet

Edge Layout
Carried to Inside
of Cabinet

Black Area
Chiseled Out for
Hinge Leaf

PIVOT HINGES

Pivot hinges (6–46) are used on cabinets where butt hinges might be unsightly. This type of hinge is less visible than the butt hinge.

Pivot hinges require gains on door edges. They are mounted in door gains and then fastened to the carcass.

■ **6–46.** *Pivot hinges are mounted in door gains and then fastened to the carcass.*

INVISIBLE HINGES

Hinges such as the *Soss* hinges are not visible when cabinet doors are closed. They are mounted in mortises cut into doors and carcasses (6–47).

European-style hinges are also invisible when cabinet doors are closed. These hinges consist of two main parts: a cup-shaped component that fits into a blind hole in the door and a base plate that mounts on the cabinet (6–48). These hinges install quickly and are fully adjustable. European hinges are available in a variety of configurations, allowing many mounting and opening options.

■ **6–47.** *Operating principle for Soss hinges.*

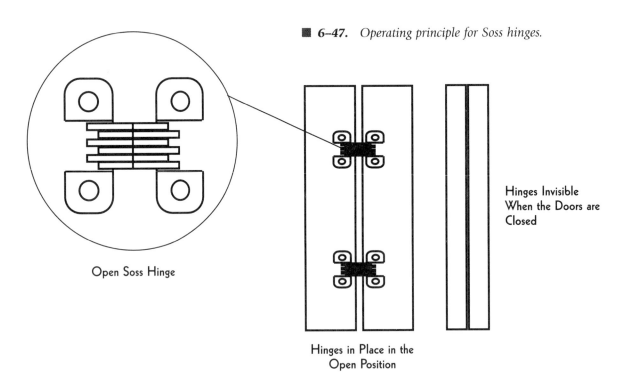

Open Soss Hinge

Hinges in Place in the Open Position

Hinges Invisible When the Doors are Closed

■ *6–48.* *European-style hinge.*

CATCHES

Catches are used to hold doors in the closed position against the carcass or frame. When self-closing hinges are installed, catches are not required. Self-closing hinges are often used on kitchen cabinets.

Magnetic catches (6–49) are popular because

■ *6–49.* *Magnetic catch.*

they are quiet and easy to install. The catch consists of a magnet and a steel strike plate.

To install a magnetic catch, do the following:

1. Fasten the magnet catch to the inside of the carcass, using the screws provided. These types of catches have screw slots that allow them to be adjusted.
2. Place the strike plate on the magnetic catch and close the door and press it in against the catch. A projection on the back of the strike plate makes a dent in the door's surface. This dent is used to locate the strike plate on the door.

    An alternate method is to place a piece of double-stick carpet tape on the inside of the door opposite the catch. When the door is closed, the strike plate adheres to the double-stick carpet tape.
3. Screw the strike plate to the door. Other types of catches are installed in a similar way, with the catch mounted on the carcass and the strike plate or the stud mounted on the door.

DRAWERS

Drawers can be thought of as sliding boxes that fit into the cabinet carcass. A careful examination of the drawers can often determine the quality of the carcass. In quality construction, drawers operate smoothly with minimum effort. They should remain level and open fully so as to allow full access.

Well-made drawers have solid-wood fronts, sides, and backs. The fronts should be at least ¾ inch thick. The sides and backs should be made of hardwood and be at least ⅜ inch thick. The bottoms can be made of plywood or hardboard.

In quality construction, drawer fronts and sides are fastened together with joints that resist pulling forces. The dovetail is an excellent example of such a joint. The backs should be joined to the sides using dadoes or similar locking joinery.

Drawers can fit *into* or *over* the carcass or frame fronts (6–50). Drawers that fit into the carcass are known as flush drawers. Drawers that fit over the carcass are known as overlay drawers.

The *fronts* of drawers can be attached to the sides using a variety of joints, including rabbet, rabbet-dado, dovetail-dado, and multiple dovetail joints (6–51).

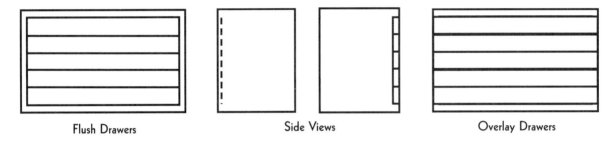

Flush Drawers   Side Views   Overlay Drawers

■ *6–50.* *Flush and overlay drawer fronts.*

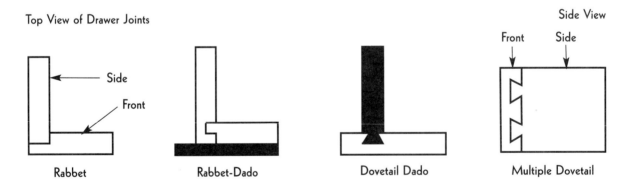

Top View of Drawer Joints

Rabbet   Rabbet-Dado   Dovetail Dado   Multiple Dovetail

■ *6–51.* *The joints used to attach drawer fronts to the sides.*

A rabbet-dado joint can be used when a separate drawer face is to be attached to the drawer, because the front will cover the joint. This type of construction allows the less-experienced woodworker to fabricate a cabinet with flush-fitting drawers. The technique consists of fitting a single piece into the carcass opening and then cutting it into separate pieces that become drawer fronts. Curved drawer fronts are usually attached to drawers of this type (6–52).

Drawer *backs* are usually narrower than the drawer sides, to allow drawer bottoms to pass under their lower edges. They can be dadoed into drawer sides (6–53).

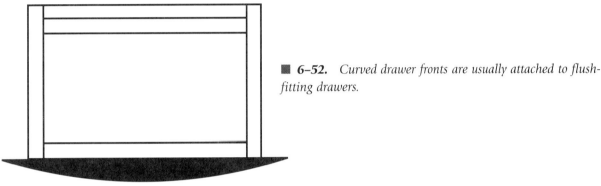

Top View of Curved Drawer Front Fastened to Drawer

■ *6–52. Curved drawer fronts are usually attached to flush-fitting drawers.*

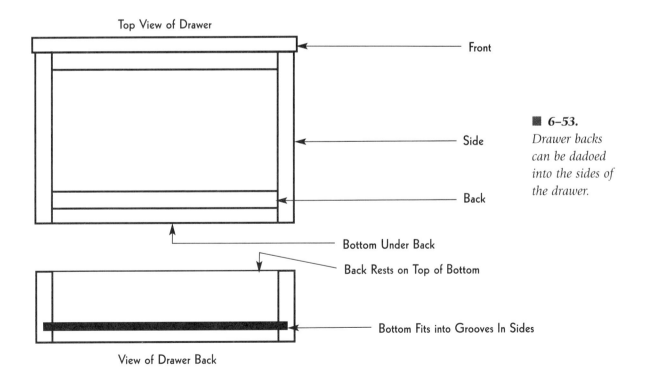

Top View of Drawer

Front

Side

Back

Bottom Under Back

Back Rests on Top of Bottom

Bottom Fits into Grooves In Sides

View of Drawer Back

■ *6–53. Drawer backs can be dadoed into the sides of the drawer.*

Drawer *bottoms* fit into grooves cut into the sides and front of the drawer (6–54). This keeps drawer bottoms clear of horizontal dividers.

Drawer *sides* are often shaped to reduce friction between the upper edges of the sides and the front edge of the cabinet (6–55).

Top View of Front and Side of Drawer

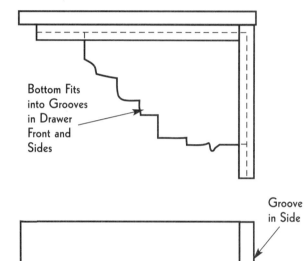

Bottom Fits into Grooves in Drawer Front and Sides

Groove in Side

End View of Drawer

■ **6–54.** *Drawer bottoms fit into grooves in the sides and front of the drawer.*

Width Reduced

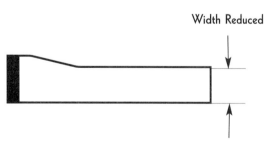

■ **6–55.** *A side view of a drawer that has been reduced in width.*

Drawer Installation Methods

Two methods can be used to install drawers into a cabinet. The simpler one involves fitting the drawers into a horizontally divided cabinet. The upper and lower edges of the drawers are supported by horizontal dividers located above and below the drawer. Single drawers in tables or desks are often installed in this way. This system works best when the drawers are relatively light and loose fitting. Drawers in small pieces such as jewelry boxes are often installed using this method (6–56).

Drawers can also be supported by wooden strips that fit into grooves cut into the sides of the drawers. The strips are fastened to the inside surfaces of the carcass sides. These drawers are easy to install when separate drawer fronts can be attached to the drawers after they are mounted in the carcass.

This technique involves inserting extra-long drawer-supporting strips into the slots in the sides of the drawers. The drawers and supporting strips are positioned in the carcass opening. Once a drawer is in position, its supporting strips are fastened to the carcass. The drawers are removed and the supporting strips are cut to length. The drawer fronts are fastened to the drawers, and the drawers are returned to the cabinet (6–57).

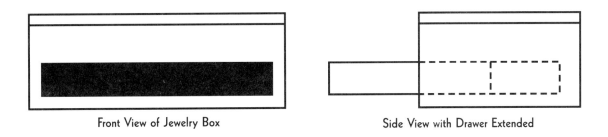

Front View of Jewelry Box

Side View with Drawer Extended

■ **6–56.** *Simpler drawers such as this jewelry-box drawer can be installed in a horizontally divided cabinet.*

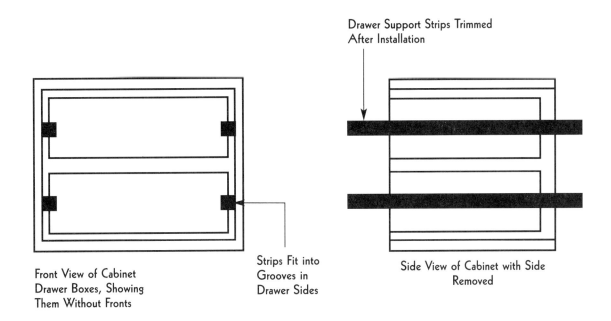

Drawer Support Strips Trimmed
After Installation

Front View of Cabinet
Drawer Boxes, Showing
Them Without Fronts

Strips Fit into
Grooves in
Drawer Sides

Side View of Cabinet with Side
Removed

■ **6–57.** *Drawer installation method using oversized supporting strips.*

Drawer Hardware

Various types of hardware are made for drawers. One of the more common types is the two-piece side-mounted drawer support (6–58). One part of the support slide is fastened to the carcass, and the other is fastened to the side of the drawer. This device provides good support; smooth, level action; and a drawer stop. The stop limits drawer travel so that the drawer does not fall out of the cabinet.

CHAIRS

Chairs offer a challenge to the woodworker. This is because chairs require relatively complex joinery. This joinery helps to make chairs strong enough to support the load provided by the typical human body. In addition, many chair joints involve parts that do not meet at right angles (6–59). A full-sized drawing of the chair to be made is usually required. This helps in the layout and design of the chair joints.

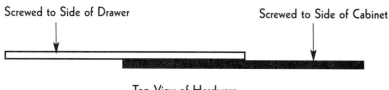

Screwed to Side of Drawer   Screwed to Side of Cabinet

Top View of Hardware

■ **6–58.** *This two-piece drawer hardware support is mounted on the side of the drawer.*

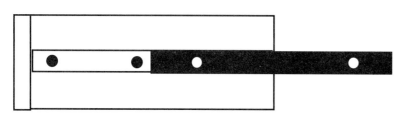

Side View of Drawer with Drawer-Support Hardware

■ **6–59.** *The legs and rails on this chair do not meet at right angles.*

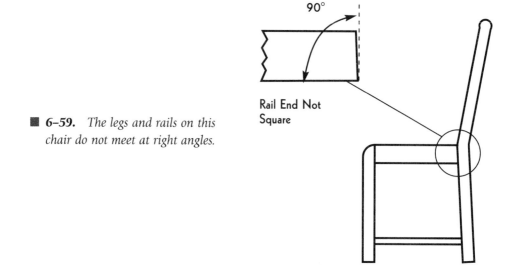

90°

Rail End Not Square

Chair Components

The *seat* of the typical chair is about 17 inches above the floor. It is usually about 18 inches deep and about 20 inches wide (6–60).

The *back* is about 18 inches long. This makes the chair about 35 or 36 inches high.

A trapezoid-shaped frame formed by the chair rails supports the seat. The corners of the frame are formed by the chair legs (6–61). The front

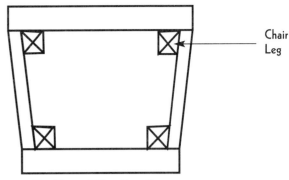

Top View of Chair Seat Frame

■ **6–61.** *Top view of a trapezoid-shaped seat frame.*

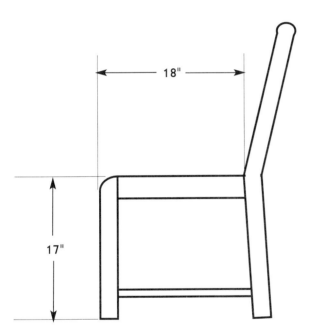

■ **6–60.** *Side view of a chair that shows the length of a typical seat and how high above the floor it should be.*

rail is usually narrower than the side rails, so that the seat can rest on top of it. This helps to make the chair more comfortable. The side rails may be rabbeted, allowing the edges of the seat to fit into the rails. The rails are often joined to the legs with a dowel or mortise-and-tenon joint. They are usually made from ¾ x 2-inch material.

Corner blocks are glued and fastened to the rails to strengthen the seat frame. Bolts in the legs fit into holes in the corner blocks.

The sides of the back frame are a continuation of the rear chair leg. This reduces the number of joints required and adds strength to the chair. (Refer to 6–60.) This leg-back piece is often curved.

The *splat,* a vertical back support, fits into the back frame. The back frame is made up of the curved leg-back pieces, the rear seat rail, and the top, or crest, rail. The ends of the splat fit into grooves in the rear seat rail and the crest rail (6–62).

In fabricating a chair, the front legs and front seat rail are assembled to form the front unit. The rear leg-back pieces, the back seat rail, the top back frame, and the splat are assembled to form the back unit. The front and back units are connected together by the side seat rails.

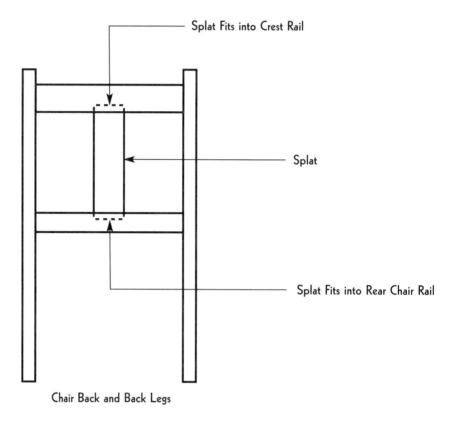

Splat Fits into Crest Rail

Splat

Splat Fits into Rear Chair Rail

Chair Back and Back Legs

■ **6–62.** *The splat is a vertical support that fits into the chair rail and back crest.*

C H A P T E R

7

FINISHING TECHNIQUES

■ ■ ■ ■ ■ ■ ■ ■ ■ ■ ■ ■ ■ ■

TYPES OF FINISH

Finishes are applied to wood for two principal reasons: to protect it and to enhance its appearance. *Transparent finishes*, such as varnish or lacquer, allow the grain of the wood to show through the finish. *Opaque finishes*, such as paint, hide the grain as well as imperfections and repairs made to the surface (7–1).

Finishing materials dry by evaporation and/or chemical change, usually oxidation. *Evaporative finishes* dry when their vehicles-lacquer thinner and other volatile solvents-evaporate, leaving the previously dissolved solids behind. Lacquer is such a finish. When additional coats of lacquer are applied, the solvents in the lacquer being applied can redissolve the lacquer on the surface. This is one of the reasons why finishes of this type are usually applied by spraying.

Brushing lacquers are formulated using materials that slow the drying process. This allows additional time for the finish to flow out and flatten before softening of previously applied coats takes place.

Water-based finishes such as latex paints also dry by evaporation. The solids in these finishes consist of small, thin particles that bond as the

■ *7–1.* *Lacquer and paint are two types of opaque finish.*

water evaporates. These particles form a somewhat flexible film that adheres to the surface.

Oils and varnishes dry slowly because complete drying requires a chemical reaction with the oxygen in the air to take place. Finishes that dry as the result of a chemical reaction are known as *reactive* finishes. If these finishes are applied too heavily, the surface layer of the finish may dry while the underlying material does not. This happens because the finish under the surface cannot react with the oxygen in the air. This can result in a soft finish that is easily damaged.

SELECTING A FINISH

Woodworkers should consider the finish to be used when planning a project, because the type of finish can affect material selection and construction methods. Clear finishes require the use of high-quality, defect-free materials. Opaque finishes often allow the use of less-expensive, blemished materials.

Even the selection of glue and fastening methods can be impacted by finish selection. Glue that leaves a dark glue line may not be suitable for use with a light-colored wood. Plugged screw holes may be acceptable under an opaque finish, but not under a transparent one.

The principal focus of this chapter will be on transparent finishes that are most often used in fine woodworking.

Finishes are usually applied after the project has been assembled. Easily removable components such as drawers and doors are often removed and finished separately.

PREPARING THE SURFACE

Before applying a transparent finish, make sure the surfaces are clean and blemish-free. An attempt should be made to remove pencil marks with a pencil eraser. The removal of other blemishes requires the use of a coated abrasive such as sandpaper. Sanding wears or abrades away some of the surface; in so doing, it carries away scratches, dirt, and other blemishes. The abrasive particles on the sandpaper leave scratches on the surface. Sanding with finer and finer grades of sandpaper gradually reduces the size of these scratches until they are no longer visible.

Sanding also leaves particles of abrasive embedded in the surface of the sanded surface. Cutting tools used on a surface that has been sanded will be dulled by these particles. Therefore, if at all possible, all tool work should be completed before any sanding is done.

Abrasives

Any material that is harder than the material it is used on can act as an abrasive on that material. Among the abrasives used on wood are aluminum oxide, garnet, silicon carbide, and flint.

Aluminum oxide (7–2) is a man-made abrasive derived from the mineral bauxite. It is usually brown in color and is most commonly used in coated abrasives designed for use on sanding machinery. Its properties make it an ideal abrasive for use on hardwoods and non-wood materials.

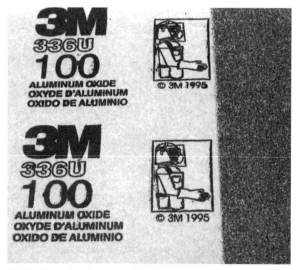

■ *7–2. Aluminum oxide is a man-made abrasive that is ideal for use on hardwoods and non-wood materials.*

Garnet (7–3) is a natural abrasive and is relatively durable when compared to the silica used on flint paper. This reddish abrasive is long lasting because its fragile crystals are frequently fractured, exposing sharp new cutting edges.

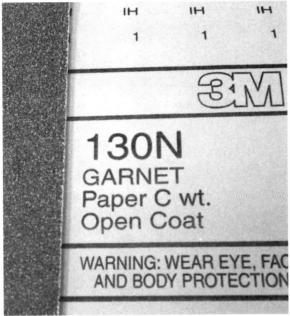

■ *7–3. Open-coat garnet, a natural abrasive.*

Silicon carbide is an ultra-hard, man-made material that is used primarily for sanding between finishing coats (7–4). This abrasive is often made in a "wet or dry," or waterproof, form that allows it be used with water. The water acts as a lubricant and slows the cutting action. This is an especially valuable quality in an abrasive used for sanding coats of finish.

Flint (7–5) is crushed quartz or silica that is used for sandpaper. This material has the same chemical properties as common sand; hence the name sandpaper. It is also the principal ingredient in glasspaper, an abrasive that is coated with pulverized glass. Flint paper is less durable, less expensive, and less desirable for finishing than

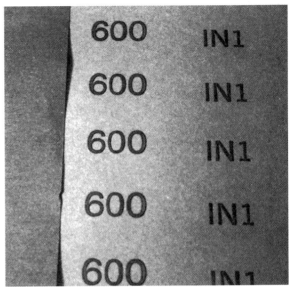

■ *7–4. Wet/dry silicon carbide, a very hard man-made abrasive used primarily for sanding between finishing coats.*

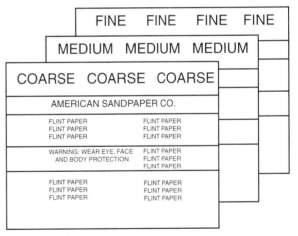

■ *7–5. Flint paper.*

the other types of abrasives. It wears out quickly and is available in a limited number of grades or grits.

Open-coated abrasives are specifically designed for use on softwoods and other soft materials.

Abrasive particles are more widely spaced in open-coat materials than they are in regular-coated abrasives. This open spacing helps to reduce the tendency for the abrasive to become clogged.

Abrasives are graded by particle size. Most abrasives are graded using a numbering system that contains the designation "grit." The number assigned represents the size of a screen, actual or theoretical, that is used to prevent the abrasive particles from passing through. Smaller num-bers represent screens with large openings that allow relatively large particles to pass through them. Larger numbers represent screens with smaller openings that allow the passage of smaller particles. For example, 40-grit sandpaper has larger abrasive particles and is more coarse than 100-grit sandpaper (Table 7–1).

Word and fractional designations are used on flint or glasspaper. Number designations are used on all other types of coated abrasives.

Designation	Number	Fractional Designation
Extra Fine	360-600	10/0-12/0
Very Fine	220-320	6/0-9/0
Fine	120-180	3/0-5/0
Medium	80-100	0-2/0
Coarse	40-60	1½-½
Very Coarse	24-36	3-2
Extra Coarse	12-20	4-3½

Table 7–1. *Abrasive-grade comparison table.*

BACKINGS

The backings used for coated abrasives include thin or heavy paper, cloth, or fiberboard.

The lighter backing papers, which are used for hand-sanding, are called *finishing papers*. The heavier grades are called *cabinet papers*.

The letter and grit designations for the backing material are usually found on the back of the abrasive sheets. Paper backings for coated abrasives designed to be used on *machines* are graded from A through D. A is the lightest and D the heaviest. Cloth backings are used for sanding belts and similar products.

SANDING SLEEVES

Sanding sleeves (7–6) are cardboard tubes coated with abrasives. These sleeves are mounted on drums and are used for sanding curved surfaces. The drums can be used on machines such as drill presses, lathes, or spindle sanders.

■ *7–6.   Sanding sleeves.*

■ *7–7.   Prior to using sandpaper, run its smooth side over a bench or table corner, to help prevent it from tearing during use.*

Sanding Techniques

One of two methods of sanding can be done. *Finish-sanding* is often done using portable power sanders, which are described in Chapter 3. *Hand-sanding* is often used to supplement machine-sanding in areas that are hard to reach with a power sander. The step-by-step procedures are the same. They are as follows:

1. Before doing any sanding, examine the surface for any crushed fibers. Some of these fibers can be steamed with a soldering iron and removed with a folded piece of wet cotton fabric. Also try to remove pencil marks with a pencil eraser.

2. Select the first abrasive paper to use on the wood. The first abrasive paper used on a surface that *has not been sanded* should not be more coarse than number-80 grit. If sanding were done before assembly, number-100 grit would be a good choice for initial sanding. Using an abrasive that is too fine for initial sanding will result in a lot of wasted time.

3. Run the smooth side of the sandpaper over a bench or table corner prior to using it (7–7). This will break the glue coating into small pieces that will prevent the sandpaper from tearing during use.

4. Whenever possible, wrap the sandpaper tightly around an appropriate block during sanding. The block will help to keep the surface from being sanded flat. Curved blocks can be made for use on curved surfaces.

5. Begin the sanding. All sanding should be done with the grain whenever possible. This requires that the sanding block be moved in a path that is parallel to the grain of the piece being sanded (7–8). As sanding progresses, gradually move the block from one side of the surface being sanded to the other (7–9). This helps to limit the depth of the scratches produced.

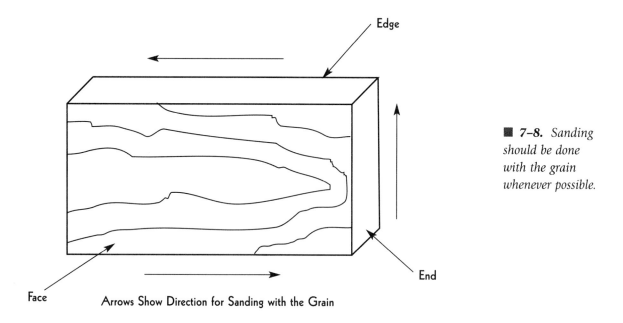

Edge

End

Face

Arrows Show Direction for Sanding with the Grain

■ *7–8. Sanding should be done with the grain whenever possible.*

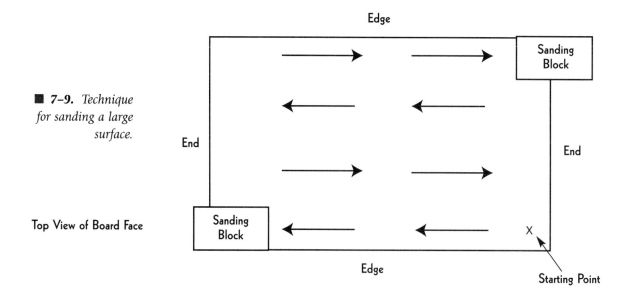

Edge

Sanding Block

End

End

Sanding Block

X

Starting Point

Edge

Top View of Board Face

■ *7–9. Technique for sanding a large surface.*

6. Once all the blemishes, dirt, and tool marks have been removed by the initial sanding, use the next, finer grade of paper available. This sanding is done to remove the scratches made by the initial sanding. Continue this process until number 220- or 240-grit abrasives have been used. Abrasives with higher grit numbers should be reserved for sanding between finishing coats.

7. When all sanding has been completed, wipe the sanded surfaces free of dust using a tack cloth or a piece of lint-free cloth saturated with a suitable solvent.

SELECTING AND APPLYING TRANSPARENT FINISHES

Safety Techniques

The materials used in finishing must be handled with care. Some are toxic, and many are flammable. Pay attention to the following safety techniques when using finishing materials:

1. Always follow the manufacturer's directions for the safe use and disposal of all finishing materials.

2. Whenever possible, consider using water-based finishing materials instead of other finishes. These materials are nonflammable and are usually less toxic than solvent-based finishing materials.

3. Carry out all finishing operations in well-ventilated locations or outdoors.

4. Perform all work in areas where open flames or spark-producing devices are not likely to come into contact with vapors produced during finishing operations.

5. Dispose of rags or paper products saturated with flammable finishing materials in approved metal containers. These containers must be emptied daily.

6. Wear appropriate eye and skin protective devices when handling finishing materials.

Applying Stains

Sanding sealers can be applied to wood surfaces that are not going to be stained. Always make sure that the sealer and finish are compatible before using a sealer. Some manufacturers recommend using a thinned-out coat of the finishing material as a sealer.

Staining is accomplished by applying a dye-like material to the wood after sanding. This is usually the first step in the finishing process. Some stains are designed to add color and finish at the same time.

Woodworkers who choose not to use stains often feel that staining is not an "honest" use of materials. A piece of pine that is stained dark brown with a walnut-colored stain will not have its grain pattern altered by the stain. The piece will look like a piece of stained pine.

Stains often highlight any blemishes that may be present, especially crushed fibers or rough areas. Glue residues, which may have been invisible before staining, will become more visible when stain is applied because most stains cannot penetrate or adhere to glue.

TYPES OF STAIN

There are three types of stain: oil-based, water-based, and spirit-based. Oil stains (7–10) are popular because they are relatively easy to use. They are available in either *penetrating* or *pigmented* forms. The solids in stains are carried in the *vehicle*, the liquid part of the stain. Penetrating stains have relatively few solids in them, and tend to stain materials uniformly. Pigmented stains carry a higher percentage of solids than penetrating stains, and streaking can occur if the stain is not wiped carefully.

■ *7–11.* Water-based stain.

■ *7–10.* Oil stain.

Stains are usually applied with a brush or cloth pad. The stain is allowed to remain on the material for a few minutes before the excess is wiped away with a lint-free cloth. Additional coats of stain do not usually intensify the color of the stained surface. Some shade variation is possible when pigmented stains are used. This can be done by leaving more of the residual stain on the surface.

Water-based stains (7–11) use water as a vehicle. Since water causes wood to swell (that is, it raises the grain), raise the grain of any wood to which water stains will be applied *before* applying a stain. This is done by applying water to the surface with a water-saturated cloth. After the water has had a chance to dry, the surface is sanded with same grit abrasive that was used last during sanding operations.

Spirit stains (7–12) use alcohol as a vehicle. These stains raise grain, so the wood to be stained should have its grain raised with water or alcohol *prior* to staining. Spirit stains are often sold in dry form and are dissolved in alcohol prior to use. They are applied using a brush or cloth pad. These stains penetrate and dry quickly, and wiping can't be used to control color intensity. A spirit-stained surface can be lightened a bit by wiping it with a cloth pad saturated in alcohol.

North Bay Paint Co.

Santa Rosa Ca.

SPIRIT STAIN

SOLUBLE IN ALCOHOL

WALNUT

■ *7–12.* *Spirit-based stain.*

Applying Wood Fillers

Paste wood fillers (7–13) may be applied to the surface of a porous wood once the staining process is complete. Fillers are applied with a folded piece of burlap that is rubbed across and into the grain. After the drying period recommended by the manufacturer has passed, the excess filler is removed with a clean burlap pad that is rubbed across the grain. When the filler is completely dry, a suitable sealer can be applied. Fillers can stain the surfaces they are applied too. It is always wise to test fillers on scrap material before using them on a project.

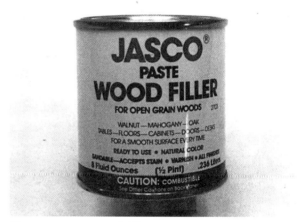

■ *7–13.* *Paste wood filler.*

Applying the Finish

Oil finishes are often used on woods such as walnut and teak (7–14). Commercial rubbing oils perform well when used as directed. One of the principal advantages of an oil finish is ease of application. Oil finishes are usually rubbed into

■ *7–14.* *A rubbing-oil finish.*

the surface with a lint-free cloth. The excess oil remaining on the surface is rubbed off after the stipulated drying time has passed.

Oil finishes take a long time to accumulate on a surface. Multiple applications are often required to develop a suitable coating.

Some oil finishes contain staining ingredients that add color to the finish. Once the desired shade develops, a clear version of the finish can be used for additional coats.

Applying some of the original oil to the damaged area can repair small scratches on oil-finished surfaces.

Lacquer finishes are widely used by furniture manufacturers. The sprayed lacquer dries quickly, allowing the manufacturer to package and ship the furniture quickly. Lacquer finishes are durable, moisture-resistant, and suitable for use on many types of furniture.

Brushing lacquers (7–15) may be used when spraying equipment is not available. These lacquers are available in a variety of finish types ranging from flat to gloss.

Brushing lacquers can usually be applied to an unsealed surface. The first coat of lacquer

■ *7–15.* A brushing lacquer.

serves as a sealer. Most brushing lacquers dry in about 30 minutes and can be recoated in two hours, if the surface is not sanded.

It is important not to add coats to missed areas until the lacquer is completely dry. The solvent-rich material on the applicator can dissolve and remove the lacquer applied earlier, resulting in a finish-starved area.

Sanding between coats is required if the surface feels rough. Sanding after the first coat is almost always necessary, because the lacquer stiffens fibers left by sanding. It is usually necessary to allow lacquer to dry for several hours before sanding.

Three or more coats are required for the buildup of a durable lacquer finish.

Varnishes (7–16) are a good finish to use when durability and wear resistance are required.

■ *7–16.* Clear varnish.

Varnishes dry largely by oxidation. They dry slowly and allow plenty of time for application. Additional coats adhere well and a completely dry finish can be smoothed by sanding.

A variety of varnishes are available to the finisher. Among these are alkyd-, polyurethane-, and phenolic-resin varnishes. Alkyd varnishes are made by blending synthetic resins with oils such as tung or linseed oil, using thinners and drying agents. Alkyd varnishes are durable and flexible. If water resistance is required, a varnish containing tung oil should be used.

Polyurethane varnishes are available in water—and oil-based formulations. The solids in polyurethane varnish are more like plastic than the resins used in other forms of varnish. These result in a finish that is tough and durable, although somewhat brittle.

Polyurethane varnish dries in about four hours. Additional coats usually have to be applied within 24 hours. Unless otherwise indicated, polyurethane varnishes are restricted to indoor use.

It is very important to follow the manufacturer's application directions to obtain good adherence between coats. It is generally necessary to sand down to new wood when using this type of varnish for refinishing. Removing a polyurethane finish by sanding can be difficult because of its hardness.

Phenolic varnishes (7–17) are moisture-proof and much tougher than alkyd varnishes. The resins used in these varnishes are also used to make spar and marine varnishes, which are designed for outdoor use. Although softer than polyurethane, these varnishes are more flexible, allowing their use in situations where expansion and contraction are likely to occur.

■ *7–17. Spar varnish. These types of varnishes are designed for outdoor use.*

Finish Applicators

Finish applicators include brushes, rollers, pads, and spraying units. Brushes are especially useful when relatively small areas are to be coated. It is important to use a brush having the type of bristle that is designed for use with the material to be applied.

Synthetic-bristle brushes such as nylon brushes work well with water-based finishes. Brushes with natural bristles such as hog or horsehair are ideal for the application of oil-based varnishes. The package that contains the brush usually lists the materials the brush can be used to apply.

Whenever possible, keep the surface being coated horizontal. This helps to prevent running.

When using a brush, dip about one-third of its bristles into the finishing material. Dipping deeper can cause the finishing material to collect around the metal ferrule at the base of the brush. Finishing material collected in this area is very difficult to wash out, and will shorten brush life.

Move the brush from the center of the surface toward the outside edges (7–18). This helps to eliminate running at the edges. Moving the brush from the edge toward the center will result in running on vertical surfaces (7–19).

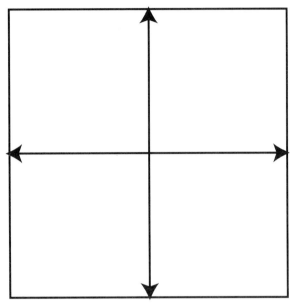

Finishing Material Applied by Brush is Moved from the Inside of the Piece Toward the Edges

■ *7–18. Technique for applying a finish with a brush to avoid drips on edges.*

Brushes should be cleaned using a suitable thinner immediately after each use. The clean brush should be allowed to dry and then wrapped in paper to keep its bristles straight.

Rollers are available in a wide variety of sizes and materials. The packages containing the rollers usually include information describing which materials can be applied with the roller and how to use it effectively.

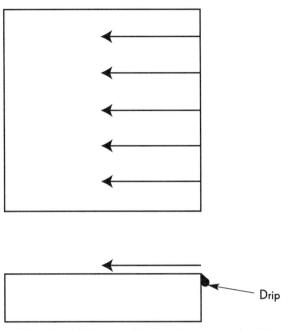

Drip

Wrong Brush Movement Results in Dripping at the Edge

■ *7–19. Incorrect method of moving the brush when applying a finish.*

Rollers can be an attractive applicator choice when large areas are to be coated. However, they sometimes leave a stippled or bumpy finish surface, so they should always be tested before use on a project.

SAMPLE FINISHING PROCEDURES

The sample finishing procedures described in Tables 7–2 to 7–5 are typical of those that might be followed in the nonprofessional woodworking shop.

Finishing should done in an environment that is as dust-free as possible. Fast-drying finishes are less likely to be affected by dust than slower-drying ones. If a woodworking shop is used for finishing, it should be thoroughly cleaned before finishing operations begin. Dry days are better for finishing than humid ones. Excessive humidity can slow the drying process considerably. Adequate air circulation will help to speed drying.

Since each situation is different, any of the procedures described should be tested and adjusted as necessary. Manufacturer's directions should always take precedence over any of the procedures described.

All of the finishing procedures described are to be carried out on work that has been completely sanded with 220-grit abrasive and wiped clean with a suitable tack cloth.

Procedure	Drying Time	Tips
1 Stain as required.	Overnight	Raise grain prior to staining if water stain is to be used.
2 Fill as required.	Overnight	Paste wood filler may be used on open-pored woods.
3 If wood is stained or filled, seal with lacquer sealer.	1 to 2 hours	If not stained or filled, skip to step 4.
4 Apply lacquer after sanding with #280-grit paper.	30 minutes	Sanded surfaces must be wiped clean with tack cloth before lacquer is applied.
5 Apply second coat of lacquer.	Overnight	Overnight is safest interval; however, two hours is the minimum allowable drying time.
6 Apply lacquer after sanding with #280-grit paper.	Overnight	Overnight is safest interval; however, 2 hours is the minimum allowable drying time. Repeat step 6 until desired finish buildup is attained. Three coats minimum.
7 Apply paste wax and buff if desired.		

Table 7–2. *Finishing procedure for brushing lacquers.*

Procedure	Drying Time	Tips
1 Stain as required.	Overnight	Raise grain prior to staining if water stain is to be used.
2 Fill as required.	Overnight	Raise grain prior to staining if water stain is to be used.
3 Seal with an all-purpose sealer or thinned coat of varnish.	Overnight	Sanded surfaces must be wiped clean with tack cloth before finish is applied.
4 Apply varnish after sanding with #280-grit paper.	Overnight	Sanded surfaces must be wiped clean with tack cloth before finish is applied. Repeat step 4 until the desired finish buildup is achieved.
5 Rub with a moistened felt pad coat with pumice.		Rub with the grain. Wipe clean with paint thinner when finished.
6 Rub with a moistened felt-pad coat with rottenstone.		Rub with the grain. Wipe clean with paint thinner when finished.
7 Repeat steps 5 and 6 to create satin finish on glossy coat of varnish.		

Table 7–3. *Finishing procedure for alkyd varnishes.*

	Procedure	Drying Time	Tips
1	Flood surface with oil.	30 minutes	
2	Reapply oil.	15 minutes	Wipe off excess.
3	Reapply oil after 6 to 8 hours.		*Repeat steps 1 to 3 until desired buildup is developed.

*The manufacturers of some tung-oil products recommend smoothing between coats with #0000 steel wool. If steel wool is used, it is important to clean the surface completely in order to avoid finish contamination. Moving a strong magnet over the surface can be useful in this process.

Table 7–4. *Finishing procedure for rubbing-oil finishes.*

	Procedure	Drying Time	Tips
1	Apply varnish.	4 to 8 hours	Sand lightly between coats with #280-grit paper and wipe surface clean with a tack cloth.
2	Apply additional coats within 24 hours.	4 to 8 hours	Repeat steps 1 and 2 until at least 3 coats have been applied.

Table 7–5. *Finish procedure for polyurethane varnishes.*

METRIC EQUIVALENTS CHART

INCHES TO MILLEMETERS AND CENTIMETERS
MM—Millemeters   CM—Centimeters

Inches	MM	CM	Inches	CM	Inches	CM
J	3	0.3	9	22.9	30	76.2
G	6	0.6	10	25.4	31	78.7
K	10	1.0	11	27.9	32	81.3
H	13	1.3	12	30.5	33	83.8
L	16	1.6	13	33.0	34	86.4
I	19	1.9	14	35.6	35	88.9
M	22	2.2	15	38.1	36	91.4
1	25	2.5	16	40.6	37	94.0
1G	32	3.2	17	43.2	38	96.5
1H	38	3.8	18	45.7	39	99.1
1I	44	4.4	19	48.3	48	101.6
2	51	5.1	20	50.8	41	104.1
2H	64	6.4	21	53.3	42	106.7
3	76	7.6	22	55.9	43	109.2
3H	89	8.9	23	58.4	44	111.8
4	102	0.2	24	61.0	45	114.3
4H	114	11.4	25	63.5	46	116.8
5	127	12.7	25	66.0	47	119.4
6	152	15.2	27	68.6	48	121.9
7	178	17.8	28	71.1	49	124.5
8	203	20.3	29	73.7	50	127.0

INDEX